GOD AMONG

THE SHAKERS

GOD AMONG THE SHAKERS

A Search for Stillness and Faith

at Sabbathday Lake

SUZANNE SKEES

HYPERION

NEW YORK

Library of Congress Cataloging-In-Publication Data

Skees, Suzanne, 1962-
God among the Shakers : a search for stillness and faith at
Sabbathday Lake / Suzanne Skees.—1st ed.
p.   cm.
Includes bibliographical references.
ISBN 0-7868-6237-8
1. Shakers—Maine—Sabbathday Lake. 2. Spirituality—Shakers.
I. Title.
BX9768.S2S54   1998   97-7814
289'.8—dc21   CIP

Book design by Holly McNeely

FIRST EDITION
10   9   8   7   6   5   4   3   2   1

FOR

JONAH, ISAAC, AND BENJAMIN

LIGHT AND INSPIRATION OF MY LIFETIME.

CONTENTS

God among

the Shakers

PROLOGUE

I went to the Shakers to look for God, who lately had been absent from my harried, distracted days. Time, there seemed never enough time to complete all the tasks screaming for my attention. To summon the energy to conquer each day seemed insurmountable. Leaping from bed in the morning, back muscles already tense, I ran here and drove there, snapping at my children as I juggled laundry and cooking and telephone calls and diaper changes, glaring at the clock, grasping for coffee and scrambling to achieve, acquire, produce, accomplish.

Stillness, which the Shakers would say leaves room in one's heart for the Spirit God, slowly had gotten crowded out of my life. Stillness, which hovered like mist over the waters of Sabbathday Lake, Maine, the last Shaker haven on earth, found no place to linger here.

I was living the American dream. Striving to build a career, family, and home. Along the way, however, hope had been lost to frenzy, and my spirit had dried up like mist burned off a lake by the harsh morning sun.

I longed to reach out to something beyond my arbitrary world, yet I no longer knew if I believed.

Belief in the God of my childhood had withered many years ago. The Great White God of Christianity, the old man with blue eyes and a beard, had watched over my early years from his almighty throne in the sky. He held all the power of floods and plagues, and he played the earth like a puppeteer from above, sinister sometimes, choosing sides in wars and striking down those who would not kneel before him.

I held tightly my songbook in the crowded pew of our Catholic church and sang songs about God's swift hand of justice, his mighty eye of omniscience. And it seemed to me that God watched me, no matter where I tried to hide, and saw all the shameful or selfish things I did—like Santa Claus at Christmas. Yet God kept watch all year, and meted out not merely toys but great blessings and curses due to my actions.

More imperfect than most, I learned to become sneaky under the constant glare of that righteous eye. My mother, after all, hid stashes of money and candy from us children, and burrowed books about sex in her lingerie drawer. Both parents hid their carefully balanced checkbook from us, and rushed to cover their bodies if we saw them dressing. So I, too, learned to hide things—my childhood desires, deep primal feelings, budding sexuality. Inner and outer selves formed—the wild urchin under constant reproach from church, parents, and parochial school, and the good Catholic girl I tried so hard and hopelessly to be.

When I reached adolescence, people at my church began to talk about "agape," Christian love. They said God was forgiving and loving, Jesus was my brother and best friend. And to this notion I clung. Still, the new claim of gentleness in God perhaps came too little, too late. It stung in my eyes, as when my mother used to spank me and then hug me, saying, "Oh, this hurts me more than it hurts you. I love you so much."

My breasts began to swell, my period came, and suddenly I felt not only imperfect but utterly female as well. The God of my Catholicism loomed more and more remote from my view. God. Jesus. The sheer maleness of them, and of the disciples and scripture writers and priests and bishops and pope, set them far apart from the feelings and experiences I was having as a young woman.

Desperate to cling to belief, I began a series of meetings with a priest. "How can Jesus be the deepest part of my heart," I asked him, "when he is male and I am female? How can I be male at the core of my self?"

"When Jesus lives in your heart, he goes beyond gender," the priest nodded wisely from his comfortable fake-leather swivel chair. "Think of him as being androgynous." Well. This stuck like a lump in my throat. I could not swallow the idea of someone so physically tangible that I weekly ate his body and drank his blood, so physically male that an entire church system of patriarchy had been modeled after his anatomy, suddenly losing shape to androgyny.

Meanwhile, my double life continued. I studied hard for my classes but disobeyed my parents every chance I got. I served as senior class president but drank beer in cars on weekends. Turning to Mary, the Blessed Mother, for some connection woman to woman, all I saw was the looming distance between us: She, glowing with purity, was a virginal vessel of God; I, reeking of cigarette smoke, was a confused rebel who let boys touch me. Mary Magdalene, the biblical prostitute, and I had more in common, yet no one ever prayed to her.

Cloistered in a Catholic college, which my parents hoped would shield my faith from corrupt culture, I lost all hope. I stood before an outside shrine of the Virgin Mary, on the lawn of my small Midwestern campus, and wept. I tried to reach her, to reach God, reach anyone beyond who would listen to filth like me. And no one did.

Years of agnosticism followed. One night during graduate school, as I drove my rusted-out Volkswagen to the night-shift job that paid my rent, I shook my fist to the dark sky and bellowed from the bottom of my lungs, "Are you there or not? Why won't you answer me? Goddamn you, I hate you! I don't believe in you!"

Tears poured down, spilling into my lap. I tried not to wreck the car as I swerved along dim curves to work.

Jewish people say that one can never stop being a Jew—no

matter how one might rage against God and deny having faith. And this is what happened to me.

My intellectual mind, having read psychology, evolutionary science, and creation physics, saw God as merely the burning human need for more, for meaning, for eternity. Still, my heart hungered for someone to listen to my prayers.

Some years later, bored with my perfect job in book publishing and still hungry for more, I entered divinity school to study world religions. It seemed clear, by then, that my whole life would be a search. In books and Bibles I searched, in art and dreams and music and the faces of diverse peoples. The Allah of Islam, the Yahweh of Judaism, the Great Spirit of Native America, the nirvana beyond the Buddha, the Savior of Christianity, the Brahman of Hinduism—I searched the faces of gods all over the world. After divinity graduation, my daily work in theological writing continued the search. I dug out stories of people and their faith, like an archaeologist discovering precious fragments of truth that, in the end, may all fit together to create a whole.

Gradually, my idea of God evolved. My God began to resemble the tenderness in a mother's eyes when she first beholds her newborn child; the quiet strength in a father's shoulder as he holds his child in the deep, tearful night. My God looked like the wilted dandelion my small son picked with reverence, the streak of glorious color in a sunset, the benign welcome of a round moon in the twilit sky.

This benevolent force of Good became for me more abstract, less humanoid. A great leap of belief had taken me from the Almighty God of my childhood to the strength of love that pulses through earth, the power of goodness from the mightiest forces of the universe to the smallest act of kindness by a stranger, the miraculous beauty that occurs when life is nothing but itself.

Yet the departure I made from a traditional white male God already had been made, 250 years ago, by a radical Christian sect called the Shakers. They turned their God inside out, casting off the shell of human likeness and claiming that God was all spirit. Shakerism said this God encompassed all qualities of male and female humans, yet surpassed our slightest understanding. Suddenly God became literally, immediately, available to all.

First in the mid-1700s in England, then in Revolutionary America, the "shaking Quakers," as people jeeringly called them, declared that Christianity had seen only one side of God. Christians claim to believe that God may reflect both female and male, that all nations and peoples are equal in God's sight. But most Christians still paint their image of God as a white male, and many recoil from inclusive language. They send their missions to ignorant peoples, to enlighten poor unsaved souls to their right way. History oozes with the blood of peoples they have slaughtered in the name of religious superiority. The Christian God takes sides.

Shakers, meanwhile, have long understood that we human beings are a literal people, and we must give more than lip service to a Whole God. The Shaker God, pure spirit, looks like no man yet reflects every person. God may be pure spirit, yet God contains all the plump nurturing of a mother's lap, all the powerful protection of a father's arms. And Shakers know that we human beings need tangible symbols, so they pray to a Father/Mother God.

I could pray to this kind of God, I began to realize. This God looked like me, and then again looked like the Whole of God's creation.

This God inspired founder Ann Lee to follow her visions across an ocean, to seek in free America a home for her fledgling faith. This God inspired early Shakers to cast off all material property, family ties, sexual relations, and worldly goals to come and live together as a spiritual family. The Spirit God led Shakers to establish an equal ministry of women and men, to reduce diverse new members to one communal status, to buy African slaves to set them free, to welcome orphaned children and broken families, hungry and homeless (who often later abandoned them and returned to the world). Shakers sang of the ever-present Spirit of Christ that dwelt in the hearts of all peoples they encountered in the New World that, in turn, branded them witches.

This God, claimed Ann Lee, wanted me to hand over all feelings of shame and inadequacy, to confess my shortcomings and then be done with them. The pivotal role of confession in Shakerism was, I discovered, one of unburdening of the soul. Other Christians hold onto their sinfulness like a grudge, be-cause it brings them back to a saving God whose mercy they crave. Shakers, rather, thrust away their sins on a regular basis. They are left pure, clean, not perfect but whole, and ready to begin again.

The powerful figure of Ann Lee looked nothing like my meek, mousy Immaculate Mary, and that drew me to her. Ac-tually, the historical Mary of Nazareth may have been a pretty average teenager who just happened to say "yes" to God at a moment when the universe opened to her. She may have been deified by her loving faithful until there was no human substance left of her. But I still could not get close to her. I would never be so perfect, pure, untouched.

Ann Lee, however, was all human. She brought from En-gland a chipped porcelain tea cup and a basketful of psycholog-ical hang-ups. She was not beautiful. She could not read nor write. She lost her temper, she blasted into other people's Sun-day church services, and she claimed to have regular conversa-tions with the dead.

The radical, rebellious human figure of Ann Lee speaks to my twenty-first-century soul. Lee was a woman of extremes. She leapt into Shakerism with an obsession that still reeks today in the pages of Shaker history and theology, in the stories of en-counters people had with this strange woman.

She preached until she got thrown in jail. She preached from jail.

She traveled three months in a rickety boat called the *Snow Maria* that had been condemned; she brashly informed the captain that God would never sink the boat while she and her believers were aboard.

She built a religious system that, in America's revolutionary days, freed her in ways women dared not dream. She renounced all sexual relations with her husband, thus freeing herself from housewifery and childbearing, and set herself up to govern a growing flock.

No one owned her.

She declared herself equal in the sight of God, declared slavery to be an abomination, and refused to participate in the Revolutionary War. For although she supported America's struggle for independence, she saw the world as a whole of equal countries, none of which ought to war with another for any cause.

She probably either adored or detested everything she tasted in life. Lee knew no middle ground.

I looked at her today, from the perspective of an educated woman in a technologically advanced, relatively liberated society, and I bowed down to her. No stars dazzled my eyes, because I saw Ann Lee from without, from the objectivity of a non-Shaker. I revered her as the equal to me that she said she was, the fierce woman who re-imaged God and founded Christian egalitarianism, the woman who embodied Christ and dared to say I could do so, too.

I could feel the presence of Ann Lee even now, almost palpably. She stirred to life in the pages of Shaker history; I could see her burning eyes and hear the fervor in her voice. And I suspected that she lived on at Sabbathday Lake, where I had heard that the last sisters and brothers would speak of her as though she had just left the room, and sing her praises till their meetinghouse echoed with her spirit. She seemed to stir the quiet waters of that little country lake in Maine, a continent away from my reality of shopping malls and high-rise offices, hundred-dollar shoes stepping over the homeless, people scurrying from work to gym to errands to day care, tense with tasks undone, wishes unmet, pain unforgiven, differences battled, lives survived.

Maybe it was Ann Lee who beckoned me to the shores of Sabbathday Lake. Something called me to come and see, come and see. See more deeply than the ripples on the surface that books barely touch. Hear more closely than the echo of voices from the library across the lake, the official statements of Shakers in interviews and texts. Feel with my hands the wooden bowl into which apple peels go. Witness with my eyes the tears of a flesh-and-blood Sister who sorrows over her struggle. Know with my heart the Savior Ann, the Mother-Father God, that lifted these eight last Shakers up off the ground and halfway to the heaven they strive so hard to live in the here and now.

Whatever it was that called me, it came from deep within. My head could have tried to hush the call, but my soul would not rest until I followed its own path, in its own time. The chance had come. It made no sense now, when my body was weary from birth, night nursings, and day nurturing, and my little children needed so much from me. Yet the soul works in its own time, wishing to lead us to the meaning of our life, if we will but listen. For some the soul may lead to soaring high in a hot-air balloon, or leaving corporate safety to launch a business of your own, or falling in love with someone you never imagined. For me it was to take this chance, when the eldress of the Shakers said "yes" I may come and stay a while. It was to continue the search for God I have walked for half a lifetime, to see their God for myself and then tell the story that emerged.

Maybe this journey to the Shakers had something to do with my own desire to escape the sterility of agnosticism. As I plunged headlong into research, I began to want more than books can tell. To go deeper than the dry amalgamation of facts and quotes I had written into divinity papers—I wanted the guts of this story. I wanted to know, from the deepest pit of my being, what it was like to *be* Shaker. Yet they seemed so different from me that I doubted I could ever really know.

Shakers symbolized all that I was not. They lived a rural existence for which I would have no patience nor physical stamina. How could I run a farm when the one tomato plant I attempted last summer leaned over in a scraggled mess? How could I bear the monotony of woodpiles and apple pies when I have known the glittering glamour of Boston, Chicago, and San Francisco; all the variety of books and clothing and art my wallet can afford; all the fast-paced freedom of cars and subways and airplanes?

I knew I had not the quiet of soul that these eight people possessed. My lust looms too large: I want the world. I want to travel, to learn, to eat and drink and love. I want rich colors and soft fabrics in my home, strong coffee wafting into a hot early-morning shower, the nuzzle of children's hair against my cheek. I want sexual bliss again and again. I want to absorb knowledge from all sorts of reputable and questionable sources, to spend a lifetime discovering books, art, music, wine. I want to roll on the soft grass of my own backyard, yet journey to the farthest corners of the wonderfully tangible world in which my body lives.

What called me to Sabbathday Lake demanded more self-control than I ever may have had to summon. Not only would I have to lower my hemlines and hide my birth control pills, I would have to be quiet. To listen.

As I prepared to go and share a bit of life with the last eight Shakers, I expected to have to struggle to stay awake through some of the less magnetic sermons. To attempt to remain interested after the fortieth potato had been peeled, after the third hour of weeding the herb garden. To remain alert enough to hear what was being said underneath what I expected these Shakers to say, to hear beyond stereotype, judgment, romanticizing. To clear the clutter of my overcrowded American mind from desires and distractions. To be still.

I expected to spend many hours engaged in small talk with people decades older than I. To learn skills I would never use again: how to bake mincemeat pies with buttered crusts, how to bend strands of elm for a Shaker oval box. Yet unless I went and listened, how could I see their God? Unless I "put my hands to work and my heart to God," as the Shakers say, how would I know?

Maybe I dared this journey so I could do more in this world than just procreate and domesticate, do more than dabble in the theologies of people so different from me. Something profound in Shakerism drew me to a way of life that starkly contrasts with that of my own. Something deep in my soul believed the Shakers had answers to questions I had not even bothered to ask.

The vast difference I perceived between us could serve as my bridge to the world. I felt deeply inadequate to be among these people, to try to work their work and pray their prayers and then to have the audacity to tell their story for them. Yet what happened was that the story became my own, that of the encounter of one cynical, worldly woman with simple, utter faith.

As I made plans for the journey, I hoped to see the nit and grit of everyday Shaker life. I wondered what compelled these people to choose their rare path. Frederick W. Evans, a New Hampshire elder in the mid-1800s, chose Shakerism partly for its liberal philosophies but largely because he underwent three weeks of visions that convinced him the spirit world beyond the veil of earthly life was real. An eldress of the same era, Antoinette Doolittle, heard a voice at age fourteen telling her to leave her loudly protesting family and "Go to the Shakers, and see for yourself." She arrived for a brief visit and stayed the rest of her life.

And so, what if I went to the Shakers and fell in love? By going to Sabbathday Lake with an open mind and heart—the only way I knew how to go—I risked losing my life as it was, forsaking my family, orphaning my children, and throwing away everything I have loved in this life to embrace the Shaker way. One cannot open up to let in new views and new truths without risking a soul-shattering conversion. Others had, after all, come to visit Shaker communities and never wished to return to the world. And with the kind of spiritual power these Shakers supposedly wielded, who knew but that I might fall under their spell?

So, here lurked the greatest risk: I could come back Shaker. Rationally, this seemed unlikely. I was a grown woman with a developed philosophy of life. I had encountered many appealing religions through my theological studies and, much as I revered each one, had remained in the roots of my Catholicism. This, however, felt different. This journey went far beyond the most engaging text or invigorating lecture; it took me to real human beings in a beautiful place living the noblest life. I could fall madly in love with all of it. Yes, the risk was real.

As I held my husband in my arms, the last night before my journey, I told him aloud and laughing that this could happen. "Then we could all go and live in community," I proffered as a joke, "give our money to the Shakers and live chastely as brother and sister." He laughed, too, with fear in his voice. He had read my heart and knew how open it was to this Shaker faith. Perhaps for him willingly to let me go anyway was the ultimate act of generous love.

Risking, then, that my children may suffer long-term damage from maternal deprivation, or at the very least fall off the jungle gym and have no one to hold them through their primal screams; that my husband could storm off in a fit of rage at this silly spiritual quest that consumed his wife, or at least learn to live contentedly without me while I was away; that I may be sucked into conversion by some mysterious magnetic spiritual force, or at least open my mind and find its logically structured ideologies irrevocably altered; I packed a bulging suitcase and flew three thousand miles east.

The witness of eight people on a farm in Maine who believed firmly enough to give up the world for Shakerism, to pray their way into a seemingly certain extinction, would stand for itself. If these eight human beings really practiced the simple devotion their myth resounded, if Ann Lee could be found whispering among the fields of Sabbathday Lake farm, if God reverberated from the soil of the last Shaker farm on earth, then I would see and hear and know for myself.

This book tells the faith story of the Shakers from their radical revolution to now. Rather than rely only upon historical sources considered verifiable by society, I also have entered into Shaker sacred literature, to attempt to see God as Shakers themselves see God. Voices from eyewitnesses, scholars, and Shakers speak herein their often opposing sides of the story—accusation, doubt, awe, and devotion.

My own voice speaks throughout, of my fleeting glimpse into Shakerism and its impact upon my heart. It echoes with the sound of my own limited history: that I began life as a liberal Catholic who went to divinity school and came out an intellectual universalist, that I live deeply within worldliness and love intensely my husband and children, and that I hold a political passion for equality, freedom, and compassion for all human beings.

Shakerism may be no more and no less biased and flawed than all other religions of the world. Still, it may possess truths about the human soul startling in their beauty, aptness, and purity. And so I labor on, telling a faith story that will attempt to do justice to the quiet conviction by which thousands of Shaker people have lived and died. Biased and flawed as my story may be, it may contain bits of startling truth.

CHAPTER ONE

SURVIVAL

What saith the Spirit to the poor and oppressed?
"Come unto me and I will give you rest.
Are ye heavy laden, have ye fallen by the way?
Jordan hath the power of healing.
Brave ye the billows now and again,
Healing from blindness, sorrow and pain,
Oh be persuaded the waters to try,
God in his mercy is dealing."

—*"What Saith the Spirit?"*

As I prepared to go and spend time with the Shakers, to learn something about the fierce beliefs that have sustained them into a third century, I felt more than a little trepidation. The journey stood at the pinnacle of all the book knowledge I had gathered during my study of Shakerism, beginning when I was a divinity student and continuing through my writing on international people and their faiths.

Here beckoned the chance of a lifetime: to dwell among a community whose truths had so infiltrated current culture that

their song "Simple Gifts" blared out from television car commercials, their antique furniture auctioned off to such figure-
heads as Oprah Winfrey at $220,000 per table, and their
museums drew thousands of people clamoring to see clever tools
and time-saving devices, barren beds and haunted meetinghouses. Something in the life of these people had touched the
soul of culture today.

During my years of research into the lives of these people,
I had heard the same question asked by friends and librarians:
"Oh, Shakers. Aren't they just like the Quakers? Or is it the
Amish?" Well, I discovered that Shakerism had similar roots,
but also critical differences.

Born in an era surging with new religions of the spirit, Shakerism shared much in common with other sectarian faiths, such
as the French Camisards and Quakers. Their fire-and-brimstone
founders all denounced conventional churches, condemning
their clerical hierarchies and ecclesiastical practices. They proclaimed that the end time had come, the apocalypse was now.
They dared to place the spirit, the feeling of God and personal
experience of the divine, above all else, even scriptural authority
and papal infallibility. And they had the audacity to claim that
women and men, poor and rich, seminarian and illiterate, all
shared the same power of access to the Spirit.

Knowing how radical such claims to equality sounded even
now, I could only imagine how fanatical such Christians must
have seemed in the eighteenth century.

Shakerism sprang up from the same English soil and spiritual
ground as Quakerism, and both faiths stress personal access of
the individual to God, without the need for elaborate hierarchies of church, meticulous following of creed, or literal salvation through the Bible. Still, Shakerism differs. Only eight
celibate Shakers remain on earth, while some 250,000 Quakers
thrive around the world. Shakers give body and soul to union
within their community—relinquishing their families of birth,
giving up marriage and sexual relations, individual ownership
and self-will—to live as one with other believers in the striving

toward heaven. Quakers marry and have families, and they live in society. They dwell deeply and equally within both realms, meditating quietly to "touch the light within" (God), then moving actively into worldly work in social justice, peace, and charity.

Shakers also differ from the Amish, who have 112 settlements in the United States and beyond but live primarily in Pennsylvania, Ohio, and Indiana. While Shakers gather members through conversion only, Amish numbers grow through marriage and the births of large families. Amish share a brotherhood in Christianity, as do the Shakers, but they read the Christian Bible with a more literal eye. Standing against culture, the Amish spurn electricity and machinery, modern dress and transportation. Meanwhile, Shakers have given American society dozens of inventions, such as the flat broom and washing machine. They gladly embrace technology, from microwaves to computers, that can facilitate their work.

Initially, society held great contempt for this nascent sect. The dusty books I read voraciously in my little upstairs office told tales of scandal, hatred, and fear. Shakers had been persecuted since their early days in colonial New England. Their dances of the spirit, communication with the dead, power to pray in unknown languages, and ability to reach religious ecstasy convinced their frightened neighbors they were witches. Their insistence against marriage and procreation inspired protests that they were undermining the natural order of family. Their pacifism, and staunch refusal to fight even for the cause of the Revolutionary War, got them labeled Tory spies from Mother England. And no one could ever believe the Shakers were actually celibate, so there were rumors of naked forest orgies and jokes about how Shaker women were too ugly for romance.

Over the centuries, however, Shakers have come to symbolize the heart of American freedom. Meeting with great resistance in their early years, they slowly proved themselves merely by living what they believed. Outsiders witnessed their tidy farms and pious prayer, their nonviolence toward people and beasts, and their quiet dedication to work, and slowly learned to accept the Shakers.

I could see in the history books the growing respect for, and even a romanticizing of, the Shakers. "They are an orderly, industrious sect," wrote historian James Fenimore Cooper in 1828, "and models of decency, cleanliness, and of morality, too, so far as the human eye can penetrate. I have never seen, in any country, villages so neat, and so perfectly beautiful, as to order and arrangement."

Some visitors described Shaker communities as though they were literally bits of heaven on earth. I wondered, as I read, how much these views were colored by the writers' own rosy perception. "The very dust in the road seemed pure," Benson J. Lossing told *Harper's* readers in 1857. And Hepworth Dixon echoed this sentiment in *New America* in 1867: "The streets are quiet . . . and every building, whatever may be its use, has something of the air of a chapel. The paint is all fresh; the planks are all bright; the windows are all clean. A white sheen is on everything, a happy quiet reigns around. . . . [Shaker Village] strikes you as a place where it is always Sunday."

Despite its heavenly appearance, Shaker faith has changed— perhaps as drastically as any Christian faith—since Revolutionary times. The hostility that Shakers held for the world and its lustful, sinful ways has mellowed into acceptance for people "where they are" in their spiritual journey.

The heterodox sect that denounced all other religions as false now forms close bonds with Christian monastic communities all over the country, welcomes visitors of all faiths, is studied in schools and universities as an orthodox branch of Christianity, and is revered by antique Shaker furniture collectors and artists, philosophers and travelers.

Slowly, Shakerism has become embraced by the very world it rejected. As historian Stephen Stein wrote in the mid-1990s, "Once feared, hated, and persecuted, the Shakers are now the darlings of American culture," surrounded by "a mood of collective nostalgia." We so love their furniture, their simplicity, their down-home purity, that "the contemporary Shakers are in danger of becoming symbols, living icons," Stein warned.

Yet under the surface, Stein insisted, their values still rub against the grain of American culture: absolute celibacy, communal sharing of goods, unquestioning obedience to higher spiritual authorities, and the struggle toward humility and self-denial could not be more "out of step with the individualism and consumerism" of America today.

And herein I began to see the irony: Current society loves what we perceive as the simple, pure life of Shakers because it stands in stark contrast to everything we have become.

Hundreds of eyewitnesses before me had glimpsed the interior of Shaker life and tried to convey what they saw. Journalist Tim Clark, writing for *Yankee* magazine in 1980, was one of them. He admitted that "We all come to the Shakers with certain preconceived notions. We carry an image around in our heads of an austere, highly disciplined, perhaps fanatical sect, living in nearly bare rooms with pegs on the walls, speaking in stilted Old Testament English, refusing to have any truck with the corrupt and worldly twentieth century."

Yet in one short day at Sabbathday Lake, Clark discovered that "Shakers strive for separation from the sense and feeling of the world, not from the world itself. After all, 'God made the world. The world is a good place,' one member told me. Today's Shakers live in the present." His stereotype "Shaker" shattered, and he began to talk with the community as one human being to another.

A friend of the Shakers for several decades, New York lawyer and museum director Gerard Wertkin wrote of an early experience attending Sunday Meeting at Sabbathday Lake. He discovered that, to be among Shakers, one must simply, profoundly, be oneself: "I felt free to stand among the Believers and repeat the ancient Hebrew words of a prayer from my own religious heritage," he wrote in his 1986 book, *The Four Seasons of Shaker Life*, "knowing that they did not want me to be anything but myself, just as they were true to themselves. Years ago,

Brother Ted observed that there were no masks among Believers. It is a Shaker principle that only in stripping away artifice and conceit can true freedom be realized. Simplicity, as mediated for us by the Shakers, is not some form of cold austerity, but a continuing process of self-discovery."

Now, I look at the Shakers and see all we have forgotten at the root of our homeland. They wear plain clothes and put on neither makeup nor airs. They labor each day in honest work, harvesting sheep wool to spin and dye yarn, then coax a hundred-year-old loom to weave a rug of the earth's richest colors. They tend rows and rows of apple trees in an orchard behind the meetinghouse, then pick and store and peel and slice and bake apples into pies whose steam wafts all through the dwellinghouse. They bow their heads in prayer three times a day, together reading scripture and raising their voices to the heavens, then take that moment's peace back to the barn or laundry room, humming through chores for the sheer joy of knowing God.

They call themselves family, yet American colonists accused the first Shakers of tearing apart family structure. Indeed, all who remain at Sabbathday Lake have, I learned, forsaken their families of birth to come and live in the spirit. They marry the Christ, pledging body and soul with an intensity that leaves no room for nuclear family. They live as one in the Spirit, striving ever toward intimacy of the soul while, through a lifetime of celibacy, employing the body merely for the chores of this realm.

Telephone calls to scholars, friends of the Shakers, and the current eldress herself, began to build for me the history of the small family remaining at Maine. I learned that the four eldest sisters (three at the farm, one nearby in a nursing home) came to the Shakers as children, in the twentieth-century era before government assisted struggling families, when their desperate parents gave them away to the hands of loving strangers. Shaker communities had a reputation for moral upbringing, quality education, and hearty food. And when foster children came of age, they freely chose whether to stay or go. These four were the last of a generation who signed the Shaker covenant without having seen the world beyond, and they have stayed at Sabbathday Lake all the decades since.

The other four, one sister and three brothers, grew up in suburbs and cities near and far, and only as adults came to choose the Shaker way. One brother simply enjoyed his experience as a teenage farmhand at Sabbathday Lake; another had mystical visions that called him away from his worldly urban life to semi-monasticism at Shaker Village.

Only through conversion does this family survive. The conversion process takes place slowly. First one visits, then corresponds and returns, asking and listening and learning the faith. When the elders say the time is right, one spends a year as a Shaker, trying the life. Even so, conversion can backfire: hundreds of letters each year flood the little community, from seekers of truth who pick up and then set aside Shakerism like a book off the shelf. They write or call or even come to visit, yet balk at the enormity of the Shaker covenant. The door to the dwellinghouse at Sabbathday Lake freely swings both ways. Only recently a young and "very promising" sister relinquished her vows to return to what the Shakers call "the world": the realm beyond.

This family, as fluid as any today, has known its share of on-lookers and dabblers: those who felt called to join despite wrenching pain of what they left behind, and those who broke their hearts to leave the Shakers once again. The past echoes with stories of star-crossed lovers running off in the night to marry, scandals of administrators squandering community money through bad debts and get-rich schemes, even rumors of spiritual mediums using their powers to wield their will through alleged messages from the dead. Shakers of the past have not been perfect.

All the darkness and light of human nature lives on in today's Shakers, who struggle daily to overcome what they see as flawed, weak selves striving toward God. And because the door swings both ways, they know the persistence of their freedom to return to the world of ego, lust, control, and attachment.

Even before I left for Sabbathday Lake, I saw clearly in books, letters, and conversations the level of commitment these last Shakers upheld. Every day, as they awakened in the chill of the Maine morning to dress and join their spirit family for the moment of silence that opened their day, eight Shakers consciously chose their covenant again and again.

A handful of Shaker brothers and sisters kindled the fire of a faith that, with no marriage or procreation, no creed or ordained ministry, has survived for two and a half centuries. For them the end time is now, the kingdom has come, and the spirit of Christ dwells deep in the hearts of all people. We in the world have only to wake up to this truth, and touch the divine within, to know the salvation that awaits.

The Shakers living today on a farm in south central Maine pray daily for the world, that we might recognize the quiet way in which the kingdom already has come. They believe to the root of their being that the voice of Shakerism still speaks truths to the world at the turn of the third millennium. Undaunted by the small size of their community, they point out that Ann Lee began with only eight believers—the same number they now have—when she first arrived in America. Moreover, Shaker prophecies declare that when numbers dwindle to that which can be counted on one hand, a great resurgence will occur.

Though we may not choose to live like Shakers, engaged in repetitive farm tasks far from the fast-paced world, something about the values they actually live by appeals to jaded Americans who remember the hardworking, Puritan, God-fearing, devout, freedom-fighting rebels of this land's past.

Something about their unquestioning devotion to God chokes in our throat like uncried tears. Maybe it is the memory of a childhood time when we, too, believed so fiercely that all our reality was built around the Friend who lived in our heart. Somewhere along the way, we have transformed from a country of religious rebels to a place of wanton wealth, where money is God and God gets fed in the church collection basket on Sunday mornings if at all but no longer lives in our crowded, busy hearts.

This was the two-sided truth I faced as I crammed my suitcase for Maine: Our culture loves that for which the last eight Shakers stand: purity, simplicity, labor, and faith; yet we cannot give up all we have gained to go back and live where they do. Years of skyscrapers and subway trains, computer networking and electronic banking, sexual liberation and material abundance, have wired us to this realm until, even for those of us who do the Sunday God thing, we lose sight of intangible realities simultaneously in our midst.

Today's Shakers give it all away, toss out their car keys and house deeds, paychecks and promotions, to live in a community in which no one owns anything. They relinquish their rights to own property—except maybe a toothbrush—and to have their way. There is no running off on a whim to see a movie or to fall in love, no matter who walks through the door in the years to come. They also give up cynicism, which rates so highly today, and agnosticism, the fickle freedom to unbelieve for a while in the face of insufficient evidence.

As for me, I thought as I tried to close the suitcase overstuffed with all the material objects I knew I absolutely could not live without, I was too attached ever to be a Shaker.

I was also utterly attached to the family I had created. My heart yearned for the little arms of children I had not yet even left. My eyes welled up at the thought of not checking them in their beds at night, not being the one to kiss their bumps and bruises. Just before my trip to Sabbathday Lake, my husband had left for three weeks' business travel and I wept at the airport—something I rarely do, as he and his briefcase constantly flit in and out of my life. What if something happened to one of us on our journeys, and we never saw each other again? I felt I must embrace him and then wholly let him go, trusting that he may return safe, or that calamity might crash us apart. If so, nothing I could do could stop it.

Loss of control: that is what inspired the fear that welled up within me. My husband's health, luggage, energy, physical safety, and morale seemed much more worrisome when he was so far out of my reach. And I feared going to Maine, because for all I knew I would lose my soul to the eccentric group of believers who awaited me there.

I feared entrusting my children to nannies and preschool teachers, because I would lose the ability to make sure their lunch boxes contained all four food groups, that they got hugs when they felt tired and crabby, that they wore their jackets on cold mornings. The pain of leaving tore at me. It felt like amputation.

The deep attachment was, however, as much my own as the need I perceived in them.

Granted, I believed my children needed to know without a doubt the depth and staying power of their mother's love. That kind of surety comes not from grand birthday presents nor exciting Disneyland trips, but from the ordinary moments of a shared life. My children knew my love every time I stopped what I was doing to hug them through their toddler tantrums, every time I cuddled them on my lap to read a nice long book, every time I looked deep in their eyes to really listen to what they told me.

And I knew that our youngest, then six months old, needed to nurse and needed my presence in a more fundamental way than did the older two. So I took him along, arranging for my younger sister, Sally, to drive over from her home in Vermont and meet us in Maine, to stay with us and care for the baby while I spent time with the Shakers. She was his godmother, and had spent time with him at birth and Christmas. Having been married a few years, she longed for a baby of her own, and so she would give all that tenderness to my son.

Eventually I hoped that my children would find mothering far beyond myself: in the pat of an understanding teacher, the extra good-bye kiss in the morning from daddy, the giggly shoulder ride on a strong and careful uncle, the offer of a consoling toy from a young friend. I hoped my sons would find nurturing from many sources, and that ultimately they would learn to find it within. Striving to learn how to love without attachment, I tried to give love more freely when I was present with them, and yet to trust their ability to thrive without me when I was not. The last thing I wanted to do was create the illusion that they could not survive without Mommy.

They *could* survive. They could flourish. When I boarded that airplane for Maine, they were surrounded by people who loved them: They had their smart, intense dad and their huggy, surrogate-grandma nanny. They had their gentle preschool teachers, who knew all about my trip, my belaboring over it, and the boys' anxiety about it. They had their sweet, fun-loving aunt, my older sister, Sandy, who lived across town and would come check on them, and their pal-cousins Elisabeth and Christina, who were as close to them as sisters. They had surprises to open when I left: a long recorded cassette tape for each of mommy reading their favorite storybooks and telling them about my love for them, homemade "love books" with photographs of our family and a story of our belonging to one another, a calendar with days to check off till mommy and the baby would return, and a basket full of fruit and animal cookies and their favorite morning cereal. They had the promise of several adventures while I was away and things to look forward to right after my return: a family trip, a birthday party, and summertime activities.

Oh, I knew in my head that they would be just fine. It was the heart that cried as I left. But when, having made all preparations for their well-being, I still wavered, I saw that it would be wrong not to follow my dream because of them. Of course, if a dream took me away forever, or caused them unquestionable harm, that would be different. But this took me away for only a few weeks, and, in fact, I would find when I came home stronger, more self-assured little boys who realized they could succeed on their own and who saw firsthand that grown-ups can follow their dreams.

They had learned a little song, in their church play program, called "Follow Your Heart," and they would sing this at the breakfast table or in the bathtub. What I did, in my work, showed them the legitimacy of that, for them as well as me. I did not want to be, twenty years from now, an embittered wife and mother who subverted her dreams and then unconsciously blamed her family for it. That would be cowardly. To go now, to trust them to carry on without me, required more courage than staying.

Life tries in many ways to teach me nonattachment, I realized as I typed pages and pages of instructions for the nanny. How can human nature love without clinging? Zen Buddhism teaches nonattachment as a path toward compassion. But can couples and families really share personal love in this detached manner? Most Christians cling to one another so hard they believe their bonds will outlast death itself, holding them together in heavenly reunions. Shakers, meanwhile, shun this kind of exclusive love, the ownership of people we call "family." Turning from their blood kin, sacrificing the chance to build families of their own, they form a spiritual family that, they believe, leaves their hearts open to love all people.

Still, I wondered if the possessive feelings I held for my husband and children would be, for the Shakers, transferred to members of their spiritual family. Shared philosophy and daily life would breed a deep kindred love, would it not? You cannot know whether someone puts pepper in her soup, how off-key her voice goes on a certain song, and how frail she looks when sick, and not learn to love. You cannot bend side by side to pick tomatoes, read a lifetime of books, and share generations of conversations, without feeling your heart fairly wrench out of your body when that person dies.

The day for departure came. My bulging suitcase sat somewhere in limbo, while the plane was late for the first leg of the journey.

Control, I told my husband over our last lunch together, is merely an illusion. He disagreed. "I could stop the very world from spinning if I set up enough atomic bombs to counteract gravitational forces," he calmly informed me. Then our baby, perched on his arm, leaked poop all over my husband's pristine, starched-white executive shirt, and we had to run home to clean up before heading off to the airport. So much for his notion of being in control.

Now I emerged into the unknown, leaving nothing but the unknown behind. Who knew what would happen to my family while I was away?

Being attached, one wants everything right now: to have one's children in one's arms even while pursuing life's work. Choices do not allow this, however. Once I married my husband, I closed off the possibility of exploring how much I might love another man, even, perhaps, one to whom my heart felt a strong yearning. Or, if I had chosen to be Shaker, I would never have known the primal bond of mother and baby as my infant suckles my breast and holds my hand, both of us knowing we are wholly there for each other. If I chose not to take this trip, I could never see the truth of life as this group of believers sees it.

So I went into the unknown. I left the illusion of control, of my lovely little life, in search of reality.

Did the Shakers have it? I had built up quite a fantasy in my mind. I fancied they lived without the temptation we feel when surrounded by glittering goods at the local shopping mall, the craving we hide when chatting at a party with a very attractive married man, and the jealousy we suppress when a co-worker gets the promotion.

Shakers seemed beyond the reach of attachment, while we other Americans lived immersed in material goods that lost their value almost as soon as they were acquired, scrambling in a flurry of activity that amounted to less than nothing at death.

Really, I thought as I boarded the plane, what did I, the

antithesis of these pure, big-hearted Shakers, hope to find at Sabbathday Lake?

Maybe I hoped to find out that they were right.

I entered Maine in the dark, blindly. Only by sheer luck did I get there. My first flight took off quite late, so to catch my connection to Portland I lurched through the Cincinnati airport, pushing my baby's stroller and tugging heavy bags full of his diapers and my work. Plopping heavily into my chair, I buckled my seat belt just as the plane rolled away from the gate.

We flew through increasing clouds and rain in the middle of the night. Later I learned that we should not even have been up there: The flight was supposed to have been canceled due to stormy weather. We flew by faith alone, trusting the instrument panel to guide what the pilots could not see. The turbulence turned my stomach. I gazed at my sleeping baby and wished fervently only to get to Maine alive.

Clouds thickened the night sky so that it seemed we would never descend, and then suddenly we cleared them at no more than twenty feet above ground. Amid drizzling rain we jolted down hard onto the runway, and a planeful of people breathed sighs of relief.

Blinking through the bright lights of the Portland airport at 1:00 A.M., I stumbled toward baggage claim and gave thanks again when all my hefty, seemingly essential luggage appeared. There was Sally, faithful and true, having waited hours for our delayed flight. She cooed at her godson, carried the overpacked black bag, and then led us in our rental car out onto the foggy Maine turnpike.

Unable to see more than a few feet in front of me, I carried on, trusting that these roads would lead to the little motel near Sabbathday Lake where we would make our home. Sally would care for my baby during the next weeks, to free my heart and hands to try the Shaker way. We soon would settle into a rhythm: I would wake with him well before dawn, snuggle and feed him while my sister slept nearby. Then I would dress while he lay in the middle of the bed and grinned at me. Sally would then rise, yawning and sleepy, and take him from my arms when it came time to warm the rental car and get to Shaker Village before the breakfast bell rang. Throughout the day I would return at scheduled times to feed the baby. Meanwhile she sustained him with yogurt and baby cereal, played with him and his baby toys on a blanket, and took him for walks and to do laundry. The surprising, delightful effect was that my infant and I both got mothered by this loving, capable woman. And he never cried when I handed him to her to return to my work.

That first night, though, never did seem to end. Unpacking the gear and settling the baby in took time, and when I lay my head down on the lumpy pillow it was only a few hours till dawn. Dreams of the Shakers swirled through my restless mind. They seemed sharply real. They talked with me, and welcomed me in. Their faces clustered in some sort of circle, floating above my head. They smiled and their hands came out to wave me forward, to their bosom, to their hallowed land.

The next morning felt like a continuation of the same day. Already I had begun to lose my sense of time.

When I drove to Sabbathday Lake I felt I was coming home to a place I had known long ago. I had visited only once before, when as a divinity student I had come to scour the library for research. Yet from deep within, I felt familiar in this land. My car wound its way confidently around the curves of Route 26, in the northwest corner of the town of New Gloucester, in south central Maine. I passed clapboard homes and antique barns, and suddenly the cluster of Shaker buildings came into view, looking like an old friend.

I parked the rental car alongside several other cars, and made my way to the front door of the massive 1884 dwelling-house. Six stories of red brick, softened with age, towered above me. Windows gleamed all the way up to the attic, and I wondered if from behind the lace curtains some older Shaker sister may already have seen that I had arrived.

I, their inquisitor.

How must it feel to welcome politely, to feed and entertain, someone who may write in favor of you or against you—you really would not know till the book came out—but in any case would open you up for public scrutiny? Were they as nervous as I? If the roles were switched and they were the ones who wanted to learn all about my life and my beliefs, I doubt I could open my home and heart so graciously.

Standing on the steps of the dwellinghouse, I looked out over the land. All around me, the damp, chilled air of dawn swirled thickly. Fog blanketed the hushed waters of the lake, the rectangles of herb gardens and rows of apple trees, and the hilltop buildings clustered along the path from barn to dwellinghouse. Birds blared as the morning sun pierced the fog for an instant, then disappeared again. On the rural highway that bisected Shaker Village, the incessant roar of trucks barreling past awakened two dogs, who barked in protest.

Chill seeped into the dwellinghouse through its mortar and brick, windowpanes, and door frames. Inside I waited while the last "family" of Shakers on earth dressed in haste. Shivering a bit in the downstairs hall, I heard the faint sound of rushing water upstairs as someone took refuge in a moment's hot shower. Elsewhere a hair dryer whined. Nearby, a door banged shut as a brother shuffled down the path to the barn to see if an expectant ewe made it safely through the night. I waited, in silence, to begin my encounter with these unknown people.

Down in the bowels of the six-story building, two sisters danced in unison through the kitchen, in movements made graceful from fifty years of cooking. One turned the bacon, the other checked the toast. They pirouetted past one another to carry bowls of jelly and cereal through a swinging door to dining tables beyond. Plain white cups and saucers awaited coffee perking in the big electric pot. Each member's place was set the evening before. The sisters filled the water glasses and set condiments on the table. I watched, peering through a nearby doorway, and to me their eyes and movements seemed surreal.

As the two sisters finished their dance, the others stepped

into place, one by one. Brothers descended the left staircase, and sisters the right, each to separate-gender waiting rooms that flanked the dining room. Only the sleepy voices of the brothers in greeting broke the silence. The two large dogs, who happened also to be male, lounged at their feet, knowing well the bell for breakfast soon would ring, as it did at the same time every day. Down the hall in the sisters' waiting room, a small, smiling sister shivered, wrapped her sweater more tightly about her, and dreamed of the upcoming day.

Precisely at the moment of the signal, all rose and entered the dining hall—brothers through one door, sisters through another. Their feet moved in slow procession over old wood floorboards, past rows of empty tables to the two set for their small family. Flanking the swinging door that led to the kitchen were the two cooking sisters, standing ready to serve.

I came and stood among them, though I felt like an intruder to their early-morning choreography. All paused behind their chairs, bowed heads, closed eyes, and uttered a wordless prayer to the Father-Mother God, in whose image all were created equal. Then in unison they pulled out ladderback chairs, sat down and spread napkins, and tasted the first gifts of the unfolding day.

Sister Frances, the eldress, had interrupted her cooking earlier to come and greet me. She walked forward with eyes and arms wide open, smiling a broad, warm smile and grasping my two hands in hers. "Welcome!" she said. "We're glad you're here."

Already I knew of her pleasant, polite manner from our many phone conversations and letters. And I knew she had a reputation for being a warm, gracious host who moved easily from farm duties to eldress responsibilities to mediations with the world.

Still, I think I was not prepared for her presence. She loomed rather tall and hearty in size. Her face, and the way she carried her body, seemed many years too young. I knew from reading her autobiography that she must be around seventy, yet she fairly bristled with vitality.

And happiness.

Not everything was perfect at Sabbathday Lake: Likes and dislikes abounded, and many of the family felt tired, having just returned from a trip to Philadelphia, where they had spent early mornings till late nights studying and praying with another small Christian community.

Yet the same essence that bubbled out from Sister Frances's voice in greeting also shone in Sister June's eyes when she, a tiny woman of sixty in a snap-front apron shift, a khaki skirt, and white socks with lace-up shoes, peered up at me to shake my hand and introduce herself. And that essence flowed throughout the dining room as a dozen of us later shared noontime dinner in a spirit of fellowship, pleasure in the taste of home-cooked food, and luxury in the hour away from chores.

I think it was peace.

Later, walking past the well and haystack, past the woodworking shop and pile of chopped firewood to the barn beyond, I felt as though I could be at any farm in New England. The weather forecast had called for more chilling rain, so the surprise of mild spring sun lifted everyone's spirits. Walking to the barn to feed the animals became a stroll, not a chore.

Two brothers bent to feed their baby sheep, and as they suckled them they stroked their fur, called them by nicknames, and haggled over the personality traits of each lamb. Brother Arnold, a wiry man with dark hair and a trim beard, fed them one at a time with an old plastic Diet Coke bottle topped off with a black rubber nipple. Lambs clambered around him, trying to climb atop his squatting legs and hoping to nudge each other out of the way.

"Wait your turn, little one," he said. "Just a minute. It won't be long."

Meanwhile, Brother Wayne, in coveralls and glasses, had rigged a bucket with several nipples all around it, and was feeding three lambs at once. "See how efficient this is," he said.

"You can get all of them fed at once." He bent down to tousle their fur and talk with them.

The two brothers debated the welfare of a new mother of triplets, being kept separate in a small penned-in area of the barn. "What would happen to her if you let her out?" I asked, imagining the mother disowning her babies or other lambs stealing her milk.

"Nothing," Brother Arnold laughed, and nodded toward Brother Wayne. "He's just being overprotective."

"Maybe I am," Brother Wayne replied. And they left it at that.

As that day wound on, and the days and days after spun together like strands on the loom in Brother Arnold's weaving workshop, I began to understand the real human beings behind the shining eyes of photographs and fervent convictions in the history books.

Eldress Frances A. Carr arrived at Sabbathday Lake in the 1930s, at the age of ten. She came from nearby Lewiston, Maine, having been brought up Catholic. Her mother could not provide for her, and already had placed several of her children with the Shakers. The high-spirited Sister Frances grew up alongside her blood sister Ruth and several close friends who later left the community. She knew the firm, loving care of older Shaker sisters who served as aunts and mothers to her.

To Sister Frances, the mischief of youth meant stealing a supply of maple sugar intended for the Shaker store, losing a sock among the piles of community laundry, sneaking out of her room at night to gossip down the hall with the other teenage girls, and getting a crush on a cute boy from the world who attended Shaker school.

Teachers, sisters, and young people came and left, but by age twenty-one Sister Frances committed herself to Shakerism as a fully covenanted adult. She learned the Shaker way from a genteel generation of sisters from the past, and has carried on the kernel of their tradition while adapting to widespread changes at the dawn of a new millennium.

Now it is she who leads the little group, serving as their spiritual mother, wielding her strength as financial administrator, confessional counselor, property manager, sermon preacher, diplomat to the world, and kitchen head chef. True to Shaker tradition, even the elders do physical work every day. "I have done some sort of work in the kitchen every single day for fifty years," sighed Sister Frances, as she spread a colorful array of dishes for the upcoming meal. She has written an autobiography on her experience, *Growing Up Shaker*, and a cookbook that shares the recipes and philosophy of hearty Shaker cooking.

Three other women came to the Shakers in their youth. Ninety-year-old Sister Minnie Green lives in a nursing home in the nearby town of Gray, Maine. She has Alzheimer's disease and so her needs surpass the caretaking capacities of the community, whose members still visit, hold her hand, and talk with her several times each week.

Sister Ruth, also about ninety, lived with the Shakers as a tiny child, then went to the world for some years—to care for her infirm sister—and returned in her old age. She had resided, for many years, in the trustees' house because "She wants her independence," explained Sister Frances. She and her miniature poodle, Mitsy, spend their days knitting baby blankets for the Shaker store and chatting with close friends of the community, who often stay in the guest rooms across the hall. She walks slowly to the dwellinghouse well before meals to sit in the rocking chair in a warm corner of the kitchen and watch the comings and goings. And when her turn to lead daily prayers comes up, she raises her trembling voice high and loud to her Lord.

Sister Marie Burgess has spent a lifetime in service at Sabbathday Lake. She wears an apron over her rugby shirt and elastic-waist skirt, and a constant look of curiosity from behind her polished glasses. Near seventy, she makes her rounds in the gardens, for hours of weeding in summer; to the birdfeeders, where she keeps her little feathered ones well stocked; to the kitchen, where she spends whole mornings on her feet peeling, paring, kneading, baking, basting, steaming, cleaning. Friends have called her "the salt of the earth." She balances the headiness of Shakerism with her zest for the human qualities of animals, subtle nuances of changing weather, and the latest score of her favorite Boston Red Sox.

The other four chose Shakerism no more or less deliberately, yet at a more mature stage in life.

Elder Arnold Hadd grew up in Springfield, Massachusetts, met the Shakers at age eighteen, and has spent half his lifetime in this place where his soul found a home. Having come from a "pretty normal, pretty typical middle-class family," Brother Arnold joined the Shakers at the very cusp of transition, when he was young enough to be the son or grandson of a frail group that, rather than die out, surged forward. He has seen membership grow, the farm flourish, and spirituality begin to reach out to the world beyond, and he has graduated from the punk who shoveled smelly barns and snowy walkways to the co-leader of the Shakers.

He now writes for the *Shaker Quarterly* on history and tradition of the faith, creates Shaker rugs on the loom and Shaker oval boxes out of poplar, and reprints books on Shaker theology in the basement print shop. Working on the office computer, balancing budgets or managing restoration contractors, baking his famous lemon pie or speaking the quiet surety of his prayers, Brother Arnold brings to each task of the day the devotion that Shaker founder Mother Ann Lee commanded: "Do all your work as if you had a hundred years to live, and as if you were to die tomorrow."

There is a quiet conviction about Brother Arnold that I noticed right away. "How did you know you wanted to become a Shaker?" I asked him, after the sheep had been fed and we walked the dirt path back from the barn.

"I just knew," he said. "It's a leap of faith, really. But you know if you feel called, if the Spirit calls you in a clear voice—actually, it's as if you can listen deep within for the Spirit."

"But what about Sister Meg—didn't she feel a calling?" Meg was the young sister who had come to the Shakers and seemed an integral part of the community, then left them a year ago to return to the world.

"I don't know what she felt," he sighed. "I cannot read anyone else's heart, so I can't know what they feel, or how strongly they feel it. Some are just called to this." He gazed out over the hundreds of acres stretched before him. "It's not an easy life. I would never say that it's easy to be Shaker. But it is a leap of faith: If you believe, then you just jump into it, and any sacrifice you have to make is OK."

The voice rippled quietly and steadily across the afternoon air, yet firm conviction rang clear. This was a masculine voice, using language of today; yet suddenly I felt as though it were Ann Lee talking to me.

The Shakers might say that her spirit lives on, through them, and so naturally she could communicate to me via Brother Arnold's voice. Or maybe what I heard was the passion they share—the same do-or-die conviction with which Lee lived her life over two hundred years ago—that fires the daily belief of this man who walked beside me now.

Brother Wayne Smith, who oversees the many agricultural cycles of the farm, began as a weekend farmhand at the community, pitching in to earn high school pocket money. His Baptist family, from the suburbs of coastal Portland, knew the Shakers fairly well by the time "it dawned on me, one day, that I should try this life," Brother Wayne said. He moved in for a one-year trial period right after high school, and has stayed fifteen years. His days orbit the hands of a clock in never-ending tasks that sustain the life of the farm itself: feeding the sheep, plowing the fields, harvesting the herbs, cleaning out the barn, planting the vegetables, feeding the dogs, mending fences, buying supplies, weeding gardens. And when Brother Wayne stops his work at the sound of the bell, he comes to prayer with the same gusto, the same embodied energy, the same straightforward loyalty. He is known for his sense of humor, passion for politics, and penchant for perfection.

Sister June Carpenter, born a Baptist in 1938, once lived a life much quieter than even the Shakers' before she came to Sabbathday Lake. As an only child whose father died when she was a teen, Sister June lived with her mother in a small apartment in a Boston suburb. She studied to become a librarian, and then spent thirty years commuting back and forth to her job at Brookline Library and caring for her aged mother. She never fell in love, never had a dinner party, never wanted children.

Since the dark nights of childhood bedtime prayer, Sister June had felt called toward something. But only after her mother died did the Baptist woman feel free to explore readings on the Catholic sisterhood, which led her to the Shaker order and to Sabbathday Lake in 1989. Just then the Shakers were restoring a library in great need of a cataloger, and Sister June suddenly had a daily vocation as well as a spiritual mission for the rest of her life. She is small in both stature and humility, and she smiles up at everyone in her path, from a persistent joy that seems too blithe to be real.

Brother Alistair Bate, a young man of some height and just a bit of paunch, was born in Dublin, Ireland, in 1964. He left the small Anglican parish village of his birth, and his family, and went to England at age eighteen. He craved an emotional relationship with God, and searched for it in religions and monasteries, social work and city life, that eventually led him to discover a rare faith born on the very soil on which he stood. He began writing to Sabbathday Lake and had a series of visions that convinced him that he was being "called" to this life. When he came to Shaker Village, he had never been to America, never lived on a farm, never met the people with whom he would form a spiritual family. Yet he knew he would stay.

The youngest and newest member, he had been at Sabbathday Lake only six months.

"Brother Alistair is a novitiate," Sister Frances explained.

"He lives with us and carries full responsibilities of the Shaker life, yet has none of the decision-making power yet." It would take at least one year, "sometimes more," of full immersion into their community before he would be permitted to take Shaker vows. Sister Frances and Brother Arnold later told me they were "quite pleased with him" in his spiritual progress. If all continued well, he would become fully covenanted before the next winter.

Brother Alistair donned a white apron after dinner and prepared to tackle the pots and pans. He chuckled at the sight of a greasy, globby sinkful. "Just dump them right in there," he called to me as I lugged in more dirty dishes from the dining room.

Brother Alistair helps around the farm in whatever way is needed, with a certain cheer shoveling out the dung on the sheep-barn floor or spending hours a day washing up dishes after meals. As a young child, he learned tailoring from his father and now uses a workshop to sew small trinkets and household items for the on-site Shaker shop and the annual Christmas fair. Though he approaches village visitors with great warmth and social grace, he prefers the retreat of monastic life and reads countless volumes of philosophy and spirituality.

Eight Shaker brothers and sisters could not seem more akin when viewed from a distance—their shared values, skin color, Christian background, rural homelife—nor more diverse when seen as individuals with pain of the past, skeletons in the closet, idiosyncrasies that chafe the others, and religious convictions that clash beyond their shared Shaker faith. The members of Sabbathday Lake, it would become more and more clear to me, stood not as symbols of some dying sect but flesh-and-blood adults who had chosen a difficult path toward an elusive goal. How could they be so certain they would reach their God, I wondered. And what sustained them through the effort and monotony of everyday life till then?

How long could one scrub the same dishes, day in and day

out, with such joy? Perhaps a year, if one felt loved in these surroundings and derived personal satisfaction from one's work. But for a lifetime? Still, I scrubbed my own messy kitchen at home three times a day, with varying degrees of eagerness but always with a sense of service toward the four people I loved most on earth. Was it the feeling of family that sustained Shaker brothers and sisters? When you live long enough together, and share the deepest convictions, does a love take root that nourishes all the mundane tasks of farming, cooking, cleaning, and mending?

It was that same joy in Brother Alistair scouring the pots that I had seen in several of the sisters earlier that day, and I eyed it suspiciously. I come from a world in which joy flutters in and out, never to remain. You can work years for it, building a business or home or family or garden. You can spend thousands buying it, taking lavish vacations or upgrading your automobile or launching that long-desired boat. Yet joy is here today gone tomorrow.

Spontaneous joy, that which alights when you sit down to lunch at a picnic with your children, or when you stand back to absorb the color of the sunset from a mountain you've just climbed, flits away too, as quickly as it came.

And so I squinted harder at these people, determined in my time with them to try and uncover what lay below their glib surface of apparent contentment. If they really were happy, what could they possibly be so happy about?

CHAPTER TWO

REVOLUTION

Oh, Mother is calling for souls to come
Into the waters of healing love
Gently she's calling;
Oh, will you hear,
Cast off all doubting,
And gather near.

—"*Oh, Mother Is Calling*"

The fiery-eyed founder of Shakerism, a woman whose first followers believed was literally the Second Coming of Christ, never set foot on the holy land of Sabbathday Lake. She traveled months aboard a condemned boat from Liverpool harbor to New York harbor, traveled upriver to build the first Shaker community in the forest near Albany, and later spent two years on New England roads, walking from village to village to spread the new gospel. Yet she never traveled to the place later known as "the least of Mother's children in the East," Sabbathday Lake, founded in 1794, just ten years after her death.

The least has now become the last. Today all other Shaker

communities have petrified into museums, where time stands still. Ghosts fill the meetinghouses where Mother Ann Lee's children of yore once danced. Only Sabbathday Lake village stands, at the crest of a gently sloping hill, along a rural highway that looks like any other, in the northeast corner of a country that has all but forgotten the passion of colonial religious conviction that founded these United States.

Sabbathday Lake remembers. The memory of that holy woman, who Shakers now believe was no more than human but no less than a vessel of pure Spirit, lives on in the echoing hallways and billowing gardens, the lined faces of believers and the fire of faith that lights their eyes.

Now, at the last Shaker haven on earth, the work of the day awaits. I grab a dish towel and begin to wipe the dishes, freshly washed from breakfast. I watch as the long, productive day ticks by with the same precision as when Ann Lee scheduled her first converts' labors.

Sister June crosses the street to the Shaker library, where she will carefully catalog Shaker archives and source documents. Brother Arnold, the Shaker community historian, also staffs the library as a research assistant, writer, and printer. Brother Alistair cleans out some cluttered old built-ins, then hurries to his workshop to sew a few trinkets for sale at the Shaker shop.

Sisters Frances and Marie no sooner wash the breakfast things than they begin preparation of the noonday dinner, the Shakers' main meal. They use produce from their garden in summer, canned fruits and vegetables from their stores in winter. Then, Sister Frances turns from domesticity to administration, working in the Shaker office on correspondence, accounting, and trustee duties. Outside, Brother Wayne tends the farm's animals and weeds the vegetable garden.

The sisters and brothers, in blue jeans or long skirts, emerge from the barns and offices and workrooms at midday to come together again for a brief prayer service and then dinner. Afternoons, their specialized work continues. Evenings, except when lawns need mowing or gardens need tending, become havens for relaxation, study, quietude, prayer.

"We feel that we are, hopefully, forming a heaven on earth today," said Sister Frances, explaining to me the purpose of the precise daily schedule. "By the way we live, by the way we conduct ourselves, hopefully our lives will show other people"—but here she stopped, and apologized in her quiet, steady voice. "We're human beings," she admitted, "and even though we try to live the life of Jesus, the life of Christ, we don't always succeed in that.

"But we feel that while there is certainly a spiritual realm, known as heaven, that we are forming that heaven while we're still on earth. And hopefully, other people may see that and find hope in it."

Now that the family has shrunk back to just eight members, many buildings at Sabbathday Lake have been razed. Yet still there is a great deal of room for individuality. Each Shaker has her or his own room in the dwellinghouse. The rooms, which in populous times housed two or three each, now shelter the privacy of one. Except for Wednesday evenings and Sunday mornings, when the community worships together, members retreat after supper for private prayer, meditating, and required religious reading in their rooms.

Then, late into the slowly settling Maine evening, lights glow from the rooms in the dwellinghouse where the children of Mother Ann Lee sew or carve, write or doze, read or dream. One light clicks off just past sunset; others burn into the night sky well after the air has grown thin and cold. Deep into the night they sleep, alone, with their God, in rooms where hundreds have lived and died for Shakerism and where no one knows how the next century will tred upon their old, creaky floorboards.

Shakerism began with the ordinary birth of a woman who would become an extraordinary religious leader. She had been born on a day when time undergoes eclipse: Leap Day, February 29, 1736. Soot from nearby textile mills and smoky factories thickened the air of Toad Lane, a crowded urban piling of row-houses in Manchester, England, where an infant named Ann Lees (later shortened to Lee) was baptized, six years later, on June 1, 1742.

Ann Lee was the second born to a poor blacksmith and his God-fearing wife. Cramped together in one bedroom, the Lees somehow managed to beget six more children, for a total of eight. Some say Ann never recovered from the childhood shock of witnessing her parents' late-night lovemaking, and that what appeared to her a violent act which wore down, impregnated, and eventually killed her mother, repelled her for the rest of her life.

I found, in a book given to me by Brother Arnold, the tale of a little girl who had been terrified of sex since childhood. The *1816 Testimonies*, a posthumous account of Ann Lee by her first followers, reports that in childhood Lee "had a great abhorrence of the fleshly cohabitation of the sexes." She begged her mother not to do it; her father heard of this and tried to whip her, "at which she threw herself into her mother's arms and clung around her neck to escape his strokes."

Her mother died early, leaving Ann Lee to bring up the younger children.

In an eighteenth-century England flooded with waves of puritanical righteousness, Ann Lee would have learned shame early on regarding her bodily functions, her swelling womanliness, her physical being. She may have lain awake at night, hearing her parents move and breathe to create yet another baby they could not afford to feed. Perhaps her mother, not a liberated woman of our century, passively served her husband in bed, in acts of self-sacrifice rather than pleasurable ecstasy. Like other young women of her time, Lee would have watched her mother undergo the nausea and aches, swelling and pain, primal fear and searing birth of numerous pregnancies that resulted not from choice but from wifely duty, in a society in which women had no feasible choice but to marry and procreate.

Left motherless as a young woman, Ann Lee saw that the drama between her mother and father at night had sapped her mother's energy, ravished her body, and eventually killed her.

The bold prophet who would end up quoting scripture in the streets grew up illiterate, working in her neighborhood's mills by age eight, cutting velvet, looming cotton, and shearing fur twelve hours a day. Trapped in a place where excrement ran through the streets; where factories glowered all night and day under the toil of broken women, children, and men; where the pittance of wages was squandered in pubs on the cold taste of temporary escape; Ann Lee mentally ran away.

Poring over the shelves of the Sabbathday Lake library, I rediscovered a book I had read as a divinity student. It gave a view of Ann Lee as a strange, clairvoyant person who seemed destined for a life of the spirit. "She was a very peculiar child from infancy," read the book *The Aletheia: Spirit of Truth* by Shaker Aurelia Mace. Ann Lee "often told of having visions of supernatural things."

Ann Lee turned not to gin but to the realm beyond. Living in eighteenth-century Manchester, Lee saw many religious sects trying to break away from the state religion of Anglicanism. One group, the Quakers, led by George Fox, had long been known as "Shakers" because of the way devotees' bodies shook in spiritual ecstasy. Their heads moved so fast one could not see their faces; they screeched and whirled and sang and danced to exhaustion.

Neighbors of Lee, a couple named Jane and James Wardley, founded a new sect people jeeringly called the "Shaking Quakers." Rooted in Quakerism, Shakerism shared the same unheard-of notion that God possessed both female and male characteristics, and that women and men could equally receive inspiration from that God, who worked through the individual spirit rather than collective history.

Shakers shared roots with Puritans, too, many of whom also ended up fleeing to the New World to seek religious freedom. Both stressed simplicity, hard work, and denial of the physical life in order to achieve a fuller spiritual life. Yet Puritans married and had sex and children—little as they were meant to enjoy it—while Shakers remained celibate and relied on converts for new membership. Puritans never dreamed of dancing or singing, yet Shakers relished such celebration.

Many of the sects emerging from the frustrated lower classes of England believed in the imminence of God's judgment: The world soon would come to an end, so people had better repent now. This kind of message was delivered with great fervor by the Shakers when they regularly interrupted other Christians' Sunday morning worship services to shout their apocalyptic warnings above the drone of the preacher's sermon. "Amend your lives!" Jane Wardley cried. "Repent, for the Kingdom of God is at hand!"

Joining the Wardleys at age twenty-two, Ann Lee fell to her knees with them, three times a day, and joined them in worship services in which "the Spirit" infused them. She took solace in the meditation and confession she discovered in Shakerism. She found a cause, a reason for living, a way to rise above a life of suffering. She found spiritual mentors, perhaps even parents, in the Wardleys.

I read far into many nights the tale of Ann Lee, told with great drama and piety in the stilted English of long-ago Shakers. Here, in the texts of their own hand, I found a story only partly verifiable in the world's history books. The rest was, like Shakerism itself, a matter of faith.

Shakers said Ann Lee rather preferred not to marry, but she succumbed to her father's pressure and wed, at age twenty-six, Abraham Standerin. He worked as a blacksmith, as an apprentice to her father, and the two lived in the cramped Toad Lane house with her relatives and four children of their own, all of whom died in infancy or childhood.

Shaker history makes it clear how reluctant she had been

to marry. By then, she had joined the Wardleys' Shaking Quakers; perhaps she would have wished to devote her life to prayer. But no woman had access, in the slums of Manchester, to birth control nor childbirth anesthesia, education nor professional work, the seminary nor the pulpit. Women labored in the textile mills and bore children till they died.

So Ann Lee put her illiterate "X" on the marriage license at Christ Church, bending before a fate from which only religion, years later, could save her. She then birthed and buried four children. She toiled to bring forth life, as her mother had done, only to have life taken away again. Life's unfairness? God's punishment?

Whatever sense Lee tried to make out of the loss of her innocence in the dark shared family bedroom of her childhood, the loss of her mother and then of all her own children, we know only that she looked at her life and saw lust as the root of all evil.

And if she took a look around her, she could see the consuming destruction of lust. Lust produced too many babies. Lust fueled the factories with the sweat of thousands of poor so that England's aristocracy could summer in lavish countryside mansions. Lust spent meager paychecks on another and then another glass of whiskey, blinding a man to the wife who waited, wringing her hands, at home; or a woman to the hungry waif who wailed on her lap.

Lust meant, for Lee, not just sexual craving but over-indulgence in earthly life. Non-Shakers raise eyebrows of disbelief at the celibacy Lee chose for herself and her followers, yet we nod approvingly at the temperance Shakers practice with money, alcohol, clothing, and ornamentation. Americans love the functional simplicity of a Shaker dresser or chair, but we must know that the clean severity of its lines is carved from the same self-control as Shaker celibacy.

Ann Lee believed that "if you had sexual intercourse, you were going to hell," declared feminist theologian Marjorie Procter-Smith, in a book I had read in the months of research before coming to Sabbathday Lake. Procter-Smith thought that Ann Lee built a religion directly related to her horror of sex: "Lee suffered alienation from and bondage to her own body, in particular its sexuality and the terror of giving birth," she said. And Lee used religion to flee the kind of drudgery few women then escaped.

Celibacy got Lee out of her covenant with housewifery—a life that would have left her overshadowed by the man who legally owned her; eclipsed as a mediocre, second-class citizen with no civil rights; drained by the everyday caretaking of an alcoholic husband and perhaps more children. Celibacy gave her, literally, her freedom, her birth control, her bodily autonomy, her independence.

And only by the dictate of the Lord could she have managed this.

As in youth, when not dulling alcohol but mystical visions lifted her from the surrounding stench of poverty, during her adult religious leadership Lee turned to the realm beyond this world for solutions. This life, one that she had known as sorrowful and straining, could not possibly be the pinnacle. There must be more, God must wish more for us. Many other people born into war, affliction, and hunger have reached the same religious conclusion, then simply waited through a lifetime for the death that would bring relief. Lee, however, decided that salvation, heaven on earth, could be possible in the here and now.

Ann Lee was not the only one in her family drawn to the Shakers: Her father, her husband, and at least two of her brothers joined the nascent sect. She was the one, however, who rose slowly to towering strength within the group. She prayed all night, she sweated and toiled to hear God's word, she had nightmares of her own sinfulness and visions of the mercy of God. She blasted others' Sunday services. When thrown into the Manchester jail for disturbing the peace, she preached from her prison cell.

"They put me in a stone prison," Ann Lee later told her

first followers, "and there kept me fourteen days, where I could not straiten myself. The door was never opened through the whole time. . . . I had nothing to eat nor drink."

Ann Lee described something that sounded to me like seizures—fits of the spirit that manifested in the body. "I suffered great persecution, in England, on account of my faith. Sometimes the power of God operated so mightily upon me, that numbers would try to hold me still; but the more they tried to withstand the power of God, the more I was operated upon," she marveled.

At thirty-four Ann Lee saw God, from the tiny solitary confinement cell in which she had been placed, without light or food or room to stand up, by English officials who hoped she would learn her lesson at last. When she stumbled forth two weeks later, miraculously still alive, she declared that she now knew "the depth of man's loss, what it was, and the way of redemption." Humanity, believed Lee, had lost its spiritual union with God by wallowing in earthly lust. And she seemed certain that only through the purity of Shakerism could redemption occur.

Shaker members spilled the sins of their souls to one another openly during religious meetings, and mere women—especially Jane Wardley—preached to the congregation about the new era soon to come.

That era, the Shakers dared to say, would begin when God sent a second child to earth, one who would reveal the half of God utterly unknown to humankind. Christ would come again, in the form of a woman.

That woman would be Ann Lee.

The vision Ann Lee had in her solitary jail cell in Manchester showed her that the spirit of Christ lived in her. She was the female embodiment of God come to earth. Although she never called herself the Daughter of God nor the Savior, she made remarkable claims: "I feel the blood of Christ running through my soul and body! . . . It is not I that speak. It is Christ who dwells in me."

The first generations of believers thought Ann Lee literally the Second Coming of Christ; hence their previous name, The United Society of Believers in Christ's Second Appearance. To them, she loomed large: "of a strong constitution, rather exceeding the ordinary size of women," with a "light complexion, blue eyes, light chestnut brown hair." The female body of Christ was "majestic." She "commanded the respect" of everyone around her. Early Shakers claimed that her eyes could pierce through to one's very soul to read all the secret passions and hidden sins festering there. What an intimidating presence, I thought as I read these accounts. I probably would either obey or flee a woman of such power.

A second vision, received when she was thirty-eight, convinced Lee that she must bring the new faith to the New World. She saw "a vision of America" as "a large tree, every leaf of which shone with such brightness as made it appear like a burning torch, representing the Church of Christ which will yet be established in this land," recalled Lee's Shaker successor, James Whittaker, in an 1859 compendium of Shaker beliefs.

Ann Lee felt so compelled by God that she boarded a condemned ship, whose wages the Shakers barely could afford, to travel three months on the chance she might get there alive.

"God would not condemn it while we are on it," she boldly informed Brother John Hocknell. So, huddled aboard the *Snow Maria* for months of half-rotted food, no cabin ventilation nor toilet facilities, Lee and a straggle of eight followers prayed their way across the ocean. Their feverish worship services and whirling dances so unnerved the crew that the captain threatened to put them all in irons, and if that did not quiet them, he would cast them into the sea.

Then one evening, the ship suddenly sprang a leak. Water gushed in faster than the crew could bail it out. "The captain turned pale as a corpse, and said they all must perish before morning, for he saw no possible means to save the ship from sinking," followers later reported.

Lee told the captain to "be of good cheer," for she had just

seen "two bright angels of God standing by the mast." The angels had promised her that "not a hair of our heads [shall] perish." The Shakers set to work alongside the crew. Soon a mighty
wave struck the ship and forced the loosened plank back into
place. The leak was stopped.

The first American Shakers docked at New York harbor on
August 6, 1774. They had to earn their bread and save for the
haven they would build, out beyond the earthly dangers of the
city. So they scattered, each seeking manual or domestic labor.
Ann Lee and her husband, who had converted to Shakerism
and grudgingly accepted her pledge of celibacy, took positions
in the home and blacksmith shop of a local family.

The Shaker leader would not take a backseat, even on unknown roads. Having just landed on American soil, Lee marched
her gangly group up the middle of Pearl Street, New York, to a
particular house. The audacious woman, according to F. W.
Evans's 1871 book, *Shaker Communism*, called its owner, Mistress
Cunningham, by name, and informed her that "I am commis-
sioned of the Almighty God to preach the everlasting Gospel
to America, and an Angel commanded me to come to this
house, and to make a home for me and my people." I noticed
the parallel to Jesus' arrival into Jerusalem for his last Passover:
He sent a scout ahead to a particular house, claiming that God
wished him to lodge there.

Amid the brewing storm of the Revolutionary War, the
Shakers later took refuge on a farm northwest of Albany. They
called the settlement by its Native American name, Niskeyuna,
and set about to clear the land, raise crops, and await converts.
Ann Lee's husband, Abraham Standerin, did not come with her.
He had, by then, reportedly turned to alcohol, fallen ill, and
been nursed through a prolonged sickness in New York by Lee
that he repaid only with what Shakers termed *very ungodly* behavior. His threats and sexual intimidation finally forced an end
to their marriage.

Standerin created a scandal that still mocks the foundation
upon which Shakerism stands. I read the horrified words of early

believers: "At length, he brought a lewd woman into the house to her," wrote Shakers Calvin Green and Seth Y. Wells in *A Summary View of the Millennial Church* in 1823. Standerin "declared that, unless she would consent to live in sexual cohabitation with him, he would take that woman for his wife. . . . He soon went off with the woman."

Shakers presented the marriage of Ann Lee to Abraham Standerin as a sort of dichotomy of two worlds: she of spirit, he of flesh. Poor old Abraham just had no stamina for the sacred life. The figure of Standerin became a sort of symbol for the world left behind, the reluctant families and the protesting spouses, who had big hearts but little self-control. He looked a lot like me and you: We glance with interest at the spirit life but then remain in the world.

Now forty years old, Ann Lee worked long hours with her Shaker brothers building cabins with crude tools, clearing and draining the land, and planting crops. "The place being then in a wilderness state," says *A Summary View*, "they began, with indefatigable zeal and industry [to build a retreat] where they could enjoy their faith in peace, amid the tumults of the war in which the country was then involved."

Ann Lee made strong impressions on people in the colonies. How could she not? Now dwelling in a rural area next door to some of the reportedly most fierce Indians, Lee "put on her bonnet" and went to call upon them. She sat down to smoke the peace pipe with them, asked their advice about growing crops, and ever after was nicknamed the Good Woman by New York's Mahican tribe. Others thought that, because she claimed pacifism and refused to allow her community to take up arms in the Revolutionary War, she may be a British spy. Still other colonists, who saw or heard of this strange, prophetic woman whose people whirled and howled, became convinced she was a witch.

The Shakers waited in frustrated anticipation for several years, and then, finally, converts began to come. I wondered what would bring colonists, so suspicious of the Shakers, to their strange new religious community—first in straggles, then "flocking like doves" as Mother Ann Lee had predicted. A biography of Ann Lee by Nardi Reeder Campion explained that it was people who were "discouraged by the grimness of frontier life, frightened by the wreckage and havoc of war, guilt-ridden by feelings of sin, all were looking for the same thing: escape from a hard life. They wanted absolution for their sins and assurance of a better life in the next world."

All rose or fell to one level, to become equals. They pooled their goods to become of one class, and they lived as celibates to become one family.

Members relinquished rights to private ownership when they became convenanted Shakers, so neither rich nor poor existed. Men were stripped of their role as autocrat of home and family and their right to own money, goods, property—and women. As theologian Susan Setta put it, Shakers "reduced the status of men to the status of women" in order to achieve social equality.

Shakers lobbied all along for animal rights, medical freedom, labor rights, temperance, and sexual and racial equality. They bought African slaves in order to free them. Shakers Anna White and Leila S. Taylor boasted in 1904 that the world was only just now catching up with progressive Shakerism. The world was "beginning to ring with the reverberations of the Divine Messages" that Shakerism had offered since the dawn of their spiritual revolution in America. And the message resounded across the land: "If you will take up your crosses against the work of generation," as Ann Lee said, "and follow Christ in the regeneration, God will cleanse you of all unrighteousness."

Shakerism may have flourished then and survived till now for no reason other than the dynamic character of Ann Lee herself. After all, Shakerism fizzled out in England after Mother Ann left that country. She governed in America with such strength that, after her death at age forty-eight, not one but two Shakers, Lucy Wright and Joseph Meacham, ended up replacing her as head. And half a century later a spiritual revival inflamed thousands of Shakers now spread across America, who had visions of their deceased leader and received prophecies and artistic "gifts" from Lee.

People who met Ann Lee did not soon forget the encounter. In an 1827 edition of the *Testimonies*, I found an account by a young woman named Thankful Barce, who came to visit the Shakers in 1780 and never left:

"She sat down in a chair, and I sat by her side. Her eyes were shut, and it appeared that her sense was withdrawn from the things of time. She sang very melodiously, and appeared very beautiful. . . . Her countenance appeared bright and shining, like an angel of glory . . . singing praises to God. As I sat by the side of her, one of her hands, while in motion, frequently touched my arm; and at every touch of her hand, I instantly felt the power of God run through my whole body. . . . Could I then dispute the work of God in this woman? Nay, in no wise," she said.

From the shelves of the Sabbathday Lake library, where I read in the afternoons and borrowed books till next morning, echoed the voices of many Shakers past who claimed the mystical power of Ann Lee. Valentine Rathbun, who joined and later left, claimed that they viewed Lee literally as the biblical woman foretold in Revelations Chapter 7, who was clothed with the sun, with the moon under her feet, and on her head a crown of twelve stars. She was "the mother of all elect," Rathbun wrote.

"No blessing can come to any person, but only by and through her," he asserted. These claims were no small matter: They appeared to be blasphemy in the eyes of many. Shakers upheld Ann Lee as "the queen of heaven, Christ's wife"; she had "the fullness of the God head."

People all around her felt the power of Lee's conviction, whether or not they agreed with her zeal. Ann Lee smashed social hierarchies to the ground, equating former slave with former landowner, teacher with laborer. She stripped members of their money and possessions, chopped off their hair and dressed them in the most modest clothes. She toppled the institutions upon which Western civilization had been built: sexism, racism, capitalism, nationalism, elitism. Yet Lee's mandates came from God above, in a new country claiming religious freedom. Perhaps she retained just enough orthodox Christianity, reading from scripture and praying to the same God and Jesus as did her neighbors, to escape a national ban on her new religion. Perhaps just enough people saw the merit in her efforts toward personal piety and universal salvation to save her from being burned at the stake.

Just ten years after her arrival in what she considered "the promised land," Lee died. Shaker historians Edward Deming and Faith Andrews wrote in their 1975 book, *Fruits of the Shaker Tree of Life*, that her death was "shrouded in mystery" because later, when her remains were disinterred and moved to a Shaker cemetery, it was discovered that her skull had been fractured. Indeed, she had received many harsh beatings in the few years preceding her death, when on a missionary tour throughout New England. She may have died due to injuries sustained from mob violence. According to Shaker legend, the death of her younger, beloved brother, William Lee (who had become a devout Shaker) broke her heart earlier that year.

She was forty-eight, tired, and sad. According to the *Testimonies*, she knew of her death two months before it happened, and spent the time preparing her followers for the inevitable day. When she died, on September 8, 1784, she told the faithful who surrounded her deathbed that she saw her dear brother William "coming, in a golden chariot, to take me home." Having lived a life of controversy and strife, Ann Lee died peacefully and without struggle, believing she had arrived in her lifelong climb toward heaven.

Psychologists may say that Lee turned her pathology into theology: sexual frigidity becomes holy chastity, enforced shame becomes open confession, strict discipline becomes compulsive cleanliness, sexist persecution becomes radical egalitarianism, the death of her own family becomes the creation of the religious family.

The devout Shaker may say that Lee, from the depths of pain her earthly life had brought, opened her heart so wide to God that the healing of the Father-Mother's wisdom rushed in. Lee had not the merit of today's self-help books nor therapy, yet her revolutionary visions resolved her grief and laid the framework for a faith that would last for centuries to come. As Ann Lee said, "Live together, every day, as though it was the last day you had to live in this world."

Today's Shakers appear moderate next to the fervid whirling and stern rules of yesterday's believers. Cleanliness, still a respected value, has become part of the rhythm of daily life rather than a shackle imposed on corrupted earthly flesh. Dance worship, once done in a feverish frenzy that reflected, perhaps, both the charisma of Ann Lee and the sexual energy of the chaste early Shakers, has been reduced to a few placid hand gestures and languid footsteps. Harsh attitudes toward sinfulness and confession have softened. Most of all, the image of the Shaker God appears far less radical than before.

Time has tempered the view of Ann Lee as the literal Second Savior. "Some of the early Shakers," admitted Sister Frances, "did look upon Ann Lee as literally the Second Coming of Christ, and I think that's because of the condition of the world that they were living in at that time. It was a very bleak existence; and when this charismatic, very spiritual, very Christlike woman comes along, I can see why some of them did indeed think she might be the Second Christ."

Shakers seem to have changed their minds about the divinity of Ann Lee. "There was a real transformation from early Shaker writings to the later Shaker writings," explained Susan Setta, author of *Unspoken Worlds: Women's Religious Lives*. "In the early biographies, Ann Lee calms a storm at sea, and saves everybody on board, just like Jesus. She can heal; she looks into your eyes and she can see into your very soul. [Shakers] say, 'As Jesus was the Son so Ann is the Daughter.'"

A hundred years later, however, Shakers had changed their tune, saying no one ever really thought she was "Ann Christ."

"I think as time went on, they just had difficulty with that concept, and so they watered it down," Setta concluded. If early Shakers had not seen Lee as the literal Second Coming of Christ, they would not have joined up with this millennial community. They sought a here-and-now savior and paradise.

As Shakerism continued to develop in the early twentieth century, Sabbathday Lake Sister Aurelia Mace described a more universal view of the Christ—one that far surpassed Ann Lee. I sat in the old Sabbathday Lake schoolhouse-turned-library and read the journal, written by her own hand: "To us God is Father *and* Mother and has been from the beginning."

"Jesus was an inspired man," Mace wrote. "Ann Lee was an inspired woman." Yet "inasmuch as Jesus became the Christ, so may all be in possession of the same spirit."

Jesus was no more God's sacred child than was Ann Lee. Blasphemy? Perhaps it rings so to some Christians. Mace, in fact, dared to claim that the Christ-Spirit had come to earth not once or twice but that "Christ has appeared in the thousands."

Twentieth-century Sister Mildred Barker, who died at Sabbathday Lake not many years before my visit there, extended the image of the universal Christ: "The spirit of Christ, which is nothing more esoteric than a spirit of truth, has entered the earth through the lives of such charismatics as Plato and Buddha as well." So the Christ-Spirit, first thought to be embodied only within the historical lives of Jesus the Son and Ann the Daughter, eventually took on a more abstract quality. What Ann Lee lived still stood at the foundation of Shakerism, but she was no longer seen as savior. Rather, she was a teacher of beautiful spirit and great courage, who led the way to a goal that all Shakers could reasonably hope to achieve.

Today, the woman who governs the last Shaker heaven on earth, gentle Sister Frances, seems to have little in common with her Mother Ann Lee. Ann Lee was described as maternal yet quite severe, authoritative. Early Shakers remembered how she would "wring noses" to grab the attention of spiritual wayfarers. In contrast, I saw in Sister Frances a real warmth with people, an acceptance of them, no matter who they were. And she seemed comfortable with the world, neither frightened nor repulsed by it.

Having read intimidating biographies of Ann Lee, I sat face-to-face with the woman who now embodies all the authority of the Shaker gospel, and I asked her straight out: "Are you, in many ways, the opposite of Ann Lee?"

The eldress bent her head sideways a bit, and clasped her hands together. "Mother Ann," she began, "lived in a very difficult time in the world, when everybody was looking on another person with somewhat suspicious feelings." She referred to past witch-hunts of Shakers, when the faith she held dear had been held up to scorn and scrutiny. Now, she told me, the situation was reversed. Now it was the world—a myriad of people from it—who knocked upon her door, seeking to share a spirituality they could not find elsewhere.

"As we have progressed along in our sacred journey, we very literally keep in mind always," Sister Frances nodded to herself, "that we have to greet every one who comes to us as though he or she or it could be the Christ. And I truly try to remember that. Whoever comes to me, whoever comes to us, I try—and that is a teaching of Shakerism that Mother Ann certainly portrayed, too. She welcomed everyone who came to her." Sister Frances told me a story in which Ann Lee gave up her own bed, not once but often, to visitors who filled the first Shaker community beyond capacity.

"She had more of an in-depth relationship with them than I do with many people who just come in and leave again. So she must have had a very warm, welcoming, charismatic manner.

"And she could be very stern," Sister Frances admitted. "She was dealing with very difficult times. And people were really looking up to her. I can understand."

Ann Lee clearly stated her position, according to the *Testimonies*: "While the Shakers were living in Harvard, a wild rumor began to spread that the world was coming to an end. Many people sought Mother's help. Over and over she told them she was not concerned with the end of the world. 'I am only concerned,' Mother Ann said firmly, 'with the end of worldliness.' "

The second day with the Shakers, I awoke with a start at 5:30, thinking it much later. Rubbing my head, I scrambled to the bathroom, bumping into things along the way. I had written far too late into the night before. My sleep again was thick with dreams of the Shakers, and now I worried that I might be late for our appointed meeting time.

Soon I realized my mistake, and tried to doze again for half an hour to store up energy for the day, but it was no use. I was too excited and nervous. I tossed and turned, then jumped up again to grab a half cup of decaf and step into the shower.

At dawn, as my rental car grumbled onto the gravel of the Shaker farm driveway, I saw that some workmen had begun to gather. Contractors had been here two years already, and several more years' refurbishing still awaited them. A couple of men perched atop the museum building next door to the library, and one more scaled the scaffolding against the brick dwellinghouse, their paintbrushes slowly stroking fresh white over old. Other men chipped away old, crumbling foundation cement and shored it up with new.

Landon, the German shepherd, lumbered toward me as I approached the front door. He looked at me sideways a bit, then approached to nuzzle my hand with his nose. Later I learned that this was some sort of triumph, as the Shaker dog usually barked viciously even at "his own."

Lenny Brooks, longtime director of the Sabbathday Lake community and museum, once again answered my bell at the front door. He wore tan chinos, a plaid button-down, and a certain air of formality, nodding one diagonal nod at me when I greeted him, "Good morning, Mr. Brooks."

"Right this way," he offered, and led me to the "prayer room," a sort of formal parlor with assorted chairs surrounding a woodstove, where I had waited yesterday to meet my fate.

"I'll go and see what's to be done with you," he clipped in an efficient voice, and off he went, his round belly bobbing a bit below the plaid shirt as he walked.

I sat down, folded my hands, and looked about with some impatience. After all, I had already explored this room, examined the wood rocking chairs (not Shaker), the worn tweed sofa, the carved walnut upright piano, and the Shaker drawings and prayers framed on the walls. My hurried Western self wanted to get on with it, to hurl myself into the next bit of life, to learn what was to be learned and do what was to be done.

My hands clasped and reclasped, not for too long, then Sister June came shuffling into the room. She walked as though she were wearing slippers. We told each other, "Good morning!" with exclamation points, and her face beamed as though she wanted for nothing at all in this world.

We climbed down the sisters' stairs together and went into the "waiting room," a small room lined with a couple of benches where sisters and any other assorted women must apportion themselves before all meals. We two sat and exchanged small-talk about how we slept, how the weather seemed today, and what schedule awaited us.

"Do you work in the library every day?" I asked her.

"Oh, no," she replied, her voice lilting with carefree musicality. "Sometimes I work over there, and other times I just go wherever I'm needed." I got the feeling that this woman would be just as happy scrubbing a toilet as filing her beloved library catalog cards.

A bell rang somewhere, and Sister June and I shuffled over the linoleum floor down the hall toward the dining room. We passed by jackets and windbreakers hanging from hooks along the wall. She opened the door and we entered, the last to arrive for breakfast.

The sisters waited at their table, and the brothers at the other. Everyone stood with hands resting upon the top of the chair-backs, and then, once we stragglers arrived, all sat down in unison.

I noticed that they eat in this unified way, waiting till all have finished before clearing; and pray this way, reciting psalms with one chordal voice. The sheer civility of this struck me. I, on the other hand, had not sat down to a meal since my first baby was born.

I fed the children as I ran. For the few moments when they sat relatively still and picked at their four food groups with their toddler forks, I rushed to wash the pots, pack tomorrow's lunches, return telephone calls, spoonfeed the baby. My dinner consisted of bites shoved into my mouth as I scurried about.

Perhaps the Shaker system would not work in a home with small children, yet something about it seemed so convivial. One chatted with one's tablemates, and now and then questions and answers got flung across from the women's to the men's tables, especially between Eldress Frances and Elder Arnold. And one watched surreptitiously for the well-being of one's dining partners, passing homemade pickles, offering butter, and then waiting quietly while the others finished.

Everyone cleaned his or her plate. Should this have surprised me, when I knew of Mother Ann's admonitions against waste? Yet the manner was so unlike that of most Americans, who heap on what looks good and dump the remainder into the garbage disposal after every meal. The Shakers serve themselves, buffet-style, and then clean their plates ("Shaker your plate") so that nary a crumb remains. This makes cleanup easier, too, as the step of scraping can be avoided. And everyone appreciates the chore of cleanup, for everyone helps. Again, in unison, all rise and clear the table, stack the plates, fill the washtub, and wrap the leftovers.

This morning there were scrambled eggs and sausage for the brothers, who dug in their forks with gusto, and cold cereal with bananas for the sisters, who wished to meter their cholesterol levels.

For just an instant Sister Frances looked longingly over at the eggs; then she sighed at her raisin bran and sliced her banana with resolve. Sister Marie poured milk over her cereal and dipped in her spoon with methodical purpose. Sister June, beside me, bent over her bowl, her back slightly hunched, and nibbled a child's portion of flakes.

Not knowing what to expect for the day, I gobbled up more than I usually do, in case I ended up digging for fence posts or hand scrubbing the floors. Shakers worked hard, I had read in all the books, and I was prepared to pitch in for all I was worth.

All rose together after the morning meal, and we carried and stacked the dishes. Just as I started to fill up the sink with suds, Sister Frances informed me that "We'll do that later. Right now we pray, right after we clear the table."

Again we stood at the backs of our chairs, and now red Psalter books had appeared where our plates used to be.

Together we sat, together we opened to the same page. The strong voice of the eldress rang out the first couplet, and the rest read together the next, and so on, one and then all, one and then all. The focus of attention was here and now, on the prayer, on the words.

I was used to seeing men snooze in church, and women balance their checkbooks, and children play with toy cars they smuggled in. These people seemed to be here because they wanted to be. Yet they did this every day, by prescription. How could they honestly *want* to do this each and every morning?

Sister Frances read from Numbers in the Hebrew Bible, then Luke in the Christian Bible. She gave a prayerful sort of sermon, spontaneous, yet I would soon learn that this woman often speaks in free verse. When she prays, poetry spills forth. It sounds powerful, pure, as in the trembling style of Martin Luther King, Jr., yet it draws from specific Shaker teachings on gratitude, humility, love.

"We have so much to be grateful for, perhaps more so than any other group in this land," she said. "The legacy handed down to us, through the hard work of many, many Believers who came before us, has left us this beautiful farm and all the material blessings that surround us. May we ever strive to be worthy of this heritage, of this Chosen Land."

She prayed for those who have no food or shelter; and even this sheltered, rural Shaker sister knew that of which she spoke: She had just returned from a visit to a community in urban Philadelphia, where the group drove an hour each way through gang-ridden slums to get to church.

"You know, Sister," she told me she had confided to the sixty-nine-year-old white woman who, with her black husband of fifty years, had founded their society on principles of Christian love and racial integration, "you really shouldn't drive through these city streets alone at night."

"What do you mean?" replied the woman. "I am never *alone*."

"Now that," said Sister Frances, "is faith."

Today the Shaker offices would be moved from one building to another, so a large yellow truck and crew arrived right in the middle of prayers. The dogs, who had been resting quietly at the brothers' feet, leapt up and began barking so loud Sister Marie clapped her hands over her ears. Brother Wayne marched Landon right out of the dining room, and Brother Arnold tried to clamp shut Jason's drooling mouth.

As soon as Brother Arnold turned back to his prayer, the dog broke out barking again. Clenching his jaw and fists but moving in slow control, Brother Arnold rose and tried to pull the dog toward the door.

"Jason, I am very upset with you," he muttered. "Get over here, right now." He sounded just like me when my children disobey, only my voice usually gets several decibels louder.

The dog refused to budge.

Brother Arnold lunged for him, so Jason burrowed deep under the table, among the chair legs, and hunched down. He tried to look remorseful.

The others laughed, but later they scolded the dogs for interrupting their morning prayer.

Now Sister Frances resumed her sermon, trying to pull together the threads of her thoughts into a conclusion. Next came special intentions, prayers for loved ones who were in need of physical healing or spiritual guidance, and the list was long. She read from a typewritten, alphabetized list in orderly Shaker fashion. Then she threw in "and for all those who have asked us to remember them in our prayers," just to be sure no one got missed.

She looked down at her placemat and thumped her forehead. "Think, think, think," she commanded herself. She looked over at Brother Arnold, next table over, and joked about how difficult it was to concentrate amid the noise of contractors and movers and feisty dogs.

Then she nodded to herself, and began to sing a Shaker song. All voices joined together as they directed themselves to "More Love, More Love":

> If you cannot love one another in daily communion,
> How can you love God whom you have not seen?
> More love, more love,
>   the heavens are calling,
>   the angels are blessing,
> Oh, Zion, more love.
> If you love one another, then God dwelleth in you,
> ... For true love is God.

After morning prayers, the brothers filled their milk bottles and went off to feed the baby lambs, as usual. The sisters hurried over to direct the moving crew.

The office move touched Sister Frances deep in her memory, for she had grown up as a child in the same building they were now clearing out for work space. She had sewn school dresses, studied Sunday school lessons, and formed deep friendships with other young women and several older caretakers, in the building now sterilized for corporate use.

The community had reached the decision together because this would shield them from growing intrusion from the world.

Telephones ringing all day, doorbells demanding attention, laborers seeking direction, and library researchers seeking information, all would now go next door. The Shakers' private life could remain more private during prayer, meal, and rest times, and meanwhile, next door, the business of the day could bustle away at an increasing pace.

Still, Sister Frances's eyes glistened as she talked about boxing up old books and dishes, carting away sofas and crates of the past. Something from her tradition had been relinquished today.

The boundary between utopia and world had, in fact, crept gradually inward at Sabbathday Lake. In the 1960s, members there began to accept converts who did not, according to old Shaker law, meet criteria necessary to become official, covenanted Shakers. This was a break from tradition that Sabbathday Lake sisters and brothers gladly made. "Mother Ann said the door must always remain open," Sister Frances told the local Maine newspaper, and so they did.

Later, the land itself began to give way. The vast acreage owned by the Shakers—the history books cite 1,900 acres, while some recent surveying has led the brothers to believe the number to be closer to 1,700—has, for the most part, been leased out to orchard growers and lumberjacks. And, down the sloping hills by the shore of Sabbathday Lake itself, "We have a rather interesting arrangement with some local families," Sister Frances told me. "We lease the land to them, but they own their own cottages. They built them with the understanding that, if we should ever sell out (which we never will!), they will have the first rights to buy that land."

Now, the boundaries within the shrunken Shaker Village itself had begun to loosen and shift. Growing attention from the public, as well as ongoing refurbishing and research projects, had forced the Shakers for the first time to create an entire building dedicated to interacting with the world.

Meanwhile, the annual summer season soon would begin.

From Memorial Day to Columbus Day, onlookers from the world would stroll about the grounds every day, guided by volunteers, through many of the family's barns and workshops.

Also, the Shakers recently had hosted a large musical entourage from Boston, who recorded dozens of their sacred songs onto compact disc. The group used some of the community space for resting and tea drinking. They recorded in the actual meetinghouse where Shakers have for more than two centuries worshiped and sung their songs. That sacred building now sits right at the edge of an increasingly busy, noisy rural highway. So the operatic group recorded late into the night for several weeks, keeping a watchman outside to warn of oncoming trucks and keeping Brother Arnold up till the wee hours to lock up behind them.

Now, this summer the Shakers would host artists of a different type—ten visual artists from around the world planned to come and stay three months, living among the Shakers, taking breakfast and noon dinner with them, and working all morning in the garden and around the farm, in exchange for afternoons off to paint, sculpt, and photograph. Living in such intimacy with the Shakers, their artistic coordinator hoped, would surely result in some influence upon their art. Still, in what worldly ways would they influence the spiritual people they would leave behind in autumn?

The sheer number of people milling about the place, even now in the off-season, tingled the hairs on the back of my neck. And I was even one of them! I, after all, though permitted to eat scrambled eggs with the group and peel parsnips in the kitchen, was an intruder, too.

"You must feel you live under a microscope, no? with so many people milling about all summer," I asked Brother Arnold, as we walked the gravel path alongside the trustees' house.

"Well, it's not really that bad," he replied.

I was learning quickly that if one asked Brother Arnold, one would get the straight stuff.

"After all, it's not as though I wear some elaborate uniform or something," he glanced down at his blue jeans and gym shoes. "So how do they know I'm a brother? I could be a painter, or anybody else. I just go on about my business. And thank God for the volunteers who take them around—I don't think I would have the patience to do that."

Later I noticed Brother Alistair smiling and talking with a couple in their sixties who had stopped by, perhaps hoping to get an off-season tour.

Maybe they saw the big brown sign on the Maine turnpike at Exit 11: SHAKER VILLAGE. How would I feel if my home were announced to all who passed on the highway, and became open to the scrutiny of eyes both sympathetic and hostile?

"Oh, there'll be reports now," joked Sister Frances about the moving truck that lugged boxes from one building to the next, "that we're finally selling out. The phones will be ringing off the hook."

As in the days of the earliest believers, still the Shakers struggle to balance between being in the world and keeping worldliness at bay. For me, on the farm at Sabbathday Lake, the hysteria of the world seemed far, far away. Time stood still, when I found myself sweeping the kitchen floor in the Shaker home. Although Ann Lee never actually swept this floor, and it was now covered with linoleum, still I knew I was in a place where work was worship. The walls were painted a cheerful, lemon yellow, and hooks from the wall combined with built-in cabinets to remind me of the heritage that underpinned the microwave and dishwasher of today.

And so I swept, in long, even strokes, knowing full well that if Ann Lee were here she would look at me cross-eyed. Even at my best I could not hope ever to live up to her standards, for housecleaning nor for spiritual purity. Yet the Shakers had changed, and maybe the benefit of letting in more of the world had been tolerance. For when the sisters saw my effort at sweeping, they smiled instantly, and I knew that anything I did with genuine love in my heart was good enough for them.

CHAPTER THREE

WITCHCRAFT

At Manchester, in England,
This blessed fire began,
And like a flame in stubble,
From house to house it ran:
A few at first received it,
And did their lusts forsake;
And soon their inward power
Brought on a mighty shake.

The rulers cried, "Delusion!
Who can these Shakers be?
Are these wild fanatics,
Bewitched by Ann Lee?
We'll stop this noise and shaking,
It never shall prevail;
We'll seize the grand deceiver,
And thrust her into jail."

—*"Mother"*

Twilight creeps in quietly at Sabbathday Lake. In the distance a sheep bleats, raising high its head to break the hush in the barn. No one answers its pleas. Lights blink on in the dwellinghouse; sisters and brothers move slowly now, pulling on nightclothes, bending toward books. Outside, I lean against my car for one last look before nightfall takes me back to the motel. The sky turns orange to blue to black, color swirling into darkness, shrouding the hills of Shaker Village in mystery.

Inside the house and up, up the double staircases, across the wide hall and in through double doors to the music room, portraits of dead Shakers glare down from the walls. It is as though I can see from here their unblinking eyes piercing the thickening night. White faces with black features; yellowed edges of photographs and daguerreotypes curl with age behind gleaming glass frames that flash the last rays of light across an empty room, across the road from where I stand watching.

Their mouths purse in stern lines of the determined lives they led. Their eyes shout the single goal toward which they strove all their days so long hence. These are the faces of believers once branded witches and traitors, spies and drunks. These Shakers of the past clung fiercely to their faith, and baked their bread each day, and cried out to their God each night, in years and centuries of steadfast surety in the Shaker way. Long since dead, they keep watch now from the walls in the upstairs music room, over the sleeping bodies of the few who carry on, to the sloping hills of the village that remains. And still their eyes burn with a power so frightening the world called it witchcraft. Shakers called it simply the Spirit God.

Shakers of the past lived regimented lives of toil, as did many colonial Americans. Only in prayer did their mysterious power break through. Days and days would tick by in strict order: sisters and brothers filing down separate staircases to silent dining rooms to begin the day with breakfast and prayer, then moving about the fields and buildings like clockwork, curing foodstuffs, crafting Shaker goods, and preparing meals, all in harmony, all in restraint.

Shakers in long, dark dresses and high-buttoned shirts kept careful control of their work, their rooms, their time. Passion and emotion surged well below the surface, not even evident.

Then, only when they danced, the Shakers would lose control.

They would begin with prayer in the meetinghouse: Bible passages, recited verses, perhaps a sermon. Then, silence would follow. From the orderly rows of bonneted women and bowing men, the sound of utter silence would fill the room until it fairly needed to burst out the shining windowpanes and spill into the New England fields beyond. Tension rose. The white walls and gleaming wood floor swelled with the energy of the room.

Then, perhaps, a Shaker brother would begin to moan unheard-of prayers in a tongue not his own. A sister would bend, groan, then twist. Stepping out from her row, eyes closed in a spiritual ecstasy all her own, she would writhe and dance, flail and hurl her body into a wildness that seemed to go on and on, seemed to take her far beyond the plain room into a realm no human has seen.

Minutes later, the sister would collapse into a skirted puddle upon the floor, humble and weak, spent. She had reached a climactic sort of union with her God. She would smile through her dazed eyes as her sisters firmly lifted her back up into the straight line of believers in prayer. Together, their voices would ring out:

> We love to dance, we love to sing,
> We love to taste the living spring,
> We love to feel our union flow,
> While round, and round, and round we go.

In early days Shakerism was shocking, and Ann Lee appeared to be a witch. Her band of believers made front-page news in Virginia five years before they even landed on American soil. A correspondent from Manchester, England, wrote to the

Virginia Gazette in 1769 that a religious sect had "lately made a great noise in that town." His eyewitness account describes religious practices that might have frightened me, too, if I had been there to see:

"They hold theirs to be the only true religion, and all others to be false. They meet constantly three times a day . . . and converse . . . until the moving of the spirit comes upon them, which is first perceived by their beginning leisurely to scratch upon their thighs or other parts of their bodies; from that the motion becomes gradually quicker, and proceeds to trembling, shaking, and screeching in the most dreadful manner; at the same time their features are not distinguishable by reason of the quick motion of their heads. . . ."

"These fits come upon them at certain intervals," reported the eighteenth-century journalist, "and during the impulse of the spirit they disturb the whole neighborhood for some considerable distance, and continue sometimes whole nights in the most shocking distortions and commotions, until their strength is quite exhausted."

One man, a Baptist minister from Pittsfield, Massachusetts, joined the Shakers and stayed one year, long enough to gather up incriminating evidence he later published in a pamphlet meant to warn the public against this sect of "witches." Long before I approached Sabbathday Lake, I had read this scathing document by Valentine Rathbun, called *Some Brief Hints of a Religious Scheme, Taught and Propagated by a Number of Europeans Living in a Place Called Nisqueunia, in the State of New York.* The pages, written in 1781, still sizzled with the heat of his anger and fear. And I read his version of the truth in the same way I read unproved claims of the Shakers: I held in my mind the possibility that what this man claimed might be true.

"When any person goes to see them," Rathbun wrote, "they all meet him with many smiles, and seeming great gladness; they bid him welcome, and directly tell him they knew of his coming yesterday. . . . [T]hey get the person some victuals; then they sit down and have a spell of singing. . . . After singing, they fall to shaking their heads in a very extraordinary manner, with their eyes shut and face up."

Rathbun reported that Ann Lee prayed in tongues, in seventy-two different languages, after which a Shaker brother "pretends to interpret the woman's prayer" to the newcomer.

Soon "they come round him, and touch him with their fingers here and there, and give him a sly cross, and in a very loving way put their hands on his head, and then begin to preach their doctrine to him."

Gathered round him they would then begin their "shaking" worship, which included whirling dances, "a spell of smoking, and sometimes great fits of laughter."

Rathbun described Shaker worship as an uncontrollable frenzy of fits. "They fall a groaning and trembling . . . one will fall prostrate on the floor; another on his knees and his head in his hands . . . some will be singing, each his own tune; some without words, in an Indian tone; some sing jig tunes; some, tunes of their own making, in an unknown mutter, which they call new tongues; some will be dancing, and others stand laughing, heartily and loudly; others will be drumming on the floor with their feet, as though a pair of drum sticks were beating on a drum head; others will be agonizing, as though they were in great pains; others jumping up and down; others fluttering over somebody, and talking to them; others will be shooing and hissing evil spirits out of the house; till the different tunes, groaning, jumping, dancing, druming [sic], laughing, talking, and fluttering, shooing and hissing, makes a perfect bedlam: This they call the worship of God."

Imagining a meetinghouse full of such thumping, groaning, and fluttering, I could see why the neighbors felt more suspicion than enthusiasm for early Shakers.

Rathbun learned that the fall of humanity's parents, Adam and Eve, came about because of carnal lust. Their copulation had literally "ruined the world." Worse, anyone now living who engaged in sex was reenacting that dreadful sin over and over again. This key Shaker concept showed the corruption of the world, and the urgent measures people must take to stop their lustful destruction of it.

Shakers alternated their treatment of converts, from "great flattery" to "great severity" in an attempt to cultivate absolute dependency in them. Their leaders exerted "a very extraordinary and uncommon power" over the followers, who had a "strange infatuation of the mind to believe all their teachers say." Rathbun saw believers collapse into twitching and convulsions, as overtaken by the body in the power of God as a machine under the newfound power of electricity. However, he did not see such Shaker power as benevolent. "The person believes it is the power of God, and therefore dare not resist, but wholly gives way to it," he warned.

Reading through Rathbun's testimony, I realized that this account came from an embittered man who had once embraced and later shunned the faith. His viewpoint must be biased. Still, much of what he said had parallel accounts in the Shakers' own literature, though of course the events were explained differently. And, whether alleged drinking and debauchery or prayerful groaning and writhing, much of what the early Shakers did must indeed have looked ominous to those who suspected the worst.

Rathbun wrote of strange religious rituals, such as one in which Shakers would lie down on the ground and trace a circle in the dirt with their finger, "double their fist at it, run away from it, come at it again, show the looks of vengeance at it, threaten it with postures, then run and jump into it, and stamp it all to pieces." He explained that these actions were meant to show the Shakers' condemnation of the world, and their wish to end its influence over their lives.

Townspeople cried out in protest against the Shakers, as their family foundation crumbled at the feet of Ann Lee. "Men and their wives have parted," wrote Rathbun; "children ran away from their parents, and society entirely broke up in neighbourhoods; it makes children deny and disown their parents, and say they are full of devils."

Many began to look upon these strange sectarians as a malevolent group. Rathbun's description of their midnight frenzies, true or false, gave local colonists something to waggle their fingers about:

"They meet together in the night, and have been heard two miles by people, in the dead of the night. . . . They run about in the woods and elsewhere, hooting and tooting like owls; some of them have stripped naked in the woods, and thought they were angels, and invisible, and could go about among men and not be seen, and have lost their clothes, and never found them again."

He concluded that the group were all witches. "I am very sensible, that the spirit which leads on this new scheme, is the spirit of witchcraft, and is the most powerful of any delusion I ever heard or read of. . . . Multitudes have fallen in with [them], and are so infatuated in their senses, that they are deprived of their reason . . . the leaders of this dreadful catastrophe . . . are ever vomiting up their sulphur; like wild fire it flies, and catches at a distance, and spreads like a plague."

Their power scared the knickers off this God-fearing Baptist man. The Shakers would inflame the world, he predicted. "It is as impossible to fully set forth the power and effects of this new religion," he warned, "as to trace the airy road of the meteor."

During the years that followed, others accused the Shakers of frenzy, corruption, and witchcraft. A Connecticut newspaper reported in 1796 of "the wild vagaries" of the first Shakers, "the drunkenness of their old first mother and foundress" and "her known lasciviousness." Early Shakers would kneel about Ann Lee, according to the account, and "kiss the hem of her garment" when she was drunk.

The newspaper report went on. I knew that Shakers denied such allegations of drunkenness and debauchery as slander, yet

I wished to see clearly both sides of the Shaker story. "The Bacchanalian dances she instituted," said the article of Ann Lee, "of naked fathers, mothers, brothers, and sisters . . . guided by the Spirit, through quags, briars, hedges and over mountains, their agonized groans, twitchings, whirling around, talking in unknown tongues, prophesying, working miracles, &c. while excessive[ly] drinking," created a "blind zeal" that was shocking to behold.

Another colonist, Benjamin West, protested in 1783 that he had been "deluded by them, to the great injury of himself and family." After his "sorrowful experience" he denounced Ann Lee as the "Strange Woman," and charged her with witchcraft and deceit. West said she enticed converts with flattery and threats. Women and men did not lodge in one bed, nor did women remain submissive to men, as in outer society. "Thus women become monsters, and men worse than infidels in this new and strange religion," he declared.

As the movement began to take hold in the burgeoning United States, a collection of those who tasted the faith, only to spit it back out, grew. Apostates claimed that Shakers used alcohol excessively, danced naked in the woods, burned books, and exorcised demons. A 1787 essay called "Some Account of the Tenets and Practice of the Religious Society called Shakers" declared that "it is notorious that they call rum the Spirit of God!!! and account it a piece of devotion to be filled therewith." A Christian man named Barton W. Stone called the Shakers wild enthusiasts who "made shipwreck of faith, and turned aside to an old woman's fables."

Two other Rathbuns also made claims against the eighteenth-century Shakers. Daniel Rathbun charged that Ann Lee "pummeled the private parts of her followers" in a frenzied act of ascetic discipline. And Reuben Rathbun, who lived with the Shakers from 1780 to 1799, later wrote that the Shaker teachings were "repugnant to the Gospel." He reported that Shaker men and women stripped naked and went into the water together. They engaged in ascetic practices so severe that men sometimes lost physical control and were subject to "involuntary evacuations" of the "seed of copulation" (ejaculation). Rathbun claimed he saw drunken brawls between Ann Lee and her brother, William Lee. He heard blasphemous language used by the founders, and witnessed "whoredom" committed by Brother James Whittaker. The Shakers dismissed all this as an outrageous attack.

Other reports claimed that the Shakers "castrated all their males, and consequently exposed their necks to the gallows; or divested of all modesty, [they] stripped and danced naked in their night meetings, blew out the candles, and went into a promiscuous debauch."

The Shakers had been in America not even a decade, and already a body of literature had condemned them as witches. "There is no witchcraft but sin!" protested Mother Ann Lee, and the group carried on. They prayed through their days and labored to cultivate their land, and they believed they were progressing toward heaven on earth. They believed they could discern helpful from harmful spiritual gifts. "I have not been following a drunken woman nor a harlot," as Sister Hannah Cogswell put it: "Can an evil tree bring forth good fruit?" For Shakers, the fruit of their work, and of their lives, has always been the measure by which they would have others judge their intentions.

And people did judge. Neighbors of the fledgling communities of Shakers formed mobs and launched attacks on the eccentric faithful. Some of these mobs were provoked by local clergy. Dwellings where Shakers lodged were stoned; houses where they worshiped were gunned; and local disciples were clubbed, caned, and beaten with "cudgels and large whips."

Once, a mob decided to check and see if Ann Lee might really be a man underneath all those modest clothes. How could a mere woman, after all, command this magnetic leadership that pulled people away from their families and their churches, into a new and strange life?

Lee, on a missionary tour in the Northeast, had set up headquarters at a Shaker residence called the Square House in Harvard, Massachusetts. It was there that a group of drunken townsmen, calling themselves the Blackguard Committee, broke in and searched the house till they found Mother Ann in one of the bedrooms.

"They immediately seized her by the feet," the report goes, "and inhumanely dragged her, feet foremost, out of the house, and threw her into a sleigh, with as little ceremony as they would the dead carcase of a beast, and drove off, committing at the same time, acts of inhumanity and indecency which even savages would be ashamed of."

The mob drove three miles on a cold winter's night to Peckham's tavern, where, upon delivery of the Shaker Mother, they were to receive from the pub's owner all the free rum they could drink. The Shaker report offers no graphic detail of the search under Mother Ann's dress, but she did lose her cap and handkerchief, and her clothes were "torn in a shameful manner." Lee, brought back in the middle of the night in her tattered clothes, "came in, singing for joy, that she was again restored to her children," reported the 1816 *Testimonies*.

In his autobiography, Shaker Issachar Bates wrote of another time when a mob in Indiana made many threats, including one that implied castration:

"A mob of 12 men came upon us on horseback with ropes to bind us, headed by John Thompson. He stepped up to me and said, Come prepare yourselves to move—Move where? said I—Out of this country, said he, for you have ruined a fine neighborhood and now we intend to fix you—Your hats are too big, we shall take off part of them, and your coats are too long, we shall take off part of them, and seeing you will have nothing to do with women, we shall fix you so that you can not perform."

The Shakers suffered much persecution for their faith, certainly, but the attacks from without seem only to have strengthened the resolve within. Ann Lee may at times even have resorted to fistfights. An 1854 account from a Petersham, Massachusetts, history book said that the Shakers had been "violently assaulted" and that "Mother Ann Lee is said to have fought valiantly against the assailants in person." I would not be surprised if this woman of mighty resolve lost her temper and succumbed to physical retaliation. To me, history that looks pure is false. No group—not even one of devout religious followers—can conduct whole lives committing no mistakes.

What early colonists did to Shakers—violence against people based on what they believed—seemed to me the antithesis of the very basis of the new nation of freedom that was forming. Still, the fear of the unknown prevailed against the Shakers. And if a collection of unrelated, eccentrically dressed, religiously feverish people moved into the suburbs of America today, they may receive the same reaction.

Yet, in the 1770s, most everyone believed in the power of magic, and the presence of spirits. So then, neighbors of the Shakers would have all the more reason to fear the new faith, to brand them witches. If Shakers could see and hear spirits, could they also influence them to wage voodoo harm against innocent people? Such possibilities seemed plausible then.

Now, in our time of science, the tangible reigns supreme. What cannot be seen cannot be proven, thus has no existence. Many today would scoff at the early Shakers' belief in the spirit realm.

As for me, I am no mystic. Yet I thought I saw Mother Ann once.

It happened in the stillness of late evening, one night in the months before my journey to Sabbathday Lake. My children slept deeply, peacefully. My husband worked late at the office. I got up from my bed, where I had been perched while I worked, compiling research for this very book.

I rose and turned to walk to the bathroom. In the corner of my eye there flitted a figure in the next room. I thought it was a woman—she seemed clothed in a sort of short cape and blouson sleeves and long, full skirts from another century. She wore navy or black, with perhaps white as the blouse and petticoat underneath. She stood in the middle of the room, bent over the baby's cradle, and as I turned she seemed to vanish into the mirror of the large walnut armoire.

I did not want to see this.

I do not believe in spirits. In fact, I have an intense intellectual disbelief in creatures from another dimension. No matter how much religious training or reading I undertake, I still feel that I know for sure only the here and now. That means, while reincarnation may sound feasible, it remains for me unproved. While heaven beckons its appeal, for me it remains in the realm of myth. This body for this one mortal life is all I have. This I know.

The thing I thought was Ann Lee must have been a figment of my imagination.

"But it could have been real," whispered my gut, from the place way below my brain that feels rather than thinks its way through life. "You were not, after all, looking for such a vision. You were not thinking about her at all. What if . . ."

And what if, I asked myself later, in the cold light of the next day while my baby blew bubbles on my shoulder and began to clamor for his next feeding. What did Ann Lee want from me? Why would she be standing over my infant? Did she mean well? Was it she who had brought me to this search for the Shaker God, the writing of this book? If so, would she haunt it till my story would say what she wanted it to say?

"Nonsense," replied my well-trained brain.

Months later, on the lumpy bed with worn covers in Maine, the strange presence of Ann Lee crept in again. I dreamed that I was back in my childhood home in Ohio, a two-story suburban box with many bedrooms and baths for our family of nine. I was alone in the house—that is, I was the only human being.

The house had that gray, darkish haze of dreams. Upstairs in my brothers' old bedroom, I suddenly saw Ann Lee. She stood right by me. Although she was a spirit, she wore clothes of two hundred years ago, and her eyes bore down, painfully, into my soul.

I felt terrified. I ran from her, quickly to the next room, but she was already there, standing opposite me, challenging me somehow with her steady gaze.

Whether I feared her because she was a ghost or because she seemed so stern, I did not know. But I ran, from room to room and finally downstairs; everywhere I ran I found her waiting. I nearly bumped right into her.

I scared myself awake, and lay in bed trying to figure out this dream. Native Americans believe that spirits can visit one in dreams. Had I been visited by the actual spirit of this woman? Did I believe?

The night sky outside was still black. I knew before checking, *knew* that it was four o'clock. I looked at the travel clock on the nightstand. Four o'clock.

"Awake, arise!" I heard a voice in my head.

It was Ann Lee.

"What do you want me to do?" I said groggily to her.

"Arise, and to work!"

I still didn't know if I was conversing with a spirit, or with my own imagination.

"Let me sleep a little longer, please," I pleaded to her in my thoughts. Now this haughty woman, beckoning me to work in the middle of the night, seemed a lot like the strict, demanding Ann Lee about whom I had read. Was she the same frightening witch who had just chased me through my dreams?

I knew I could get a lot of writing done in the two hours till dawn. I could even get in the car and drive the few miles to the shoreline of Sabbathday Lake, and be there shivering in the cold Maine morning, ready to photograph the sunrise. But already the trip had taken a toll on me, and I lay curled in a nest of fatigue and warmth. This was ridiculous, I thought. I still suspected I was conversing with my own head.

And so I went back to sleep, not easily nor deeply. "I have to pace myself for the day," I thought, knowing it would be long and draining as they all had been, and that I wanted to harness my energy for kitchen chores, spiritual conversations, and group prayer.

The ghost of Ann Lee seemed to poke and prod me, chastising my laziness, while I attempted to doze a while until the safe light of morning had been switched on outside my window. All that day, the dream continued to haunt me.

Granted, I had been dreaming of the Shakers for months. Entering into this faith vicariously had begun to change me at the bottom of my soul. Even though my life still looked the same, underneath I felt the influence of the fiery believers of Shakerism past and present. And it was, after all, from underneath my consciousness that I dreamed.

Also, during the weeks at Sabbathday Lake I worked from early morning till late into the night, listening and talking, reading and writing, trying to soak up as much as I could in such a short time. I was absorbed, exhausted, obsessed. And so it only seemed natural that the work should spill over into my dream life.

The symbolism in the dream wielded great power. It meant that there was no escaping my search for the Shaker God in the world today. It meant that the persona of Shakerism's founder had seeped into my very ego—the core of my self, symbolized by the house. She was everywhere, in all the chambers of my mind/self. She demanded attention. She was a dream symbol for the urgency of my search for the truth.

If she *was* only a symbol.

The visions and ecstasies of Shakers past have subsided. No one whirls much anymore. The Sabbathday Lake Shakers hold Sunday Meetings that seem absolutely sedate next to those of many be-bopping, holy-rolling Christians today.

Only Sister Frances remembers the last time an incident occurred in the middle of Shaker worship: "One Sunday morning," she wrote in *Growing Up Shaker*, her self-published autobiography, "I was sitting in the last row in the Chapel at Meeting. We had almost come to the end of the service when suddenly Sister Eliza Jeffers, a gentle and unassuming Sister from Alfred [Maine], leapt from her place in the second row and almost without touching the floor . . . began to whirl around in a small circle.

"Eldress Prudence went to her, and without touching her gave her invisible support. The whirling lasted a brief time, and during that time not a sound was heard in the Chapel."

Sister Frances, the last of the Shakers to have seen what used to be a core experience of the power of the Spirit, believed that what she saw that morning proved the grace of God. "Without a doubt, it was the manifestation of the Spirit, and every person in the room felt it," she declared.

How could one explain the strange events of colonial Shakerism? I wondered. What they did in prayer seemed magical. Heads spinning, bodies whirling, believers collapsing in puddles of ecstasy, tongues praying in languages unknown—some of this might shake me up if I saw it today, even though I am sympathetic to their faith.

In my own church experience, witnessing the charismatic Christian renewal of the 1960s and 1970s, I had seen the kind of praying in tongues that Shakers shared. I had watched one person babble incoherently, only to have her "prayer" translated by another member of the prayer group, who seemed to know instinctively the message that God intended. Sometimes this would be a biblical passage, often a message of comfort and encouragement, always one of great love from Beyond.

Within the narrow context of my life as a Catholic, I had also heard of people of my faith around the world having visions of Mary. Someone may have been crippled, and he traveled to Lourdes and felt healed. Or a group may together have seen the Blessed Virgin floating high above them, arms held out in a merciful gesture of nurturing love.

Did these people create such delusions in their minds? Was this the manifestation of power from some spirit realm, or just a lot of hungry people longing for the power of love or of healing? Did it matter?

Later in the morning of my dream-vision of Ann Lee, in the polite quiet of the sisters' waiting room, Sister June greeted me with her perennial smile. She sat down next to me and fidgeted with fingers that curled up and clasped together in her lap. She wanted to continue a conversation begun the day before, as we had bent together over our research on the gleaming Shaker-style tables. She had started to tell me about her own modern form of mysticism: the daily power of Jesus over the events of her life.

"You asked yesterday," she began, "how I know if something comes from above or if it's just a figment of my imagination.

"Of all the things that have happened to me," she began, "one is the most striking. Years ago, I used to take the bus to work at the library. My mother did most of the driving, if we needed to go anywhere else.

"But the bus service got worse and worse, and finally I decided to buy a little used car, so I could drive myself to the train station. That would be better."

Sister June nodded in agreement with herself, and encircled the edge of her glasses with her thumb and forefinger to gently lift them up higher on her nose.

"Well, I began to get a feeling that there might be something wrong with the brakes. Of course, I didn't know—I don't know anything about cars. But I was frightened. And I said to Jesus, 'If the brakes go out while I'm driving, I don't think I could cope.' And I asked him, please, if there was anything wrong with the brakes, to make it so they'd go out while the car was in the garage or something."

She looked up now and then as she talked, and that was a lot for this shy woman. Her voice lilted high and raspy, like that of a little girl whose body grew up but whose soul never did.

"Well, some time went by, and I guess I took the car in for regular service. You know, I dropped it off at the shop and took the bus to the library. I came back after work, and they had finished with the tune-up. They said, 'Everything's OK, and we did your tune-up and all. We also fixed your brakes. See, when we finished with your car and our mechanic backed it out of the garage, the brakes went out on him all of a sudden.' "

Instantly, the shy woman forgot all her inhibitions, threw her hands up in the air, and laughed. The universe had opened for her that day, and she had seen the workings of a power that she now knew meant to protect and safeguard little, ordinary her.

"I told my friend that story, and she said, 'Jesus is holding you right in his hand!' She said, if something like that ever happened to her, she wouldn't worry about anything ever again."

Something may in fact exist, whether deep within our souls or in the divine beyond, that can move us to dreams and visions, prayers and songs, heroism and healing, far beyond our expected capacity. People of many religions and cultures have believed in spiritual power: In Native American religions, people undergo sundance and sweat lodge ceremonies to touch the beyond within; in Islam, the mystical Sufis twirl and spin themselves into a dizzying ecstasy; in Buddhism, people meditate for years in order to clear their minds so as to see bald Truth itself.

Fear of the inexplicable realm of the intangible, meanwhile, has fueled witch-hunts all along. Colonists who did not engage in such spirited practices in their own churches and homes felt suspicious of the source of Shakers' power.

All along, the Shakers claimed that it was not the devil, nor the force of the earth or the universe, but the very Spirit of God that spun them through fields and pastures without their feet touching the ground—the same spirit that bolstered their resolve to live pure lives of prayer and celibacy in the long days and years of labor.

So many scandalous stories abounded in the accounts of early Shakerism, that at first I wondered which side to believe. Could the Shakers really be having drunken orgies in the woods? A part of human nature, the part that watches horror movies and reads the tabloids, knows that darkness lurks beneath every light. We know that loneliness haunts the most glamorous Hollywood stars; infidelity seeps into the happiest marriages; embezzlement plagues the most devout television evangelists. The murderous lunatic lurks outside the window of our lovely, safe homes. Evil exists.

Someone once told me that there is no "devil," only the evil that lies in wait deep within the heart of human beings, that when unfurled leaves in its wake burned churches and bombed buildings, raped women and tortured men, massacred races and deformed countries.

I know well my own dark side, for I have seen it in the quiet of anger when I know what my hands could do to hurt others if only I let loose. I know my evil, which breaks through my mask of the benign, tolerant, faithful universalist and spills out the arrogance, pride, and fear that fester within. I live with my demons every day—I lose my temper with my children far too often, snip at my husband and snap at the grocery clerk, draw walls up around myself instead of reaching out to help others, waste precious days and years in self-indulgence instead of using the time for love and work. More selfish, more—let us say— witchy than most, I live side by side with my own dark side, which never lets me forget it is there.

But what about the dark side of Shakerism? No religion remains untouched by corruption, for no matter how divine the goal, the path toward the goal is walked by humans.

Darkness haunted Shakerism in a time when mystical powers seemed so frightening that people would burn others at the stake rather than live next door to the unknown. Darkness hovers at the edges of Shakerism today, too. But it is not the darkness of witchcraft. Rather, the speaking in tongues, the dancing into ecstasy, and so forth emerge from a force so deep within that the Shakers themselves never even have understood it. Some may call this the subconscious, or telepathy; the Shakers call it God.

No, the dark side of Shakerism has nothing to do with witchcraft, or with mystical events that cannot be explained. The dark side, much more mundane, has to do with human nature: Shakers walking off the path toward their paradise.

Doubtless there have been Shakers who tipped the bottle too often; verily pairs of Shakers have run off in the night to wed. The records show that Shaker trustees violated investment rules to make a quick buck or ferreted away money toward midnight apostasy. Shaker elders played favorites and made unwise decisions, and Shaker visionaries lied about divine imperatives to suit their own ambitions.

Much as Shakers wanted to hide away from the corruption of the world, they found through the centuries that what they wished to hide from dwelt deep inside their own hearts. Today's Shakers might now try to cover up or deny past mistakes, but they do not. Members at Sabbathday Lake understand that good and evil coexist; that we all fight the demons that try to prevent us from developing our potential and achieving our loftiest goals.

All of today's Shakers had problems to overcome in their spiritual journey toward God. Brother Alistair arrived at Sabbathday Lake a year ago with a suitcase full of demons. He left behind a family who neither understood him nor respected his life choices. He brought the haunting memory of several good friends whom he had watched die in the AIDS hospice in London where he worked for several years. He stood in the middle of the airport on the day of the trip that would bring him straight from secular life into monastic, and he parted right then with one of his demons:

"I was smoking at least twenty a day for quite a few years. I had my last cigarette at Heathrow Airport. I had a small supply of nicotine chewing gum, which lasted two weeks. And I just went cold turkey," he told me.

For Brother Alistair, giving up smoking for the purity of Shaker life proved easier than expected. "I don't think I would have been able to do it anywhere else," he said. "But in this kind of environment, it was hardly problematic at all." Here the air smelled clean, he explained; the food tasted wholesome and hearty; the work used one's energy in a satisfying way; and the people who now formed his family had welcomed him lovingly into their circle.

Living in a religious community such as Sabbathday Lake, some demons rankle rather than heal. Brother Wayne wrestles daily with his insensitivity. "Trying to live a Christian life," he told me one day in the library as the afternoon sun slanted in through windows around us, meant for him "just trying to be mindful that other people have feelings and not always to be thinking about my feelings first.

"You know," he said in the matter-of-fact voice of a man who punches down his demons with gusto, "if someone annoys me, my first inclination is to bite them back. But . . . they have feelings, I have feelings, and we're all equal in the sight of God."

He peered at me now and then from behind the crisscrossed fingers of his large hands. "By putting my feelings first, that's just selfishness," said the farmer who could bring forth a baby lamb into life and coax plump tomatoes out of rough, dry soil. "It's important to be mindful of others." Then he looked up and smiled full in the face. "And to realize that they might be having a bad hair day or whatever."

For Brother Arnold, "a horrible little devil lives inside me." He grasped his beard with one hand and tugged on it, irked even at the thought of it.

"I think I'm very willful, very unbending. I have a really hard time not being right," he said. "I mean, if I'm wrong, I would freely admit it. And that is the truth. But if I know I'm right, I just cannot back down." I suspected that Brother Arnold was much tougher with himself than with those around him.

"It never gets better," he shook his head ruefully. "It's not that I'm not aware of it, and it's not that I don't try; but sometimes I really have to try just to keep my mouth shut."

He feels the weight of this challenge most heavily in his role as elder, he told me. The Shakers still practice confession— a weekly requirement in times past, but now an as-needed informality—in which members talk over their problems with elders. Being the spiritual mentor and counselor for the brothers at Sabbathday Lake, Elder Arnold said he "would love to give up" the burden of answering for someone else's soul.

"It's a lot of responsibility," he said, "because you're judged not only for your own deeds but for that which you do for the others coming into the faith."

Here the demon of fear raised its head, and Brother Arnold looked at it straight on. "You can let your own self slide, perhaps, but you can't really afford to think about having to face God for things that you've left undone for others, especially in this kind of responsibility. . . . Yet the most important thing I have to do is to make sure that I'm available when people need me, to keep my mouth shut and keep my ears open, and listen to problems." Rather than simply be right, the quiet, contemplative elder at Shaker Village struggles daily just to be present for those around him—to be open, to be alongside, to let grace lead.

"I feel guilty about things within my own life," Sister Frances confided to me one day, "that I haven't really been able to bring to perfection yet."

She looked down at her strong hands, yoked together as though to give prayer to her thought, and I wondered what this woman possibly could do that the world would consider sinful. She, after all, probably does not steal notepads from the office storeroom, nor cheat just a little on her taxes, nor call her kids names in a fit of rage, nor have an affair just once. Sitting there across from her, I had to stretch myself to listen, really listen. Because I saw that, innocent as she seemed to me, genuine pain shadowed her face when she told me: "I feel guilt often for the things I do. I feel guilt when I say or do something to another person that separates me from that full union with them and with our Father/Mother God."

And so, herein lay her demon. She worried about the misuse of her power over others. Even the world would recognize this kind of transgression; this was no trivial confession to grabbing the last helping of pie at Sunday dinner. Sister Frances, the most powerful person today in the Shaker realm, knew how the others needed compassion alongside her authority, respect alongside her commanding example.

She had other demons as well, demons I knew full well as a woman. "I only allow myself one banana split per year!" she exclaimed in the kitchen late one morning, when the sisters' stomachs grumbled for lunch, and we all chatted about a family restaurant the next town over where the ice cream was home-made, creamy, and famous.

"Oh, why only one?" I asked, not being one to curb my insatiable lust for sweets.

"Well, look at me!" she lamented, patting one generous hip and scrunching up her eyebrows with regret.

How human you are, I thought as we all laughed woefully. Yet what had I expected? I looked around the plain kitchen, with its painted yellow walls and worn linoleum floor, and shook my head at myself. Had I come here expecting to find whirling dancers, babbling in apostolic tongues? Had I thought to see the specter of Ann Lee rocking in a Shaker chair, over in the corner, overlooking us all?

Well, yes, maybe.

It would, after all, have been quite spectacular, and it would have made a story even the tabloids could print.

Yet I stood in the midst of a people as human as I—not witches nor warlocks, just people who had carved for themselves a life on a Christian farm in which they could concentrate on what mattered most to them.

It is not being human that holds people back from being Shakers, I realized later, long after the journey when I sat staring out my window, trying to sort out the lessons of Sabbathday Lake. It was clear to me that I had returned to all the dark as well as the light of my own worldly American life. I was just as human as before I had left, and I still battled my own personal demons. I was not exempt just because I had been to the Shakers, and they were not exempt just because they were Shakers.

It is not humanness, but rather certain elements within humanity that stand between oneself and God—that, I believed, was what Brother Wayne or Sister Frances might say about the wrestling with self that continues at Sabbathday Lake, long after the whirling dances have stopped. Individual ego, sexual lust, pride, greed—these realities of human nature have led past Shakers away from the fold, and now challenge current Shakers to stay faithful to the way toward their soul's union with God.

The mighty power of early Shakerism, which neighbors called witchcraft and believers called the Spirit, has quieted— for now—at Sabbathday Lake. If today's Shakers embrace the dark side, it is in a wrestling match with the demons within: the parts of who they are that block them from union with one another, which is the earthly presence of God. The dark side may exist as long as Shakers remain in the earthly realm; for it is part of life. And part of light.

CHAPTER FOUR

GOD

Light, light is shining all over Zion!
Oh! Let us bask in the rays from above;
'Tis the loving kindness of the Omnipotent;
'Tis but a proof of an Infinite Love.
Smile on us, Father, thro' the clear sunlight,
When tears of affliction mingle with our joys;
Bless us, Heav'nly Mother, from Thy throne of mercy,
'Til we're perfected for Thy lasting choice.

—*"Light, Light Is Shining All Over Zion"*

Few people alive today know the power that hovers over the wood benches and gleaming floors of the meetinghouse at Sabbathday Lake. Ann Lee never danced there, never prayed in her languages unknown to men. She never lived to see the day. Built by the hands of the first Maine believers, who shaped their own nails and hewed 20,000 bricks for double chimneys, the gambrel-roofed meetinghouse was completed just in time for Christmas worship in 1794.

The meetinghouse was not the first building I noticed upon

my arrival at Shaker Village. First, the looming red-brick dwelling-house, built in the next century across the street and on the pinnacle of the hill, commanded my attention. And then the seventeenth-century wood-plank barn, used for storing tractors, caught my eye because its crumbling architecture speaks of a time before the Shakers, when a farmer-turned-believer named Gowen Wilson owned the land.

Among the cluster of buildings, I hardly noticed the sacred one where spirits of Shakers long dead are said to gather in the dance, especially when living believers fill the room. It hovered too close to the highway, where incessant trucks roar past, flinging dust across dual sidewalks that lead up to the sisters' and brothers' entryways. It huddled back against the edge of the herb garden and apple orchards beyond. It balanced on a teetering ridge between the quiet Shaker farm and the encroaching frantic world, the spirited singing and whirling of past centuries and the subdued and shrunken group that carries on the faith today.

Few have felt it, but those who have say that the Spirit breathes power through the vast, first-floor room where generations of Shakers have stepped and uttered their love for God. Built so that three stories could be supported without one beam interrupting the ground-floor dancing space, the meetinghouse whispers the memory of ministers who lived and died upstairs, the select few who spent all their time in this tabernacle of the Spirit.

Now, each summer thousands of tourists troop through upstairs museum rooms where ministry elders lived, but they only peek into the large space where Shakers danced. Some say they feel the history here. Some say they feel more. Is it the ghosts of Shakers who linger in this realm, or the spirit energy of the living handful who carry on the faith? Maybe it is the breath of the Spirit God itself, blowing life into a small, unnoticed building alongside an ordinary rural highway.

One way to understand why people do what they do, I believe, is to look at their God. Shakers have held firm to their convictions through two and a half centuries of persecution, ridicule, poverty, abundance, celibacy, and near-extinction. What image of God could motivate such steady devotion?

It was such a God as no Christian had ever seen before.

Shakers declared that only half of God had been seen by humanity in the nearly two thousand years thus of Christianity. Not merely male, God possessed all the essence of female and male. God radiated the full spectrum of woman and man. Shakers took this from Genesis 1:26: "Let *us* make man in *our* image, after *our* likeness"; and from the circumstantial evidence they found in dual-gender species all over the earth.

Shakers sang out their discovery:

> The Father's high eternal throne
> Was never fill'd by one alone:
> There Wisdom holds the Mother's seat,
> And is the Father's helper-meet.
>
> This vast creation was not made
> Without the fruitful Mother's aid;
> For by the works of God we know
> The fountain-head from which they flow.

God surpassed anything we humans could imagine. He/She superseded all possible human understanding into the realm of the infinite, the intangible, the Spirit. "Father and Mother," states the 1816 *Testimonies*, "are attributes of God, not separate persons or personalities."

This kind of God must have looked radically abstract to Christians in 1774. Even now, for many people worldwide, God remains a sort of superhuman on a throne in the sky. Shakers stretched their imaginations to what I would call a *Star Trek* God: a spiritual force of goodness in the universe that does not at all resemble humans. And, as if it were not enough to state that God is both Mother and Father and yet exists far beyond our limited androgynous view, Shakers also claimed that the spirit of God could exist within the soul of anyone. *Anyone*.

In Shakerism, I learned, Christ-existence is not esoteric. It waits, available, even to me. Suddenly I need not be born of a virgin nor divinely predestined; I need only open my heart to the Spirit. This is the great equalizer of Shakerism. Because no one ranks superior as savior or priest, all citizens stand before God with the same potential for holiness and leadership. And as for salvation, I sit in the driver's seat: In Shakerism there is no passive forgiveness and salvation by a merciful Other; rather, I save myself through my own effort toward openness to the Spirit.

The Shakers who landed in New York harbor in 1774 waged a spiritual revolution, of sorts, in the New World. They paved the way for current thinking on the feminine in God and Christ, equal rights for all in religious ministry and social governance, and nontraditional ways of forming families and building utopian communities.

Ann Lee told Joseph Meacham in 1780 that she was not literally the "female Christ" but, as Adam and Eve were the "natural" parents of humanity, so she and Jesus were the spiritual parents of a new and higher order of humanity. She was carrying out the work that Jesus had begun but was no longer on this earth to do. In the 1816 *Testimonies*, Ann Lee spoke of her relationship with Christ, her "husband" and "lover," in intimate terms: "I feel great union with him, and walk with him in union, as with a lover." Reading this passage from my modern perspective, I had to wonder how Lee would know what married intimacy felt like. She had come out of an incompatible marriage to devote herself to a life of celibacy. So, how could she feel with a spirit what she had never known with a flesh-and-blood man?

The 1816 *Testimonies* explains Shaker theology as originating in "the first two foundation pillars of the Church of Christ—

the two anointed ones," Jesus and Ann Lee, who were "the first parents in the work of redemption." Redemption, possible only after one confessed one's sins and turned away from lust to a life in the spirit, led to heaven—here on earth *and* in the hereafter. The Shakers felt that, as in the natural world creation was not finished until both male and female were formed, so in the spiritual realm a woman was needed to complete redemption, to complete "the foundation of a new creation."

The coming of the Christ-Spirit through the body of a woman, according to some early Shakers, reversed the mighty force of the Fall from Eden. Sister Ruth Webster wrote in *The Shaker* that traditional Christian theology endorsed the subjugation of women because it blamed Eve for leading Adam into original sin and thus eviction from the Garden of Eden. This excuse no longer held. Now, in Shakerism, humanity had been saved through a female version of Christ. We no longer could hold women responsible for our sinful condition.

"About one hundred years ago God raised up a woman," she wrote in 1876, and gave her the wisdom "by which mankind might be led *out* of sin." Anyone who refused to hear the testimony and continued in their sinful ways, she warned, had no one to blame but themselves. "If mankind," she lamented, "had been as ready to have been led *out* as *into* sin, long, ere this, lewdness would have ceased in the land, and long since, war would have been no more."

According to Shaker tradition, Ann Lee wielded the kind of mighty powers that have been compared to the miracles of Jesus. The *Testimonies* reports miraculous healings of "body and mind" as a result of "a mere touch of the hand . . . or the sound of her voice."

Preaching to large crowds that gathered around her, Ann Lee fed the throngs even when provisions were scarce. "Sometimes the people were ordered, by Mother, to sit down upon the floor, or on the ground; and a small quantity of bread and cheese, or some other kind of provision, was served round to the multitude, much in the manner as Christ fed the multitude, with a few loaves and fishes: and the power and blessing of God evidently attended them."

Ann Lee could see so deep into people's hearts that she often shocked them, at their first introduction to her, by telling their deepest secrets, hidden sins, or experiences of their lives. She and the other elders were reportedly delivered, many times, from danger by providential means—the appearance of a benefactor, warnings through a vision, or Lee's own mysterious "great power and authority."

How to explain the multiplying of the loaves and cheeses? I have wondered about it for a long time. And what of the accounts of Ann Lee "reading" people's hearts? Perhaps the crowds who surrounded Ann Lee felt so moved by her charismatic preaching and spontaneous sharing from her own lunch basket that they reached deep into their own knapsacks and added whatever they had.

Possibly Ann Lee, with her visions into the lives of people and the valley of the dead, was a genuine psychic. Certainly she has been called by some the originator of the American spiritualist movement, which surged in the century following her death. And one way Shakers always have differed from other Christians is in their refusal to separate spiritism from spirituality. Living in pure devotion to God meant, for them, also unlocking powers of intuition, opening one's inner eye to realms beyond the three-dimensional.

I remembered talking with Sister Frances in the kitchen one morning, when something she said suggested she may share a bit of the intuitive power Ann Lee possessed. She was talking of her great sadness over the loss of Sister Meg, a young convert who had spent many years in Shaker community but then returned to the world. "But you know," Sister Frances twisted toward me as she tied an apron around her waist, "I saw it coming. I *knew*, about a year beforehand, that she was going to leave."

"You knew even before she knew?" I asked.

"Yes," she replied.

I wondered what this eldress would see in me, beyond what I saw in myself, even now as we got to know each other during my stay.

The way Shakers perceived God did not just free the spirit: it literally freed people from shackles placed by society. First, Shakerism freed women. Scholars today call Ann Lee a "protofeminist," a strong leader who began to establish women's equality and rights two hundred years before American society and other religions followed suit. Shakers believed in a male-female God (the "Eternal Two"), used language in their prayer that included both genders, and established a dual-gender governance for their community.

Sister Frances said that even today, when women can own land and companies, hang Sheetrock or perform brain surgery, she feels "absolutely" freer than women in the world. That feeling of freedom has much to do with the Shaker view of God. "The Shakers see God, think of God, love God, as a Father/ Mother image," she said.

"Because Shakers believe God is all spirit, it is very easy for us not to have any sexual connotation as 'the man' or 'the woman.' But we do feel that the God-Spirit is both male and female.

"When Mother Ann came," she explained, "people flocked to her in the hundreds and thousands," hungry not just for her simple message of spiritual purity but for her radical belief in human rights. "This was the beginning of Shakerism," said Sister Frances, "and ever since that time women have been just as important in the Shaker Church as any man. There has never been the slightest—not the *slightest*—difference [in treatment] between them."

The eight women and men who will take Shakerism into the third millennium base their theology firmly within a foundation of the dual-gender God. "Recently," Sister Frances told me, "I read something about 'a church in California grappled with the idea of a Mother-God.' And to us it seems so strange that one has to 'grapple' with it—this has always been a part of our life."

To her, the beauty of Ann Lee the "female Christ" is that an average woman of this earth so opened her soul to the spirit of Christ that she came fully to embody that spirit. Lee proved that anyone could do it. Her life as human vessel of the spirit revealed for her followers that the Kingdom of God awaits only the openness of our hearts.

Shakerism also freed people of color. Shakers opposed the slavery of Africans from the time they first landed on New World soil. Ann Lee had visions of "poor negroes" in the spirit realm, finally redeemed from their loss. Next century, young Shaker sisters in Ohio had a vision in which they traveled to the City of Delight in the "spirit land." They saw slave owners serving their former slaves. Another group of people in their vision, who had owned slaves during their earthly life, refused to wait upon them, and so they were expelled from the City of Delight until they repented. "God is just," the sisters said, "and all wrongs must be righted."

When slave owners joined the Shakers, they set free their slaves. Some former slaves joined the Shakers, too. Ex-slaves in the northern communities lived as equals. Those at South Union, Kentucky, however, lived in segregation, sleeping and dining in their own "black" residence and dining room. Yet even there, a journal reports Shakers' efforts toward equality: "Today we purchased Jonas Crutcher a colored man who had been a believer about nineteen years. We kept him hired here while his owner retained him a slave. We have bought him to prevent his being sold South."

An all-African-American Shaker group in Philadelphia lived in community and, though they worked in the city by day, at home they lived out the gospel as one family. They had close ties to the group at Watervliet, New York. The group was led by Mother Rebecca Jackson, and later by her adopted daughter.

Shakers were not only abolitionists, they were pacifists. The

Shaker God inspired a feeling of equality that ran so deep that the human race became one family, so integrally one in the spirit that no war ever could solve the problems between them. Three Shaker men were arrested in 1780 for declaring "that it was their determined Resolution never to take up arms and to dissuade others from doing the same." Local officials saw them as a threat to the freedom and independence of the United States. Other Shakers were arrested, too, for refusing to take up arms.

In 1819, lawyer John Holmes, a congressman from Maine and later a U.S. senator, pleaded on behalf of the Shakers to exempt them from military duty. "This singular people," he said, "contribute nothing to the increase of mankind and very properly refuse to aid in their destruction." Moreover, he felt, "They are not of the world; they are not made of flesh and blood. They share none of the extravagances of society, and wish to be exempted from the effect of them."

The Revolutionary Shakers, though poverty-stricken, paid dearly for the privilege of pacifism. Each year male members had to petition for release from military duty, submit certification from their elders that they were still part of the Shaker community, and pay the salary for an alternate soldier in the army. Many Quakers, also pacifists, did the same.

Their firm belief in nonviolence, it seemed to me, was consistent with their claim that God loved all, equally. To Shakers, the sheer audacity to call oneself *Christian* required equanimity. As I digested Shaker tracts and then dwelt among flesh-and-blood Shakers, I began to see that their ideal is to live entirely without prejudice. If the Christ-Spirit inhabits all—even those who do not realize it or access it—and if the presence of the Spirit is held as the highest value in life, then black and white, plump and wiry, scholarly and unschooled, all become one.

And they really mean it.

For Brother Arnold, Shakerism speaks the truths in his own heart about "the presence of God in one's life, daily. The working out of salvation. The quest for perfection in this life.

"I think that the Shaker concept of the duality of the god-head is very important and makes the most amount of sense of anything I've ever heard," he told me. "That and the equality of all. The way that the Shakers believe that, as we were all created equal by God, then we have to reflect that. We have to meet people right where they are. We can't try to mold them into something that they aren't, but rather we strive by the power of God to accept them as they are."

Shakerism, a millenarian faith, claims that the end-time is now. The kingdom of God, complete and miraculous, is at hand. However, this kingdom of God exists outside of time; for, two and a half centuries later, the kingdom is still at hand. "We feel that the Second Coming of Christ can happen anytime," Sister Frances spoke in the soft, clipped voice of a Maine native, "and does happen—has already happened to most of us, can continue to happen to us.

"We don't feel—and I don't mean this as any sort of criticism of any other church—but we don't feel that the Christ is going to come back in a cloud of glory, on a mountain with trumpets sounding. It's a very quiet, unobtrusive coming which comes to us whenever we open ourselves to that Christ-Spirit."

Not all millenarians today, though, see the coming of the end of the world in the same way. This I discovered during my stay with the Shakers, when a small, unforgettable woman came knocking at the door at Sabbathday Lake.

"Brother Arnold," beckoned Sister Frances later, at noon dinner, "tell the others about that very *interesting* person who spent some time talking with you this morning."

The small woman had spent an hour trying to convince Brother Arnold to join forces with her cause. She called herself the Dolly Llama, and said the end of the world had begun. First there was to be flooding—and this already had occurred—then six more disasters would follow in the next few years, culminating in the apocalypse.

"You know," Brother Arnold nodded through his goatee, "as

we approach the millennium there are more and more people who fear this may be the end of the world.

"I don't know why, but more and more often these days, these people show up on *our* doorstep." He shook his head, and I guessed that, while he felt somewhat sympathetic for this woman's zeal, he had mostly felt eager to get back to his morning's work in the print shop.

This sort of thing apparently happened often enough that the others felt relieved it was Brother Arnold, not them, who had to speak with her tactfully and listen gently for an hour.

"She wanted to enlist our support," he continued. "She is trying with fire and brimstone to prepare the world for the end. As a matter of fact, she said, we are already supporting her cause. We don't know it, but we Shakers have been chosen by God to prepare the way for her," he smiled.

"Does she know about the real Dalai Lama of Tibet?" I asked, thinking of one of my heroes, the Buddhist leader who has spent a lifetime working for peace.

"Oh, yes, she's a very knowledgeable person," replied Brother Arnold. "She reads voraciously, and then takes a little of this and a little of that."

Unlike the Dolly Llama, Shakers do not go knocking on doors to recruit support, and they print no pamphlets to pass out on street corners. Yet they seem so open to hearing the ideas of others, even those whose theology makes little sense to them. Perhaps they look at the heart of the believer and see someone who loves God and wants to express that love, even in the unique, dramatic way of the Dolly Llama.

The kind tolerance Brother Arnold showed that day to a door-to-door evangelist counters the sort of intolerance the world held for Shaker worship since the 1700s. The way Shakers saw God was downright objectionable. And their worship, which gave concrete expression to that God, seemed curious, ridiculous, or even macabre. I saw, through the eyes of past spectators, that what happened on Sunday in the meetinghouse only strengthened outsiders' repugnance for this Shaker deity.

Who else, in Puritan New England, danced thus in church? People were scandalized. "Senseless jumping!" exclaimed Ralph Waldo Emerson in the 1850s. "This shaking of their hands, like the paws of dogs." An English lady described the dancers as flapping penguins.

An eyewitness described in his journal the way the first community of Shakers at Niskeyuna worshiped their God. "I beheld 24 men dancing at one end of the room," wrote Moses Guest, a visitor in 1796, "and 20 women at the other. They appeared to be from the age of 14 to 80 years; and were formed four deep. Two of their elders were singing a song tune, called the rose tree. They kept good time, though frequently trembled as if much convulsed."

The dancers stopped, after some time, put on their coats, and walked over to the house for refreshment. Guest heard them singing in unknown languages, which he called "gibberish." He claimed they frequently conversed with the spirits of the departed. After resting an hour, the Shakers reassembled and danced again; they trembled, sighed, and groaned, twisted and convulsed. Suddenly one of the elders muttered that they should all praise God by throwing off their garments, so the men took off their coats and waistcoats, and rolled up their sleeves. The women and men lined up four deep, and some Shakers sang while others danced in an agitated manner.

"Then they all stopped dancing and one of their elders, after violently shaking his head and arms, thus addressed them—'My dear friends, I hope you will endeavor to walk worthy the vocation to which you are called; and praise God for separating you from the wicked world.' " The elder soon began shaking violently, then sighed and groaned, and called the end of Meeting. As I read, I realized Guest would have seen Ann Lee among those in worship.

Several decades later, Shaker worship got mixed reviews. Many curious spectators from the world flocked to Shaker Meeting to get a glimpse of the strange celibates at their worship. Some, like journalist Benson J. Lossing, saw a certain beauty in the dance. He wrote for *Harper's* in 1857: "The music was unlike anything I had ever heard . . . deeply solemn. . . . Their songs and hymns breathe a pure and Christian spirit; and their music . . . captivates the ear because of its severe simplicity and perfect melody."

He watched as a mob of 400 to 500 worshipers marched and countermarched in perfect time. Had this been a theatrical exhibition, Lossing declared, even the most highly critical would exclaim at their beauty. The women wore white, he wrote, "and, moving gracefully, appeared ethereal; and among them were a few very beautiful faces. All appeared happy, and upon each face rested the light of dignified serenity, which always gives power to the features of woman."

Other visitors felt great waves of revulsion at what they had witnessed. Fanny Appleton, the fiancée of Henry Wadsworth Longfellow, came to worship in 1839. She wrote in her journal of the entrance of a flock of sisters through the "female door"; of the straw bonnets hung upon pegs looking like "huge hornets' nests"; and of Shaker women lined up on benches like "jointed dolls," moving not even an eyelash, like "corpses set on end." Appleton cringed to see the little girls of the community copying the same rigid posture.

Sermons droned on "in unconnected, drawling scraps of morality." Worse yet, the Shakers dared pity the townsfolk "for our poor, lost condition" and went on "prophesying that one day we should lament we were not Shakers!" This condescension really piqued Lady Appleton. Her version of Shaker worship, colored by vivid detail, gave others a voyeur's view into meetinghouse worship.

What they then did could not be called dancing, she declared. Rather, they "ploughed up and down, [singing in] terribly shrill" voices. As the Shakers filed round into a circle formation, "hands paddling like fins and voices chanting these wild airs," the small circle of elders in the middle seemed to her "like so many old witches or enchanters, working over the cauldron."

Appleton saw "spasmodic jumps and twists of the neck." She

felt she had descended into the lower regions or into a nightmare. "There was one woman whose horrible contortions will haunt me forever," she confessed. "She wrenched her head nearly over her shoulder on one side and the other, then jerked it nearly to her knee" for a seeming endless amount of time, shuddered Appleton.

More and more, sometimes 500 at a time, clamored to Sunday Meeting to see what strange deeds these Shakers did. The world gave the Shakers so much bad press during the nineteenth century that outsiders learned more about the sect through such horrified accounts as Appleton's than they did from the actual Shakers.

Even I, living an eon past that time, sighed with relief to learn that Shaker worship had mellowed. When I attended Meeting with the Sabbathday Lake Shakers, I did not have to watch heads bobbing nor skirts whirling. Fear of the unknown: that was it. I shared with Fanny Appleton a revulsion for that which I did not understand. And, as she and thousands before me had shown, just attending Shaker worship would not dissipate that feeling. It was joining in wholeheartedly that would. Trying to see God through Shaker eyes. Even at the risk that I might shake a bit, too.

Shakers themselves have spent much breath and ink trying to explain that they were just Christians worshiping God. Sister Mildred Barker of Sabbathday Lake, writing in the *Shaker Quarterly*, confronted the stereotype of the ethereal Shaker: "It was said that the world's people about them would attend their religious services on Sunday evenings and watch them go round and round in their dance and consider them the most impractical visionaries on earth."

However, "The next morning at sunrise, these same neighbors, who had business at the [Shaker] mill would find them hard at work warping logs to the saw frame, and carrying away boards, and their conversation and deportment were as grave and serious as their religious exercises had been strange and inexplicable the night before."

Another twentieth-century Shaker tried to explain how the physical fervor of whirling and shaking could bring one's spirit closer to God. Sister Lillian Phelps of New Hampshire said there was "a definite psychological purpose behind the Shaker marches" which had been "rarely understood by the general Public. The perfect rhythmic body motions, of a worshipper, who combined this [dance] with a deep mental and religious fervor," she explained, "developed within himself, a great spiritual inspiration, almost impossible to understand or describe, by one who has never witnessed or participated in this form of worship.

"But if one could have been present, as I was, and could have seen that perfect spiritual union . . . when a soul combined the physical motions, the singing voice, and the dedicated heart, in giving praise and thanks to God—I'm sure you would have agreed that the physical motions added a still greater dimension to the expression of Prayer." Although she struggled to explain the impact it had on her, I sensed, words failed this simple woman of faith. Perhaps I would never understand. The whirling was, after all, a phenomenon of the past.

The frantic whirling of the Shaker dance gave way to uniform dances soon after the death of Ann Lee. Elder Joseph Meacham began to alter the way the Shakers worshiped as early as the turn of the nineteenth century. He wished to maintain a sense of union within the growing community. Departing from the whirling, shaking, and leaping of the first Shakers, he adopted a simple dance in which all members could step backand-forth as one.

As new forms of dance developed, Shakers used variations on the square dance, incorporating contrasting tempos and styles. They never employed callers or the rotation of partners, and hence retained a distinctive style in their dance. The Shaker "quick dance," introduced in 1811, included singers who filled the meetinghouse with melodies while dancers skipped around in a circle.

In 1815, Mother Lucy Wright, successor to Ann Lee, intro-

duced the use of gesturing with songs, to add a physical inter-
pretation to the words. The Sabbathday Lake Shakers, as I saw
in Meeting, still perform certain pantomimes to some songs—
for example, they thrust their arms to the side to show the pushing away of carnal desires.

Historians would say that the whirling of the Shakers died
out due to the sheer increase in numbers of converts. During
the nineteenth century, hundreds of Shakers swelled meetinghouses across the Midwest and the Northeast. So many bodies
on a dance floor could not gesticulate to their own inner
rhythms, and so the spirit of the dance calmed into community
choreography. Shakers say that the dance evolved into quieter
forms because that was the direction in which the Spirit led
them in order to preserve union among members.

Union is key to Shaker life.

"This is the same reason why the marches, the dances, and
all that came to an end among believers," Sister Frances told
me. "Toward the end of that period, when they were still doing
those religious exercises, as many as two-thirds of the community was not able to partake in the very vigorous, quick songs,
and [the older members] were sitting. Because all were not able
to participate, and this does tend to break the union, that gift
was taken away."

Not only did the dancing give way to quieter singing; other
worship elements became tempered with time. Shaker worship
began to resemble that of the Protestant Christian churches
from which Shakerism had departed. A member of the ministry
or an elder would often address the Meeting: this was not called
a sermon but fulfilled the same function. Shakers read from the
Bible and used the scriptural passage as the basis for the sermon.
Liturgical elements replaced charismatic fervor, although spurts
of spiritual ecstasy did occasionally burst forth as Shakers spoke
in tongues, stamped their feet, and prayed so loud that, claimed
outsiders, neither a cannonball nor thunder could be heard a
short distance away. Elder Issachar Bates wrote that one Shaker

stamped "Till blood gushed from his nose" during Meeting, and his "heels and ancles [sic] [turned] black and blue."

Still the fervor quieted, over time.

Shakers today live without the drama of whirling worship. Though their way of praying vastly differs, the Spirit God to whom they pray is the same as for their Shaker ancestors. Thus, they remain Shakers—even if they do not shake.

The primary difference for Shakers today between theirs and other faiths, is that they see their religion as self-propelled. Brother Wayne had believed in God since his Baptist childhood in the Portland suburbs. "Yeah," he told me, "we said our bedtime prayers and we went to Sunday school every Sunday. And I paid attention. I think I pretty much got a grasp of things. As much as a ten-, twelve-year-old and then later on, a teenager, thinks about God and salvation."

During childhood, he told me, church "was something you did on Sunday, and usually by the time the following weekend went around to church again, you thought, 'What a pretty crummy life this week.' That's typical of everyone, I think, from what I've observed." Like me, Brother Wayne had lived a double life, learned early in childhood. He practiced piety on Sunday and perhaps kept up appearances at other times, but he did not embrace his deepest beliefs all week.

The decision to join the Shakers was nothing extraordinary to him. "It wasn't like I was having revelations or visions or anything," joked Brother Wayne. No thundering voice from heaven, no fit of shaking convulsions. Rather, Brother Wayne had a yearning—simply to live out his love for God twenty-four hours a day. That seemed possible at Sabbathday Lake.

"I found that I really enjoyed Shaker Meeting because it was so different from going to church and having the deacon stand up and give the financial report for the week and the social calendar of what was going on in the church that week, and then the minister lecturing you for about an hour, and admonishing the congregation or whatever." He nodded his head, thick with dark, wavy hair. "You know, it was just very mundane. You could sometimes get kind of lost in it because it became so mundane." His eyes glowed with the passion of a teacher who has discovered precious truth and aches to impart it.

Worship at Sabbathday Lake, however, felt more personal. "I think Shaker Meeting is really different because, rather than having someone standing there and preaching to you, you actively participate," said Brother Wayne.

"And I think when you have to look at the lessons and then think about them and how they really apply to your life, rather than have someone lecturing you, it leaves a little more of an impression. Because you're actually doing the work. It's like in a school having a teacher give you the answer as opposed to finding the answer for yourself," he said.

Brother Wayne pushed up his glasses and stretched his arms wide and high over his head. The body in which his spirit dwelt was not accustomed to sitting still so long, especially on a warm spring afternoon when the fields needed plowing.

"I think anyone who professes to be a Christian, you know, as we do, has a responsibility. That is true especially for Shakers, but it's certainly all through the New Testament. The gospel accounts and the epistles of Paul and Peter and John talk about the fact that Christ is present within us."

The Shaker way is to love God—and not just to say so but to let that love nuance every action—all day. "And so," continued Brother Wayne, "it's like you look at a church. And you see all these people and they're so holier than thou on Sunday. And then during the week they're just absolutely horrible. Well, what does that tell you about Jesus, what does that tell you about God? Can you really believe in a God, in a Christ who represents himself that way? I mean, how does that draw you to the Christian faith if that's what you see these people as?"

For Brother Wayne, then, the magnetic pull of Shakerism lies in its power to infuse all aspects of life. He has tried to leave behind the dual life, which Ann Lee had seen as dangerous when she implored her followers to "purify your hearts, ye double-minded."

"So I think what really speaks to me the most," concluded Brother Wayne, "is that—and certainly our own founders of this particular church talk about it—that we are to *be* those epistles. . . . You can stand up on a soapbox and preach the gospel all you want. But it is the living it, it is the example of your life that best represents it and really touches the lives of people."

For Sister June, the best part of Shaker life happens on Sunday. "You know," she said, "I think I'm most at home here during Meeting. Because we have readings from the Bible, and you concentrate on those readings so that you can give a testimony during Meeting. And I think I have learned a lot of, not memorizing, but just learned a lot of scripture and learned what God wants of people. I have just grown closer to God and to Jesus.

"And I've learned from working with the manuscripts over in the library," she added. "I get to read a lot of what Shakers have written in the past. There are some really wonderful spiritual writings. And I feel a great privilege being able to work with those materials and read them."

More than worship, daily life with other Shakers has brought Sister June's life to full flower. "I just like to be with the community," she said, "and be a part of it as much as I can. And just continue also in my personal spiritual growth. I feel I have grown quite a bit since I've been here."

Confession, the counterpoint to worship, plays a central role in Shaker life. To cleanse one's soul of sin, to unburden to God the sorrow and guilt of one's heart, leaves one free to rejoice in community—through both work and worship. Ann Lee felt that by confession and turning away from worldliness, the truly repentant creates a dwelling place for the spirit of Christ. Shakers of the past followed a regimented schedule for confession, once per week, with their spiritual elders.

Sister Frances recalled a time when, in her childhood, there were so many people living at Sabbathday Lake that "we girls, when we were eight, ten, so forth, would meet with our caretaker every other Saturday. Sister Mildred had the young adults for confession, and she would say, 'I'm going to call on you tomorrow.' And so it was more regimented in that time."

These days, the community calls on one another for confession as needed. Usually, sisters seek out Sister Frances, and brothers talk to Brother Arnold; the two elders often counsel one another. Confession has become a tool for cultivating union.

"Today," said Sister Frances, "we hopefully do not let the sun go down on a real wrong that has been done in the community. We strive very hard to live up to that adage, and that works. If someone has done something wrong, they are expected to make it right. I might have to go to Sister Marie or Sister Marie might go to June—whomever you have wronged, that is a way of confessing it to that person.

"Confession," she noted, "for the Catholics and for Shakers, really is no more than an opening of the mind. A chance to share those things. It's the same as when people pay huge amounts of money to a therapist, a counselor. It's a way of taking out of your life, out of your mind, out of your heart things that are keeping you from a full union with God and your brothers and sisters."

The current method of casual confession keeps members focused as well as harmonious. "Confession," Sister June told me, "has helped me to find out what I should be doing for the community and what they expect of me. And if I need to work on certain aspects of things. When I don't do something as well as I should, perhaps."

Talking with this placid soul, I wondered how anyone could need confession in a place like Sabbathday Lake. "Everybody in the community," she gushed, "they're really wonderful people. And it's a great joy being with them. They have helped me a lot and they are very kind and compassionate, understanding people."

Even as Shaker worship on Sunday has evolved, the Sabbathday Lake Shakers have retained their sense of tradition through several yearly religious events. Beginning with New Year's Day, the family spend quiet time in reflection but also welcome with optimism the promise of the coming year:

Listen! while we join with angels,
Who in love have gathered near,
And we'll tell you of the morning—
Of the glorious day that's dawning—
Of the new and coming year.

The end of February marks the birthday of founder Ann Lee, whose actual day can be honored only once every four years, since she was born on February 29. Each year various friends of the community send greetings or stop by to express good wishes. The Shakers bake a special cake precisely to the recipe used for centuries, and they give thanks for the spiritual presence of the woman-Christ who guides them still. The community had just celebrated this holiday not long before I arrived for my stay with them. Sister Frances beamed when she told me the prayer service that day had been "full of the Spirit" and that they felt the strong presence of their Mother Ann Lee.

Later in spring, the sisters and brothers celebrate Holy Week and Easter, important to them for the renewal of earth and spirit—but not for dwelling on the crucifixion and death of Christ. Rather, the resurrection brings joy. The Shakers engage in quiet contemplation, in-depth study of biblical and devotional texts, and a "hands-to-work" application of faith in the annual spring cleaning of the village dwellinghouse and shops. "It takes us a lot longer" these days, laughed Sister Frances ruefully. "Sometimes it goes into summer."

The community commemorate each other's birthdays, as well as the "birthday" on which each member joined their spiritual family. And they observe national holidays, such as the Fourth of July.

The day when Ann Lee and the first Shakers landed on American soil, reported to be August 6, however, is celebrated with the most gusto, a sense of the miraculous for what has passed in Shaker history and of mystery for what awaits in the future.

I sensed a fine balance, at Sabbathday Lake, between the secular aspects of worldly holidays and the conscious Shaker addition of quiet meditation, worship singing, and spiritual meal sharing, to make the day contemplative.

On Thanksgiving, the worship service at ten o'clock gets packed each year with guests from the world, many of whom return again and again to celebrate the holiday with their Shaker "family." Having met some of these non-Shakers during my time at Sabbathday Lake, I saw a deep, abiding connection between their families and this celibate one. They shared greater kinship than do many blood relatives.

Christmas, the busiest season of the year for Shakers, means also a time for a "fast day" in late November or December, and the practice of confession and reconciliation on Christmas day. Like many secular families, the Shakers at Sabbathday Lake have had annual visits from Santa in the past when children lived with them. Today no children live at Sabbathday Lake, but each year the spiritual family "adopts" several needy families in their rural Maine area. They raise money in an annual "white elephant" garage sale, get wish lists and clothing sizes from the parents, and do festive shopping and wrapping. Several members told me this is a highlight of their year: They love to play Santa.

Also at Christmas, members cook Shaker boiled fruit cakes for holiday giving and pack tins of herbs and herbal teas to fill the holiday orders of customers throughout the country. Shaker Village hosts an annual Christmas fair, attended by hundreds, at which Shakers sell baked goods and gifts. On Christmas Eve, the brothers and sisters come together for a holiday meal and then sing carols, share gifts around the tree, and reaffirm their bonds to each other and their faith. At ten o'clock on Christmas morning, they meet for worship, silent meditation, and a homily of shared personal witnessing.

Even on nonholidays, the community strives to weave worship into every day. Year-round, the Shakers spent more quality time each day with their Spirit God, I discovered, than I spent with my here-and-now husband and children. To cultivate a constant awareness of God, they gather thrice daily to sing songs, recite psalms, bless special intentions, and explicate scripture. Evenings stay quiet, usually, to allow for spiritual study and contemplation. Wednesdays at five o'clock sharp, members refresh themselves with an hour of shared prayer. And Sunday morning Meeting completes the worship that has been going on all week.

The Shakers actually come eagerly to prayer. This I rarely have seen in my non-Shaker days on earth. Through the entire visit to Sabbathday Lake, I wondered how they could be so precisely punctual at daily prayers and meetings. Do they fear chastisement? Do they discipline themselves as harshly as Ann Lee would have done? Or perhaps they simply want to show respect for the community schedule and for God. But I also noticed a certain joy in the dropping of everything to rush together in prayer. The Shaker song "Hour of Prayer" conveys the feeling.

How blest is the season when, calm and retired,
The soul is by feelings angelic inspired;
Away from the troubles of life and its care,
How pleasant and sweet is the hour of prayer.

Their hour of prayer is the worldly woman's bubble bath, the worldly man's nine holes. It does for them what we spend money and pack schedules to do: the manicures and cocktails, yoga and coffeebreaks, shopping and television that supposedly relax us. Too often, even these privileges become chores to be gotten through and crossed off our daily minders. But peace, I was learning, whether found in prayer or in the bathtub, cannot be rushed.

The believers who practice today are refreshingly human. Sister Frances told me how she tries to maintain a sense of the sacred even on days when it does not come easily for her. She has utterly uninspiring days. "Oh yea, oh yea," she laughed. "Sometimes, in our Wednesday night meetings, we all take a turn leading it. And I always say to Brother Arnold, 'Is it my turn yet?' Because I'm expected, I don't know—this is just something that has occurred over the years—I'm expected to be the first one to speak, to get the spirit, the labor of the meeting under way. And many times, I would like to be able to sit there, and be able to hear what other people are saying and to be able to respond to it, to let it find a place in my thoughts that I can bring together.

"I don't always feel well prepared when that second song comes to an end and we bow heads and ask God to bless the meeting, to bless what we are going to be saying," Sister Frances admitted. "Sometimes, it's according to what we've just read and heard in the scriptures. Some of them find a real response very quickly in me, and sometimes I have to ponder it and stumble over it. Sometimes I feel far from profound."

The Maine sun streamed in the windows all around us as she talked about worshiping her God. Our bellies were full from noon dinner, a glorious spread of buttered parsnips, home-baked bread, fresh salad, and a huge vat of macaroni and cheese (not from a Kraft box) that left me craving it long after. A sense of contentment flooded the bright room.

"How do you know that God exists?" I asked her.

As the eldress looked back at me, I suspect she wondered how, in such a simple, wondrous moment, I could ask such a question.

First she gave me a matter-of-fact answer. "I was raised in a family from birth that firmly believed in a God. And so it's always been a part of my life," she said. "I can't imagine being without it."

And then she reached down to her gut and told me what she felt. "How do I know there is a God? How do I know that the sun is going to shine? How do I know that the wind will blow? I look around nature. If I didn't have any other way of believing in a higher power, I would look around at the beautiful world and know that it could not have been created by anyone other than a God."

For Sister Frances, God transcends the teachings of her youth, the decades of Shaker practice. "When I say my prayers, I don't envision—I don't see a person. I don't see anything at all," she continued. "I *feel*. I feel a very warm presence. I know that it may not be the way I *want* my prayers to be answered, but I'm convinced that somehow or other those prayers are going to be answered. I wouldn't continue to pray every single night, morning, and midday if I didn't believe. I'm truly convinced."

She lay both large, strong hands flat on the surface of the table and leaned forward just a little. "I just *know*, Sue," she told me with a steady smile. "I've always known."

Later, I stopped by to see Brother Alistair in his sewing workshop, where he stitched small mouse toys and methodically filled them with catnip. These would be sold at the Shaker shop, to help support the community. Brother Alistair sat by the window, where a soft breeze rippled the lace curtain, and talked with me about his personal view of God.

He said that, in prayer, he often visualizes God. And his vision turned out to be quite elaborate. "I think if I could have an icon painted," he mused, "I would like the meetinghouse in the background. I would like a huge radiant light with lots of colors coming out of it, over the meetinghouse. And I would like Jesus in a white seamless garment hand-in-hand with Mother Ann, just in front of the meetinghouse. Perhaps they would have their hands together and perhaps the other hand would have rays coming out of it."

Despite the complexity of this young Shaker monk's vision, he quickly added that this would be symbol only—not a view of the actual deity.

"When I pray, it is to Father/Mother God, and our Father/Mother God is spirit. I don't think of the old man in the sky," he explained.

"I don't visualize our Father/Mother God," Brother Alistair said, "but I visualize Jesus and Ann as their representatives or the man or woman made most perfectly in their image. Or the man and woman who have been anointed with the Christ-Spirit to the greatest extent. And I see them very much as the son and daughter of the new creation, of the first among many brethren and sisters. I see the Christ anointing which they received, something which is available to all."

Brother Arnold, who grew up Methodist in Springfield, Massachusetts, learned early to pray to God. "Religion was instilled in us very early on. I mean, we were very active in our church when I was young. My mother taught Sunday school and my father was on worship committee and finance committee," he said.

As a child, his personal view of God evolved through night prayers. "Well, every night our parents came to hear our prayers individually before we went to bed. We were always inspired to have a conscience and to think about God and to have an active—I mean as active as a child would have—prayer life."

Elder Arnold came to the Shakers at the formative age of eighteen. He began by corresponding with Brother Theodore Johnson, a theologian and historian who came to Sabbathday Lake in the 1960s and helped launch what historians now call the Shaker revival still in progress among the Maine Shakers. Young Arnold Hadd came to see what Shaker life was all about, and he found what he was looking for, in the everyday love of God.

"I think it was the sense of living out the life each and every day," Brother Arnold told me. "That God calls us to a commitment that seems to me to be one hundred percent. And people who are very devout can carry that within themselves. and continue to have a worldly life and all of that. But that's very, very, very difficult to do on your own.

"I don't know why I was exactly called and chosen to this particular way of life, but it seemed to appeal to me and it seemed to answer many of the questions I had theologically. It seemed to answer, How does one live a godly life in a practical daily sense? And there is a support within the community that is not available outside the community, that allows you the strength and the courage, the example and help—all of which you cannot get when you're out there on your own."

Shakerism is not an easy life, Brother Arnold told me, but added, "I've never doubted the [Shaker] way." He looked at me with eyes that smoldered intensity. "I have never, never, never doubted this is the right choice for me. And I've never doubted the absolute veracity of the gospel and that it could not be lived out anywhere else in any other experience.

"I have sometimes doubted whether I could continue to live it," he admitted, "but thankfully those have been very short spans of time. And they're needed. You know, the dark nights of the soul are horrible, horrible things to go through, but without them you can become a spiritual jellyfish.

"And God gives us the choice, over and over again," he continued. "If our eyes and ears can be opened, there's a lot of pain that we don't need to bring upon ourselves. But, because of our own self-will and determination, we often allow pain to happen. And we have to learn by our mistakes. Which is a very sad thing to have to admit to, but it's a lot of the way I've lived my life. You know, trial and error. A lot of error."

He looked down at sinewy hands that intertwined in his lap. "I don't know that I can honestly say I've regretted almost anything I've done in my entire life, because hopefully I have learned from every mistake I have ever made. The thing I would most regret is not learning from a mistake and having to repeat it until I got it right."

Listening to Brother Arnold, again I had that haunting feeling that I had heard these words before. And sure enough, when I checked the *Testimonies*, there was his founder saying in her eighteenth-century language: "I confessed my sins to my Elders, one by one, and repented of them. . . . I felt determined not to be reproved twice for one thing, but to labor to overcome the evil for myself."

Sunday morning at Sabbathday Lake, the fog hovered over the water in hushed anticipation of the day. Somehow, the day felt different. Because Shakers uphold the Sabbath, this day's work would be minimal, to allow for resting, meditating, singing, preaching, absorbing, laughing, conversing, dining, renewing. This day felt full of possibility; for anything could happen at Shaker Meeting.

Later the sun broke through, just in time for Meeting. Cars crowded the small parking area behind the dwellinghouse. A young man from the world with close-shaven black hair jumped out of a red pickup truck, smiled a greeting to me, and strode up to the building. Except in summer, Sunday worship takes place right where the Shakers live, in the large room they call Chapel on the second floor of the dwellinghouse.

Walking to the back door, I met Brother Wayne, who was dressed almost like any other churchgoing man on a Sunday morning. He wore a bright white shirt, freshly starched, with khaki pants and a button-down vest. The three brothers did not wear ties, yet Brothers Alistair and Arnold looked more formal with matching dark slacks and vests.

The sisters, except for older Sister Ruth, wore traditional Shaker dress. All I could think of, when I saw their starched cotton frocks, was how much time and effort someone spent this morning—and every Sunday—ironing every crease and gather. These Shaker women did not shrink away from color either: Sister Marie wore bright pink in a solid fabric, Sister June wore a mottled pattern in robin's egg blue, and Sister Frances wore the deepest hue of cobalt blue. Today, they, like me, had bothered with stockings, although they still wore sensible shoes. They looked comfortable. At least I thought so, until an hour later when, at the first possible moment after Meeting, the sisters all slipped away to change back into regular clothing.

Chapel was a large, bright room with wood floors and tall, paned windows. No drapes adorned these windows; only plain green shades hung down partway to regulate the light. Overhead, simple lighting fixtures dangled. The walls were bare except for a Victorian fresco around the ceiling. Its swirling arches must have been added in a more decorative period of history.

Shaker-style benches lined the walls on either side. Brothers entered through the right-side door and took their places; sisters entered on the left and faced the men. A clearing of about ten feet in the middle contained a podium at one end, for readings, and a table with a vase of red roses at the other. With my Catholic eyes I searched the room hungrily for symbols. Where was God? Or at least the human manifestation of God? Was there no open Bible to remind us of the sacrality of the Word, no picture of Ann Lee to summon her presence, no crucifix of Jesus to commemorate his martyr's death? No. Here the only symbols were the fresh, twining roses, no doubt a gift from one of the many worldly visitors of today, and the markedly dressed Shakers themselves.

Twenty-two of us, chosen and worldly alike, filled half the benches of the room. People smiled greetings to one another, or looked down at their hands to attempt meditation. There were equal numbers of women and men and, today, no children. Later I learned that the visitors had come from all over the country, and most had been here before: a couple of students from nearby Bates College, a banker from Rochester on her way to visit friends for the week, and a businessman from Ohio come to do repairs on a home he had just bought on the Maine coast.

Two staff members, the men who lived here on-site, also attended. They, like many of the others from the world, knew Shaker songs and joined in with steady voices. Brother Arnold opened Meeting with an invitation for all to feel comfortable, to join in with song and prayer, and to give testimony "as the Spirit calls you."

We began with the Psalms, read by Sister Ruth, who looked like a chaste, elegant granny in her matching floral-print dress and jacket, stockings, and flat lace-up shoes. She read from Psalms 37 with confidence, though her voice quivered with age.

The next readings, from Hebrew and Christian Bibles, delivered a powerful message on which most members of the congregation would build pieces of a sermon in turn. From John, words of hope:

> Let not your hearts be troubled; believe in God, believe also in me. In my Father's house there are many rooms; if it were not so, would I have told you that I go to prepare a place for you? . . . I will come again and will take you to myself, that where I am you may be also. *John 14:1–3*

And from Corinthians, words of comfort:

> Since we have the same spirit of faith . . . we know that he who raised the Lord Jesus will raise us also with Jesus and bring us into your presence. For it is all for your sake, so that as grace extends to more and more people it may increase thanksgiving, to the glory of God.
>
> So we do not lose heart. Though our outer nature is wasting away, our inner nature is being renewed every day. *2 Corinthians 4:13–16*

Shaker songs framed the readings at beginning and end. Then began the communal testimony. Whoever felt the urge stood and talked briefly about the meaning of the reading in his or her life, how its message felt and how it might be applied tomorrow, after the hour of worship had done. Some spoke with a sense of their humanity.

"How many times I forget to witness," Sister Frances shook her head back and forth, "even though I have been so privileged to grow up here in this place where I can be constantly reminded of the purpose for my life.

"Yet we who live here in community must remember," she continued, "what a joy and responsibility it is to be witness to God in our daily lives. We cannot go out and tell the world, unfortunately, but our lives here may touch someone else's and the spirit may grow in that way, if we remain open to it. And we must serve as witnesses, if we dare to take in the gospel meaning, if we dare call ourselves Christian, if we call ourselves Shaker."

"We may think prayer happens only at this Sunday Meeting," added Brother Arnold, standing tall and meeting the eyes of those to whom he spoke, "but the readings today challenge us to carry that awareness with us in our daily lives, all week."

"A life of order," nodded Brother Alistair, when he stood to address the small crowd, "helps me to keep my focus on God, and it creates union in a community such as this one. When our lives are well-ordered, with work and prayer, study and recreation, we can avoid the kind of distraction that comes from scurrying about."

The young man from the red pickup truck commented that he had heard several reminders to slow down—to walk, rather than run, to God. "In the Southern Baptist tradition in which I was raised," he told us, "many people turned charismatic and raced as fast as they could go to the Lord, but then in a couple of years they burned out."

He looked down at his shoes and lowered his voice. "And that's the way I live my life, too often: running and then slacking off. If only I could go slower, and more deliberately, and get there steadily."

"Amen to everything that's been said," chimed Sister Marie,

who loathed speaking up in front of people. The others looked at her, knowing this, and chuckled with her.

Songs wove through in between testimonies:

> Break forth into singing, Break forth into singing,
> ye virgin sons and daughters of the New Creation,
> For now is come salvation, for now is come salvation,
> the great and glorious day of the Lord.

Women's and men's voices encircled one another in a round as we sang of God's hand in the harvest of life:

> The sun fails not, nor the dews and showers,
> The seasons in their order come and go;
> So we look in faith to the higher pow'rs
> For a harvest from the seed we sow.
> Let us sow, let us sow, let us sow, let us sow
> With a free and lib'ral hand; let us sow, let us sow,
> Over the sea and land.

Everyone hung around after Meeting. They shook hands and chatted until Sister Frances cheerfully shooed them downstairs to the dining room. Visitors filled tables from an earlier, more crowded era, tables the Shakers alone could no longer fill. Platters of carefully arranged doughnuts were passed. People who had never before met jumped at the chance to pour each other's coffee, pass a napkin.

We tasted Shaker life that morning. We came together with people from disparate lives and personalities, approached one another with unspoken respect, and for a time shared union with them in a way that felt at once sociable and spiritual. I caught a couple of others, young college students, gazing about them with the same bit of awe I felt, to be here on Shaker holy ground and to be welcomed so fully into the fold.

On one side of the room, Brother Alistair and Sister Frances took turns holding my baby son, whom my sister had brought over for socializing after Meeting. And on the other side, Brother Wayne held court with a heated debate about gun control and gang violence. Sister June, sitting in the middle of the commotion, listened to some of the newcomers chatting about their home lives and work, and she nodded and smiled a warmth that kept them talking. Sister Marie plopped down to devour a doughnut, but soon jumped up to wait on people again. And Brother Arnold conversed one-on-one, with several people in turn, while he folded a paper napkin into tiny squares.

When the crowd grew restless but still reluctant to leave, the brothers led them on an expedition down to the sheep barn to meet baby lambs few of the Sunday visitors had yet seen. My sister and her husband (who had joined us in Maine for the weekend) carried my little six-month-old down the path and held him as he squealed with delight over the woolly babies in the barn. This field trip, the brothers' part in the day's hospitality, allowed the sisters to finish cooking a feast for noon dinner, to which we were all invited to stay.

As I donned an apron and helped Sister June arrange heaping platters of vegetables around Sister Frances's perfectly roasted turkey, I felt festivity pulsate through the air. To feed the souls and then the bodies of a crowd of twenty or more was no small feat, I knew from dinner parties I had attempted. And the Shakers did this regularly, despite their own need for quiet reflection. The sheer expense, the lugging of supplies from the market, the hours of cooking and the mess of cleanup, were approached with good-natured cheer. The sharing of prayer and food with anyone who knocked on the door carried on the centuries-old Shaker ministry of hospitality. And the Shakers felt committed to seeing the Christ in each visitor and honoring that person for the presence of the spirit within.

But there was more to it than that. As the crowd gathered again and bowed their heads for a brief blessing, then piled their plates and found their places along the table, something sacred took place. True to the style of the current Shakers, it was quiet, unobtrusive, but steadily present if only one noticed.

It was communion.

We each brought to table the best of us—our love, compassion, joy, hope—and passed it around with the same polite manner in which we passed the pickles. We were together, in community, in union. This was no ordinary experience of a large, amiable crowd dining together. The something that had drawn us all together that day, that had caused us to linger long after the plates were cleared, pulled us together as one for a while. Maybe it was the Spirit. Maybe it was simply the hunger, the search, for spirit.

This was a far cry from the Meetings of previous centuries, when visitors flocked to the Shakers to see a spectacle, the way they would to a circus or freak show. This day, the worldly had come humbly, hungrily, hoping to share in the rich spirituality they had found here before—perhaps on a tour, or at a holiday gathering, or through the introduction of a friend. They came with respect. To them, as to me, praying in the simple Shaker way felt like a privilege. To "come down where we ought to be," as the song "Simple Gifts" says, left us feeling free.

CHAPTER FIVE

CELIBACY

Oh union, pure union, thou gift of the heavens,
In harmony blending our spirits in one;
'Tis joy and blessing as onward we're pressing,
To the bright happy goal where life's crown is won.

—*"Oh Union, Pure Union"*

Atop the crest of one plain hill in Maine, on land unnoticed by many but held sacred by a few, women and men daily battle their human nature. Lust sits at the base of it. Lust laughs at their efforts to tame it, to overcome the heat of the blood that courses through their veins.

I stood atop that hill and thought of all the ways Shakers have struggled to avoid their sexuality. Long ago, brothers and sisters could channel those feelings into ecstatic worship. Yet the frenzied dance of Shakers' past stands today as a dim, strange memory to these Sabbathday Lake Shakers. So now, where did such feelings—to me an inevitable part of being alive—go?

I imagined these Shakers sublimated their libido through demanding work or consuming creativity. Or perhaps the eight sisters and brothers who remained simply took great care to stay quiet. Rise in the morning, toil all day, read the Bible, walk gently, speak politely . . . hold it in.

The reining in of libido, an energy so powerful as to fuel the whole of our lives—according to Freudian psychology—must have some impact on Shakers. No matter how chaste they strive to be, do they not pulse with the same sexuality as do the rest of us in the world? What if libido can never be denied?

Then, perhaps, the dawn-to-dusk labor of the Shakers, in their careful crafting and self-controlled cleaning, would never deplete such power. Mopping a workroom floor in steady, precise strokes could never begin to tap the passion that pulsates within. If the serene everyday devotion of the Shakers could not mask the power of their human bodies, I wondered, then where else on the softly rolling hills of the farm, in the tidy rooms of the community buildings, did their libido leak forth?

Shakers shunned sex from the very start because, they believed, lust led one to hell. Too dangerous to even think about, sexuality got shut off as though it were a valve that could be tightly closed. They preached pure celibacy.

A young man named Jonathan came to see Mother Ann Lee at Poughkeepsie, while she was on a missionary tour. He had a sweetheart, and they both sought "gospel strength." From Ann Lee, according to the *Testimonies*, he received the harshest admonition: "God will bring down the haughtiness of man," she warned, "and stain the pride of all flesh.

"Jonathan, do let that woman alone," she implored him. "God will break into pieces the man and the maid." She minced no words. "The marriage of the flesh is a covenant with death, and an agreement with hell."

The Shaker heaven on earth involved marriage of the spirit, not the flesh. "If you want to marry," she informed the young man, "you may marry the Lord Jesus Christ. He is my husband, and in him I trust."

Elder James Whittaker, who governed after Ann Lee's death, condemned his non-Shaker relatives with smoldering language:

"I hate your fleshly lives," he said, "and your fleshly generation, as I hate the smoke of the bottomless pit." Until they embraced chastity and the true gospel, he told them, they were nothing but "a stink in my nostrils."

Even while Shakers hotly denied any connection to their sexuality, though, early believers found release in dancing. Wild, untamed dancing, that believers offered as joyful worship to God, but that I began to think of as a metaphysical form of sex.

The dance of ecstasy encircled many core Shaker beliefs. Heaven, perhaps glimpsed in the whirl of the dance, was as egalitarian as the earthly Shaker community of equals. On earth, any Shaker could whirl and dance with great spiritual potency, with access to visions. Shakers could touch the spiritual realm—the dead, the saints, even the Christ. And the physical exercises and dancing that put Shakers into some sort of trance state were means toward that unity with the spiritual realm.

And the whirling—which appeared quite strange to non-Shakers, yet must have felt so liberating to women in long, drab dresses and men in tight-collared, starched shirts—became a channel for the passion Shakers wanted to avoid at any price. Intentional or not, Shaker dancing may have functioned as sex.

Worshipers were said to have twirled and jerked, stepped and jumped, until they reached a sort of trance state and then collapsed into exhaustion. The release possible in this sort of exercise, not permissible to Shakers in masturbation or any other way, must have felt wonderful. Sweaty, in the aftermath of such release, a Shaker would feel the close connection with God that prompted the dance in the first place. The human body, still sexual although Shaker, could get some relief from the tight constraints of celibacy and order, and the soul could meet its maker for an instant in time.

Maybe that instant compared with what we in the world know as orgasm.

The sex of Shakers, which may never involve the throbbing touch of body to body, may be purely metaphysical—*metasex*, so to speak. Release of libido that takes place only in the mind, that also nourishes the soul. We in the world may have experienced metasex in sexual dreams, or ripe fantasies, or the bliss that washes over us at the top of a mountain or in the glory of a shoreline sunset. Perhaps Shakers have known all along how to channel their ecstasy into the dance and beauty of life.

From early on, I found documented cases in which Shakers seem to have experienced something like spiritual orgasms. For example, a nobleman from France, the Marquis de Barbe-Marbois, visited the Niskeyuna community and reported what he saw. "The Shakers are seized with their movements at any time, on any occasion, while they cultivate the earth, while they are cutting trees, while traveling on foot, or on horseback. We saw them in this condition during their rest, and during conversation. The convulsion does not interrupt anything; the most usual movement is to turn the head from left to right, with eyes closed or raised toward the sky, with an expression which proclaims ecstasy, anguish, and pain.

"We noticed that the women shed tears," continued the Marquis, "were pale and downcast, and that their face reanimated itself only when the convulsion was at an end. The men raised their arms, trembling; their knees gave way and knocked together. Often while all their members shook, they would seem to have a seizure under which they would succumb, but it was the end of the ecstasy. The head turned less rapidly, and when the crisis was over, they sighed deeply, like people relieved at length of excessive anxiety, or coming out of a painful swoon."

I had not witnessed this kind of ecstasy yet, in my stay at Sabbathday Lake, but I soon would hear similar descriptions from the very Shakers who now surrounded me. Although they no longer danced, several reported receiving physical experiences of bliss in their daily life that they ascribed to the washing over of the presence of God.

Two centuries after the Marquis, Robert Melville wrote for the *New Statesman* on the sexuality he perceived in Shaker dance. "The men were strong and virile," he wrote, "and it is possible that the excitement of the dance led to spontaneous emissions, giving them a kind of sexual satisfaction that could be rationalized as 'immaculate.' I do not know enough about women," he admitted, "to be able to guess at the nature of their physical gratifications."

While the bliss of the dance has subsided, today the Shaker shunning of sex continues. Sister Frances suggested that "Perhaps giving in to the sexual nature of our beings might have been the original sin." Sexuality yokes one to the earth. Careful! One may slip down into the rich soil and know the earthly pleasures of man and woman. One may succumb to the body only to lose the soul. Seen in the eighteenth century as a literal loss of one's salvation, sex is now viewed as a dangerous luring away from one's primary goal of unity with God and dwelling in the spirit.

During the spiritual revolution of early Shakerism, however, even Ann Lee admitted that someone on earth must continue to propagate. Shakers have always known that they needed the young products of marriage and family as converts, that some of us in the world are meant to marry and make babies. Today, the Sabbathday Lake Shakers have an easy tolerance for and friendship with noncelibate people, friends who embrace some Shaker values, if not the lifestyle.

And, they find, the emphasis of spirit over body does prove advantageous in some ways. Sister Frances pointed out to me that "Celibacy frees you to love equally. If we had allowed marriage, naturally I'd want my husband to hold the best position; I'd want my children to be very special." Shakers wish to avoid the deep-seated competition that comes naturally to us all when we rally for our spouse's job promotion or root for our daughter's soccer team.

"Celibacy allows me to love other men, other than I would my husband, in a pure way," she said, tilting her head sideways just a little. "Many people ask me if I don't miss that close relationship with one person that a marriage would bring about. And I would have to say, at this point, that has not really been a problem in my life. Celibacy, I feel, frees me to love a lot more people than I would be able to love had I been married to one man. I have so many friends, both male and female, and many of the males are happily married, yet we're very, very close friends.

"If I don't see them for a while, and then they come for a visit, we greet each other with a hug," said the eldress. "And I feel very comfortable knowing that their wives, their families have no fear of that, because I have accepted celibacy as one of the vows that I live by.

"Other people ask if I don't miss having my own children." Here she looked down for a moment. I knew the natural love this woman had for children, for it shone in her eyes when she talked with her four-year-old grandnephew, Ricky, and it welled up in her tears as she held my own infant son in her arms.

Then the seventy-year-old virgin looked up with clarity. "All of my life," she recalled, "from the time I lived out in the children's house, there were always younger children. I came here with my younger sister, and she was very dependent on me, so I was involved with children all of my young life. And certainly all through my teenage years, right up to the point where I am now, I have been involved with children. I did some substitute and assistant teaching here in the Shaker school. . . . I don't miss children because I've always been with children. I guess I've had all of the good points with them without any of the hardships."

She *had* mothered, I realized. She had loved with motherly nurturing, and had been loved with the same tenderness. She had shared, first with her mentors and then with Shaker children and worldly schoolchildren, a deep, if not owning, kind of love.

Still, I wondered how a person could live a whole lifetime without sex. When I tried to ask her about it, Sister Frances looked at me and squinted. Could it be that she had never been aware of her libido? "It's difficult for me to really answer that adequately," she said, "not having had a sexual relationship that most women my age would have had." Yet Sister Frances admitted that she, as a flesh-and-blood human, had "the same hormones, the same feelings, same desires that any woman in the world might have."

She smiled as she remembered her youth. "Probably when those of us who accepted celibacy were in those early years, when human hormones are working overtime, perhaps the very fact that we would not be entering into a sexual relationship with anyone [bothered us]. That is a part of the human race."

Unlike her predecessor, Ann Lee, though, Sister Frances believes that sexuality fulfills a good, healthy function in the world. "I mean, God certainly created us to have those desires," she said, smiling.

Her key to celibacy was foreknowledge. All through her childhood as an adopted Shaker, she knew she would someday choose to stay or go, and that part of the Shaker choice would be lifelong celibacy. For Sister Frances, free choice made all the difference. "Once you accept the fact that you're going to be living a celibate life, it seems to fall into place easily. Perhaps not as easily for everyone as for some of us."

She also pointed out that "There are many, many people outside of Shaker religion, outside of all the religious orders who don't marry."

And, perhaps for her the most valued payoff for a lifetime of chastity, "Celibacy frees us from being men's servants. St. Paul tells about the role that women should play in the church. And I just thank God that Shaker women never had to come under the slavery that he speaks about, that we are 'inferior' to men. Heaven forbid! We're not inferior to men. And in the Shaker church, this has never been the case."

Giving up sex, in fact, proves less difficult for most Shakers than giving up their independence. Living in a communal society, people cannot "do what they want to do when they want to do it," noted Sister Frances. Adults must be obedient, she said.

During my stay at Sabbathday Lake, one afternoon the elders hosted a group of students from a nearby college, who had come for a tour and question session, hoping to glean something for their term papers on the Shaker way. They asked Brother Arnold and Sister Frances the most frequently asked question: How do you manage to live as celibates?

The two elders looked at one another and smiled, because their answer had nothing to do with sex. Brother Arnold said that he had, over the years, seen sixteen novices come and go from Sabbathday Lake: sixteen well-meaning people of faith who tried the Shaker life only to realize that they could not commit their lives to it. And, the two elders pointed out to the eager students' faces that waited before them, it was not because of sex.

"Everyone who comes into this life knows beforehand that celibacy is going to be one of the things that they will deal with," said Sister Frances. "So they are aware of that. I think what people are not aware of until they really become immersed in community life is the fact that they're going to have to give up an awful lot of what they've been used to. Independence, their own will, their own way."

One could not plan one's own daily schedule, their menu, or their next Hawaiian vacation—not within the Shaker way. "And I think we find," continued Sister Frances, "that particularly a young man or a woman who has been used to coming or going as they please, cannot get into one of the automobiles and just take off for the day. We have to have the approval and the union of everyone. You may have noticed in your stay here," she told me, "that if I'm going to be away or Brother Wayne is going to be away, we make that known so that other people can take advantage. Not only from a financial aspect, the use of the car or the gasoline, but being away from the community. And I think that's very hard for many people to take. I'm not discounting the fact that celibacy has been the stumbling block for many young people. I just don't think it is the main stumbling block for most people.

"It's not easy," she sighed. "I think that I was so fortunate in many ways in coming here and learning about it as a child, growing up in it. And I have a great deal of admiration for those young adults who come in, because you do have to give up an awful lot of *self* in the community. This seems to be what calls people away, once they have experienced it."

Later, when she and I talked, I asked her about self-will. Did the relinquishing of it, I wondered, turn these people into clones, or robots, or saints?

"For example," I said, "what if Brother Wayne had a craving for Oreo cookies late at night? Would he be able to go down and raid the kitchen for them?"

"Oh yea," the eldress replied easily.

"And would you put them on the grocery list, just for him, if he asked?"

"Yea," she said, smiling, not really understanding my point.

But I persisted. "What if Sister June wanted to study Zen Buddhism and begin meditating in the mornings?"

"Oh," she said, nodding now. "I know, right. Yea, I do. It would disrupt the union." To her, that seemed key. Although modern Shakers have their own separate checking accounts, and Sister Marie keeps her own pet (an unsociable cat) in her craft workshop, and in many other ways members fulfill their individual personalities, still nothing is worth the price of community.

The more I read about Shakers, the more I wondered about celibacy. The reality of a celibate life I could not begin to comprehend. Of course, there had been celibate periods in my life. I had deliberately *chosen* celibacy, in my past, even after knowing the pleasures of physical love. I had chosen it and honored it, even on hot nights of my body's ravenous passion and my date's persuasive kisses.

But I had merely dabbled in it, for I knew even then that celibacy functioned only as a temporary shield against heartbreak. I stayed out of lovers' beds as an act of self-protection: against pregnancy, venereal disease, and the depth of intimacy that would leave me shattered when they left . . . which they always did.

Not until I met my husband did I completely lower the

shield and enter with trust a bed of shared soul-communion, body-orgasm bliss. Laughing with relief and happiness, I tossed away the celibacy I had borrowed, never having committed my whole life to it.

Shakers seemed to have constructed a life utterly bereft of sensuality. It was not just sex they gave up: It was the knowledge of it. Sister Frances, adopted by the Shakers as a child and covenanted as a young woman, now approached her twilight years without ever having known human love.

It was not just sex Shakers gave up: It was the warmth of it, the tenderness of skin against skin with a lover who has just brought you to ecstasy. It was the knowing clasp of hand-in-hand in a movie theater or home-mortgage office—the comforting touch of the one who has seen you in all your noblest beauty and weakest pain. It was the primal hunger of a womb for a child, and the love that later swelled one's belly, and the searing birth of the child you have created together. It was the cradling together of that child, from its vulnerable infancy to the grown-up time you both reluctantly let go.

It was not just sex Shakers give up: It was the standing power of one mature body next to another through the years and changes of a lifetime. It was the comforting presence of two lovers, side by side on the bed, through quiet or restless nights of life's twilight years. It was the familiar comfort of one wrinkled smile to another over the heads of doctors, beyond the reach of pills and heating pads, alongside the fear of decay and death. It was the tenderness with which one lover buried the lifeless remains of another, placing him down into the earth with hands lined with years of loving him, tending his grave with faithfulness that only one person in this world remembers.

Before coming to Sabbathday Lake, I spent the days reading endless pages of Shaker history and theology, and then at night I rolled, laughing in love, in bed with my husband, our bodies entwined in the easy lust of long-term lovers. The incongruity of my work and life rose up like a specter of Ann Lee at the foot of our bed.

I wondered if I would ever understand. My experience was too far removed from celibacy. How could I know what it meant not only to live without sex but not to loll naked on the bed, not to feel the roll of the ocean on one's bare skin, not even to dream of wild, uninhibited sex?

We have only the now, and now is glorious. Life has blessed me with a series of sensual moments: the crisp taste of a chardonnay as a cool breeze lifts my hair at an outdoor Italian café; the smell of an old book plucked from dusty shelves; the lush drape of a holiday dress that tingles the skin as it sweeps through a party; the sound of chortling laughter of the dearest old friends gathered to bask at the beach.

For me, life has meant lapping up those moments with great thirst. It means living inside my body, with all the physicality I can muster. I absolutely *love* living inside a body. I am as grounded and ephemeral as one can be.

The purity of the Shakers' choice to live in the spirit was, ironically, matched only by my bodily commitment to my husband and children, who drew from me sustenance, nurturing, and protection. My children ran to me for kisses when they were hurt; my husband sapped my life energy when his work burdened him or his lust encircled me; and my infant sucked nourishment from my breast when everyone else had done with me. Only as I dwelt in the polar opposite of celibacy could I begin to grasp the depth of commitment with which the Shakers had pledged their bodies to God.

Our entire culture has been built upon the material. The "pursuit of happiness" usually means money, property, food, and romance—the whole lot of which the Shakers have tossed out their two-hundred-year-old farmhouse window. We all live indelibly in our bodies. Television commercials show a smattering of personal hygiene products meant to make us younger and sexier, an array of restaurants and prepared foods to tempt our well-fed American palates, and a showroom full of cars that could polish our image. Magazines show articles again and again, each month in slightly different form, about how to lose weight, firm those abdominal muscles, style your hair, wear the latest spring fashions, have the hottest sex, get money, get power, look younger, feel better.

We live not just in but through our bodies. How to live any other way? Did celibate people really know? Because I did not see how one could open the floodgates to physicality without releasing sexuality, too. To feel the full sun on my skin was sexual, to me; to share a sumptuous meal with a man was foreplay. How could one open oneself to the experience of the moment, the body-moment, and not awaken the libido within?

I was not sure it was possible.

Shakers renounced their bodies for many reasons: to purify themselves for the spirit realm, to achieve union with God, and to come together in spiritual community. They took as their model the biblical community of the early apostles. To follow Christ in the regeneration, Shakers believed they had to give up the works of generation. That is, they had to live not as humans but in purity, as angels. They quoted Luke 20:34–35:

> The children of this world marry, and are given
> in marriage: But they which shall be accounted
> worthy to obtain that world, and the resurrec-
> tion from the dead, neither marry nor are given
> in marriage.

The Shaker editor George Lomas borrowed this quote from a sage: "Marriage peoples the earth, but Celibacy increases the forces of heaven." Elsewhere, I read his point that Jesus, the "much adored exemplar" of the Shakers, had been celibate.

As for their communal lifestyle, Shakers based this on the Acts of the Apostles 4:32:

> And the multitude of them that believed were
> of one heart and of one soul; neither said any
> of them that any of the things which he pos-

sessed was his own; but they had all things in
common.

Those incoming members who were of age and free of debt
donated all their worldly goods and money to the Shaker community, for their own sustenance and for charitable donations.
The Shaker covenant stated that all members could take according to need "things both spiritual and temporal." The system of Shaker family, I noticed, took the worldliness away from
a novice at the outset, but provided for material needs
thereafter. Like a family of children, no one advanced into adult
independence as we in the world perceive it.

Shakers denounced the families of their birth so that they
might cleave to their spiritual family with purer loyalty. The
Millennial Praises of 1813 included a song admonishing the faithful to "Love not flesh, nor fleshly kin."

Shakers' separation of families met with resounding protest.
But they pointed to the spiritual family modeled in Mark 10:
29–30, when Jesus says to Peter:

> There is no man that hath left house, or breth-
> ren, or sisters, or father, or mother, or children,
> or lands for my sake and the gospel's; but he
> shall receive a hundred fold now in this time,
> houses and brethren and sisters, and mothers
> and children, and lands, with persecution, and
> in the world to come, eternal life.

Just because the spirit family found basis in the Bible, I discovered, did not justify its existence for the many who lost sons,
daughters, wives, and husbands to the Shakers. An article by
Daniel Patterson in the *Shaker Quarterly* recounts the experience
of one young man who left his home to convert. "My father was
the greatest opposer I ever had. . . . He opposed me as long as
he could, or until he saw it had no effect on me, & then he
tried to turn me by flattery . . . but it never touched me." The

father promised that he should have all his inheritance if the son would but stay, and he "turned up his eyes & cried" when the son left anyway.

The rending of natural family ties caused great pain, for new Shakers and for those they left behind. Sometimes the tearing of one from another created conflict, scandals, even lawsuits.

Outsiders believed that the spiritual "parents" of young Shakers wielded a dangerous level of control. A group who filed an 1800 petition to the New York State Legislature claimed that Shakers had threatened their youth with physical and psychological "terror" to keep them from attempting contact with their parents, relatives, and friends. Over the years, several similar claims were made.

More scandals appeared in the accounts by worldly writers that I combed in my search for the truth. Two women of the early nineteenth century lost their children to the Shakers, when they decided to leave the community, and could not get them back. Mary Dyer wrote two books, *A Brief Statement of the Sufferings of Mary Dyer* and the 450-page *A Portraiture of Shakerism*, in her attempt to win back her children after her apostasy. She called Shakerism "subversive of Christian morality" and "detrimental to the well-being of society." Meanwhile, a New Yorker named Eunice Chapman lost her husband to the Shakers, reported an article in *New York History*, and then spent three years in court vying for divorce. Gaining custody of her three children proved even more difficult, however. The Shakers had hidden them away, and they surrendered the children only after the state granted their mother custody. New York State retaliated by passing an 1818 law declaring Shakers "civilly dead," thus without rights.

Families sometimes clung hard to members who wished to leave them in favor of the new spiritual family. A mob stormed Pleasant Hill in 1825, attempting to free a teenager named Lucy Bryant from "bondage." She and her brother had been indentured to the Shakers by their father. The brother had run away

and, with his mother, planned the attack. They meant to rescue
Lucy who, it seems, wanted no rescuing at all.

A group of up to fifty men, according to letters among Shaker archives, "armed with clubs dirks or pistols," attacked a dwellinghouse. They broke open the door and began randomly
assaulting the Shakers. After some time the men agreed to in-
terview Lucy Bryant herself. She assured them that she was
"steadfast and determined to stay."

They dispersed but returned a week later. This time a mob
of 200 to 300, armed and led by Bryant's mother, descended.
"A more savage looking set of human beings," reported the
Shakers, "never traversd the wilderness of the West." They were
full of exaggerated stories, "artful insinuations," and whiskey.
Bryant's mother, "dressed in black from head to foot," rode at
the head of the yelling mob. She looked to the Shakers "like a
fury from the lower regions." They "dragged the girl off without
mercy," the ministry wrote, "and it was a day of Sufferings for
us, and an awful sight to behold."

Although the Shakers could do nothing to get Bryant back,
they heard that a year later she was still resisting the efforts of
her relatives "to recreate her mind," for she did not wish to live
in the world.

Shakers denied charges of coercion, control, and destruction
of family ties. To them the spirit progressed toward heaven in
this new setting; the heart felt nourished by the new spiritual
blood ties formed among believers. One Shaker described his
family at Enfield, New Hampshire, in 1868: "Here in this lovely
valley you will find Fathers and mothers to caress you as all
Mothers know how to, and Brothers and sisters that it fairly
makes your heart beat with unusual velosity [sic] to even think
of parting with [those] who appea[r] to be much engaged in their
efforts to come up into a higher life."

Coming together as spiritual family meant building a life
together from the ground up. During the early years, Shaker
communities converted single-family farms to fit dozens, then

hundreds, of new believers. They built dwellinghouses and work-shops, cultivated the fields and crops, and established a system of commitment to the Shaker covenant. A new Shaker would undergo three levels of commitment: as a novitiate or "young believer," then in the "junior order" wherein members devoted their labor to the community but retained their own property, and finally in the "senior order" wherein members signed the covenant to declare full spiritual and material commitment to the society. This system had relaxed over time, as I had already seen with novitiate Brother Alistair. With so few members, one became covenanted right into the full order.

At the peak of Shakerism, some 6,000 members in the mid-nineteenth century, most communities still retained a sense of smaller family. Each village consisted of several distinct families who had their own barns, workshops, and dwellinghouses; they lived up to one-half mile away from other families in the same village. Each had its own female-male pair of governing elders, deacons, and trustees. The village elders reported to the "parent" ministry at New Lebanon, in a spiritual succession of authority that descended in a direct line from Mother Ann Lee.

From the start, individuals who joined Shaker ranks relin-quished their self will to the schedule and needs of the family. Their life seemed grueling to me, and hardly an escape from toiling humanity. Shakers rose at 4:30 in summer, 5:30 in win-ter. They did early chores and then had breakfast at dawn, din-ner at noon, and supper at six. Several members shared each bedroom, called a "retiring room," and they all had to go to bed at the same time. The Shakers' strict *Millennial Laws* forbade them to "sit up after the usual time of retiring to rest, to work, read, write, or any thing of the kind," for that might cultivate too much self-interest and waste candles and lamps.

Living within a spiritual family kindled a certain kind of intimacy that the world loathed. A Scottish visitor in 1841 shuddered at the Shakers' close lifestyle. "Their vow is celibacy; and they have everything in common," he said. "How they man-age with their combs and tooth-brushes, I did not presume to ask them." Charles Nordoff, an American journalist who visited the Shakers in the 1870s, found them to be "a parcel of old bachelors and old maids," who fixated on "personal comfort, neatness, and order." Also, I found in my research some rather humorous responses to the Shakers' close quarters. During the Civil War, a Texas Ranger was astounded to find that ninety Shakers shared one dwelling at South Union, Kentucky. "If so many of us lived in one house," he declared, "we should fight and kill each other."

Uniformity ruled. No one had better things than the rest; most Shakers had a narrow bed, a chair, and shared with their roommates a wood-burning stove, washstand, looking-glass, and towels. Although members vowed celibacy, they did not cloister themselves away from the opposite sex, as have other religious groups. Rather, they bunked in separate quarters of the same dwellinghouse. Shakers attributed this to the strength of their vows. One elder compared his sect to "monks and nuns, without the bolts and bars."

Shaker law declared it contrary to order for members to develop special, private relationships, especially between women and men. However, elders knew that the human heart needs friendships. Joseph Meacham organized Union Meetings thrice weekly, during which small groups would gather to visit informally. Several sisters would bring their chairs into the brothers' room and line up their chairs in opposite rows. They would chat for an hour or so, and sing together if they wished. To avoid cliques or budding romances, members were occasionally rotated.

Even Shakers knew, apparently, how the close proximity of bodies could heat the blood of attraction. The *Millennial Laws* of 1845 prudently cautioned sisters not to mend or "set buttons on Brethren's clothes, while they have them on."

Shakers dressed modestly, with great care to reflect their emphasis on soul rather than body. Sisters wore a long, one-piece dress with a full skirt, as did rural women of days gone by. They often added an apron and, more characteristically Shaker, a white cap and bonnet and triangular-shaped white collar. Visitors to Shaker communities often remarked on how the women's dress concealed their figures. Men wore a white shirt under a vest and trousers, sometimes adding a jacket and hat.

To my surprise, I found at Sabbathday Lake, today's Shakers do not renounce their birth families with the same vigor as Shakers past. Rather, their birth families seemed to me to have become extended families, who come and visit now and again, and exchange cards and packages on special occasions, although they have become quite secondary to the new family of spirit.

Brother Wayne came from nearby Portland, and many members of his birth family lived close enough to visit often. For him, at Shaker Village, "There's very much a sense of family here." This does not replace the "nuclear" family of society— nor would he want it to. "You're surrounded by people who share the same world views you do, for the most part. We have a loving relationship. I mean, we're very much like a family," he told me. "And who's to say that, in the nuclear family, there's more love or more security or whatever."

Brother Wayne looked me straight in the eye, and spoke about something I would discover to be a theme for him. "I mean, life doesn't hold any promises. Everything can change, whether through mishap, or divorce, or whatever. The potential for loss, betrayal, whatever is there. I think in one sense, perhaps we have a lower risk of that, because I think when you commit to something like this, usually it's not something that you really rush into."

When the teenaged Wayne Smith first came to Sabbathday Lake, he left behind two parents, two brothers, and one sister. Because he already had spent four years working and visiting there, they were not shocked when he joined the Shakers right after high school graduation.

"I think by the time I made the decision," Brother Wayne remembered, "they knew the community fairly well, so it wasn't like I was going off to join Jim Jones or something. They knew I wasn't being duped into some sort of cult."

Still, the family thought Wayne was just going through a

phase. His mother prodded him. " 'Well, don't you think you're ever going to go to college? Don't you think you're ever going to get married? Are you going to stay a Shaker all your life?' I mean, she was much more actually outspoken about it than my father was.

"You know," he said wryly, "they probably figured, he's young, get it out of his system, then he'll go on to do whatever, have 2.5 children, get a golden retriever, and I think now the right car to drive is a sport utility vehicle," he quipped.

"Ouch, you touched a nerve," I confessed, as he listed my current car as among the requirements of the typical American family. We laughed together at me.

"Eventually," he continued, "the family began to understand that it was my decision, it's my life. And if this is what I'm comfortable with, then fine."

"You've watched your brothers and your sister grow up and have that life that you're not having," I mused, probing for any signs of regret.

"Yeah," he replied. "My youngest brother has three children. You know, they come up here regularly to supper. Because they only live down in Gray, so they'll come up. The kids will see the sheep and get in an argument with my sister-in-law about eating the pigs that we raise. 'Oh, they're so cute, how can you do that?' " Brother Wayne mimicked his sister-in-law in an exaggerated, high-pitched voice, then became serious again. "But, it's not like I don't know what I'm missing, if you consider it *missing*. Again, this is what I've chosen to do. And I'm aware of what the alternatives are. This is what I've chosen to do." Far from disowned, his blood siblings and their children visit often, and one brother works full-time at Sabbathday Lake.

Brother Wayne, a young, red-blooded American man, sat before me. I could not believe he did not miss the chance to hold a woman, to sleep entangled in love, to laugh and talk till dawn. I tried again and again to ask him about this. The answer I got, not the one I expected, finally convinced me that Brother Wayne simply did not want that kind of life.

"How much love is romantic love?" he protested. "When

you're committing to a one-on-one relationship, an exclusive relationship like that [of lovers], a lot of that is— How can I say it without being uncharitable, because I hate to make it sound like I think that marriage is horrible or something. I don't. But, you know, to a degree marriage calls you to a kind of a selfish exclusiveness, which we don't embrace here."

He looked at me through glasses that reflected the afternoon sun, and tipped his head sideways to see if I was following his point. "All right? Because I've not made a vow to one particular person in saying 'I'm going to love you more than everyone else. The two of us are going to be one.' Rather, all of us here are united as a family. I mean, we're not having any sort of sexual relationship, but other than that, I think all the aspects of love we have in our relationship here."

"I've been thinking about this for months leading up to this trip," I responded, slowly, not sure of the waters I tred. "Not just about celibacy. But I've been thinking about all the other aspects, you know—just physicality. I see a lot of love passing between you brothers and sisters. But I don't see a lot of hugs, a lot of touching, you know, holding hands, just the physical warmth. No one to hold in your sleep, no baby to nurse—"

"Yeah," he interrupted. "I mean, it's not that we don't have any warmth between us. It's just that, you know, we just don't express it in the same way. And when we go on trips and stuff, we hug each other good-bye and hello when we get back—that's not forbidden or anything. So there is to that degree warmth."

And then he really let me have it. "But, let's turn the tables. What makes you think *we're* giving up something? Let's put it that way. Because everyone does everything in one way, and we do something a little different, how do you know we don't have the better way and that actually the people who choose the nuclear family life have given up something? Maybe you guys have missed out on something," he proffered.

"And maybe you guys should be looking at it and saying, 'What do the Shakers have and what have we sacrificed by choosing this life?' It's not like we're love-starved or unhappy or anything. As I said earlier, you know, this is a voluntary association and if you're not comfortable in it, it's better that you go. If I begin to have pinings for the world, the door's right there."

Living in community, according to Brother Wayne, is not a cop-out from living in society. "This isn't a place to run and hide," he said. "You know, if you have problems dealing with people or whatever, really a community is probably the worst place you should go, if you don't intend to address any of the issues that are in your life.

"Because here in a community you're confronted daily with them, and so things that may have been problems for you in the world actually [intensify], because you live closely with a group of people and perhaps are under a little more pressure to address these issues."

Brother Wayne stared out the nearby window to the herb gardens beyond. "There is great support here," he pointed out. "But, you know, no one's going to do the work for you. You have to do the work yourself."

"Do you ever, like most families, get angry at each other?" I wanted to know.

"I think we lose our tempers at times," Brother Wayne said. "Yeah. But we don't hold on to those things; and we certainly make it a point to apologize and to try to work out whatever the cause of the friction was."

Here, the contemporary Shaker family makes use of the old tradition of confession. And, occasionally, the elders help members solve personality clashes. "I think sometimes you do need mediation," Brother Wayne told me. "And certainly that's available. We're all adults here. And if we're truly striving to improve ourselves, we're able to work it out. And we do."

He smiled wryly, "We haven't killed each other yet."

One day, in the sleepy hour after Shaker dinner, when the serving table had spilled over with roast chicken and buttered bread, steamed fresh fiddleheads and boiled potatoes with home-grown herbs, when I had ladled too much upon my greedy plate,

I waddled over to the library to talk with Sister June. Although we had exchanged many pleasantries in the sisters' waiting room, I had no idea how far beyond stereotype I would soon discover her life to be. And how animated this small, shy sister could become when she talked one-on-one about her deepest love in life—Christ.

Here in the enclave of spiritual serenity, Sister June had found, when she joined at age fifty, a life packed with purpose and bustling with people such as she never had known. Having never married, she worked at the library every day until she joined the Shakers. Immersed as she was in a thriving neighborhood in the city of Boston, surrounded by sophistication and culture, June Carpenter rode the bus back and forth to work and went nowhere else. She lived five decades without, by worldly standards, ever having lived.

"In your younger life," I ventured to ask, "did you ever fall in love?"

"No. I never had any attraction to that sort of thing," she said in a voice clipped with the accent of a native Bostonian. And I knew, just knew, that she meant more than the fact that she had not felt attracted to men. This woman was trying to tell me that she simply had never felt attracted to anyone . . . any human, that is.

"I just, uh, somehow, I guess I was just more interested in the spiritual life," she said. "I remember when I was in college, I started getting interested in the Catholic Church. I think it was the 150th anniversary of the Archdiocese of Boston. I started reading about sisters in teaching orders and nursing orders, and I was interested in the life of sisters and nuns. And that is how I found out that some people did give their lives to God in some way," she recalled.

"For years after that, I read everything I could find about nuns and sisters. And I didn't have any idea of being called to the ministry, you know, like a minister of a church or like that. I'm kind of more, you know, quiet, and introverted. But this life of sisters in religious communities attracted me. I didn't know about the Shakers until later."

I asked her what had been the most difficult adjustment in the eight years since she joined the Shakers. She told me that this semicloistered life had actually challenged her "to become more outgoing and more extroverted." She, her mother, and her dog "seldom had company at home," she said, except when her cousin and husband occasionally visited. However, at Sabbathday Lake, "We have a lot of company coming here, and when it keeps going on over a long period of time it's hard for me. I sometimes have the urge to draw within myself."

What drains her energy also has enriched her, though. "As I've been here, of course, I've come to know and enjoy a lot of the people and that's a big help, after you get to know them. Everybody who comes is very nice. And, you know, they come because they're attracted to the community and the way of life and they get something out of it, too. So I can relate to them that way," she said.

For Sister June, another surprising perk of spiritual family life has been the cuisine. "Sister Frances and Sister Marie and Brother Alistair, they're all good cooks. I like most every kind of food, so that's a great joy."

She has found her library work "a great source of satisfaction." Still, for her the primary goal in life is one that "I'm still working toward—you know, giving up self completely and living for Christ and for the community."

She had begun to speak in a language quite alien to my third-millennium ears. "How does one 'give up the self'?" I asked.

"The Shakers call it 'taking up your cross each day.' One day at a time. You do things for the community or for company. If somebody comes to visit, you might give up an evening when maybe you want to read or watch television or something that you like to do for yourself," she began.

"I do the dining room work, and help where I can over in

the kitchen, too. I'm no cook, so I try to do dishes and help set up the dining room before meals. And help out in the flower gardens, too." Her upturned face broke out into a wide smile.

"I really enjoy working outside." As whenever the small woman became excited, her voice trembled and rose to a high pitch as she talked. "You know, after a long, hard winter it's such a delight to get outdoors. I've learned a lot since I've been here on how to take care of gardens—how to cut things back and clean up the gardens in the spring, how to do the weeding during the summer."

Here, too, Shaker life has extended the boundaries of experience for quiet Sister June. "I remember when I was working in the library all those years, sometimes we'd sit there and look out the window and wish we could be outdoors when it was good weather."

She has discovered, too, a joy in craftmaking. "I try to make things for the Christmas fair," she said, laughing at herself as though she and art had never before mixed. "I learned how to make little wreaths, sort of like Christmas tree ornaments."

Shaker life has opened a whole realm of possibility for Sister June's mature years. And, to this woman who had clung so faithfully to her mother in her pre-Shaker life, it has granted her a new spiritual mother.

"When I discovered Mother Ann," Sister June spoke now in a low, serious voice, "she was another mother. I have come to think of her as a great saint and as my mother in a way. And I feel that she loves me."

Quoting the passage from Luke upon which Shaker spiritual family is based, Sister June said, "Jesus said in the scriptures that if you give up everything for me you'll find mothers and brothers and sisters. You know, it's possible to have all kinds of people that you think of as your mothers and brothers and sisters. Of course, I had my own natural mother. And then Mother Ann, and the Blessed Virgin Mary, and Sister Frances. And before her there was Sister Mildred. So I have several people that I think of as my mother. They all have a special place," she said, with the soft, trusting voice of a little girl.

"And then, of course, I've got the brothers and sisters in the community. Having come from a small family myself, I'm still growing in this relationship of having all of these family members. But, you know, I really like it," she realized.

"The main purpose of our life," she told me, "is to serve God by serving the people that we meet. And you love God by loving people. That's how you express it, really, your love for God—by your love for the people around you right here."

Brother Alistair, like many people of his generation, left home as a young man and sought his own place in the world. "I haven't been particularly close to my family since I left home when I was eighteen," he told me. "At one point I moved back for a couple of months. When was that—three years ago—and quite quickly moved out again."

I lifted my eyebrows to ask him why. "I have a good relationship with them," Brother Alistair added quickly, in the lilting syllables of his Great Britain homeland. "I'd say it's a *polite* relationship in some ways. I mean, we exchange presents, we speak warmly to each other, but I wouldn't say the communication went very deep." Except for one member. "I feel closer to my youngest brother," Brother Alistair smiled, gazing across the prayer room where we sat to the portraits of his predecessors on the opposite wall. "Of all the people in my family, I'm closest to him."

His family never did "understand" his life, neither in urban London nor in rural Shaker Maine. Yet "I think in many ways they've read between the lines," Brother Alistair said. "I think we communicate without talking about things very much."

Still, now that he has found his lifelong dream of monastic Christianity, "They're very happy for me to be here, really. They quite like the idea. I know that my mother would like me to go home to Ireland more often. Over the last few years I've generally been going home for a week or two weeks a year, usually around Christmas."

His life at Sabbathday Lake has changed drastically, "for the better." Still, the ties that bind him to the past cannot be easily undone.

"Well, you know," he admitted, "I have been homesick from time to time. I have shed quite a few tears. I'm simply homesick. I have no regrets of any sort, but very homesick for friends, I would say. So I simply try not to think about it."

He welcomes the self-control he has learned among his new Shaker family. "You know," he said, smiling gently at himself, "for many years I couldn't control my emotions at all. People say that suppressing isn't healthy, but for me it's a real godsend. I've never been able to do it before, so I'm quite, quite thankful that I can now. And the homesickness is certainly becoming less. Yea, I miss friends. I have some very good, close friendships there. And I certainly would have preferred Shakerism to be in England, but as it happened it was in America and to America I had to come."

Coming to the life of celibacy and spiritual family, Brother Alistair made perhaps the most dramatic change in lifestyle of all the current Shakers. While the others joined as children or teenagers, and one spinster librarian came from a life of sheltered innocence, Brother Alistair, the newest Shaker, jumped with both feet from one extreme to another. He left apartment life in London, a secular job in social services, a smoking habit and "a busy social life," to come straight to the farm at Shaker Village.

"You were very much in the world, weren't you?" I asked.

"Oh yea," he replied, "I mean I don't think that there was anything immoral about my lifestyle, but I'm sure that if some of the community had a window on my lifestyle, the way it was, they would say it was definitely decadent. Yea."

I knew exactly what he meant.

And the same would apply to me, if I ever came knocking on the dwellinghouse door as a hopeful convert. I told him so.

"Yea, yea," he responded, nodding his head and looking at me with a compassion that welled from deep within. "Well, you know," he pointed out, "as we heard in our gospel this morning, he who is forgiven more loves more. You know."

Yea, I did.

For Brother Alistair, the radical change from English urbanite to American Shaker farmer has proved much "easier than expected." Yet even for this cheerful, easygoing brother, some aspects of spiritual family life wear on him.

"Order creates harmony, for me," he began. "And one of the difficult things for me in community has been to see that there are so many aspects of Shakerism that attract people; and we are a very diverse community and we do not have the same vision for how we would like the community to be." His brow furrowed as he went on.

"I would prefer a greater separation from the world," he admitted. Suddenly I saw that this young brother whom I had witnessed in action all around the farm, talking to visitors and restoration workers with the ease and grace of a natural host, also longed for his privacy.

"I find the ministry of hospitality of the community quite wearing," he said ruefully. "That has been a particular cross for me. I would prefer a more contemplative, withdrawn sort of life."

Now that he lived at Sabbathday Lake, Brother Alistair could look back and trace the path that brought him through the windings of other faiths into Shakerism. "You see, I believe that I made the right choice when I was nineteen, in becoming a Benedictine. I believe that this kind of life, in a contemplative sort of environment, is what I've been made for." He remembered that, as a boy of seven, he had asked his mother if there were any monks in their Protestant church. She replied that there were not, and he felt "quite disappointed."

Later, right after high school, he tried life as a Catholic monk. "But the fact is," he said in the frank, humble way in which he always seemed to speak, "I really wasn't emotionally mature enough to have the stability to stay at the abbey. I just wanted other things." He stopped to ponder what it was he had wanted. "I don't know. I hadn't had any successful relationships with people and there was a real ache of loneliness there. I had to do something about that. So that kind of loneliness propelled me out" of the abbey.

During the years that followed, Alistair Bate tasted the world, as his countryside family may never have seen it, as his Benedictine monks would not have imagined it. It was through unusual circumstances that he came to discover the Shaker faith.

"Well, a friend of mine, whom I knew through the HIV field, was an ex-Benedictine monk, and I was looking after his flat while he was away on holiday. He had a bookshelf with a few books about Shakerism and Shaker art. I looked at the picture books first and I thought, *This is just beautiful.* Something about it really drew me." His eyes lit up as he spoke.

"Then I started reading the anthology of spiritual writings from believers and I just knew at that point that I'd come home, that this was the church for me. It said everything that I believed in at my deepest levels. And my emotions all came together. I knew that it was truth for me. And it was a very healing sort of experience. But at the same time it demanded an awful lot of me. And there was still a lot of pain involved in giving things up, you know, but I really felt that it was right."

Having discovered his spiritual home, he now set out to become acquainted with the strangers who would become his spiritual family, and to prepare to leave London.

"I tried giving up the world before, and it was very painful and didn't really work. But I had never got monasticism out of my system. I'd always believed that monasticism was the best thing to do with my life. You know, I still felt called to it even though it was painful and I thought I couldn't do it. The compulsion toward it would not go away," he said firmly. "And my spiritual pilgrimage had taken me in so many diverse directions since monasticism into heterodoxy, really, for example, Quakerism and spiritualism. And I could see that in all major world religions there was monasticism of one type or another."

For Brother Alistair, the search ended in Shakerism. For him, the marriage of spiritism and spirituality, Mother and Father God, and heaven with earth, felt perfectly right.

Although elder of the community, when Brother Arnold sat across from me in our conversations, he seemed as humble and human as anyone could be. When I talked with him I felt a strong sense of a person who longed to be the best he could be, but one who viewed himself with relentless expectations.

He remembered the reaction of his own birth family when, in his late teens, he chose the Shaker family over them. "They weren't very happy," he shook his head and said it again, for emphasis. "They weren't very happy. I think if they had their druthers, I wouldn't be here. They wanted me to do something different with my life. . . . My parents always brought us up to believe that they would support us in any decision we ever made. I don't think that either my father or mother ever expected that I would put them to the test and make them live up to those words. But it was difficult. My dad took a long, long time to accept it."

Not the fact that he departed from Methodism to join another Christian church, but the monasticism, "the withdrawal from the world," anguished his parents. "No hope of a spouse and grandchildren," he said. "Success, which is laid out by the world, is not going to be there. And I also think in the end they just really wondered about how happy I could be in this life."

Although his father saw Shaker Village when Brother Arnold first visited there, the man refused ever to return to the den to which his son had sold his soul. Years and years ticked by, until "he finally turned to me and said that I had made the right choice." Still, Mr. Hadd never had a chance to visit his Shaker son: In 1988, he died of a sudden heart attack, in Florida, over a game of tennis. Meanwhile, Brother Arnold's mother, reluctant at first, has come around to a warm relationship with the spirit family her son chose. She has done volunteer work and visits often.

The commitment Brother Arnold had made to these people struck me as weighty as a marriage vow. I asked him if, as in most marriages, he ever considered divorce. "Are there ever times when it gets so tough," I said, "that you just throw your hands up in the air, not knowing how you possibly can stay?"

"There have been a lot of ups and downs," he chuckled. "In one sense, it *is* sort of a marriage commitment. But it's more a family. I mean, you're bound together in a sense by spiritual blood rather than natural genetics, but it's brothers and sisters. You become siblings, aunts and uncles, and mothers and fathers, and it's all jumbled into each other," he said.

Oh, I thought. In the world we called this a nontraditional family. But the Shakers would likely say that they are bound together by more than human love: by a divine commitment.

"The concept of the Shaker family," Brother Arnold continued, "was really to re-create or superimpose the natural family onto the communal family. The archetype being God, our Father and Mother, down to our first parents, Mother Ann and Father James and Father William, then down to Father Joseph and Mother Lucy."

Giving the actual titles of "father" and "mother" to elders conveyed their spiritual parentage. "The whole reason we use the terms *brothers* and *sisters* is to remind us of the new relationship found in the Christ family," Brother Arnold explained.

"It's a very tight, very intimate family—probably much more now than it's ever, ever been. Because, when there were a lot more people you had little cliques. And you had a lot more formality. And the members of the opposite sex didn't mingle freely. And so there was a love, definitely always a love that bound everyone together, but this love is much more tangible now."

The family philosopher looked out a nearby window and thought aloud, "So what happens with love? Well, love can deepen and love can get hard, and love can change all the way around. And in our relationships today, being so small [a family], it's much more intense. So, yea, there are ups and downs. And there are personality conflicts. And there can be problems. . . ." his voice trailed off. I imagined he was deciding how much to tell me.

"I've never known anyone to hit anybody. Certainly people do abuse each other, you know, when they get very, very angry. It will happen. It's rare, thank God, but I mean it does happen, because we're only all just human and . . . That's not an excuse."

He pointed out that members do try to resolve their problems, individually and collectively. "Mother Ann says that the spiritual ill-health of one is the spiritual ill-health of all," he said. "Everyone must be in union. If they're not in union, you can feel it."

Beyond the struggle of commitment to his spirit family, I wanted to know how this man of passionate feelings had stayed celibate all these years. Every eighteen-year-old boy I had known had little or no control over his sexuality. How could this man have mastered celibacy at such a surging young age?

"When you came here at eighteen," I asked him outright, "weren't your hormones raging?"

Living celibate was difficult, he admitted. "I think it lessens all the time," he said. "I don't know if it's all the time or not, but most of the time. The older you get, the more you get accustomed to it. You just basically redirect yourself.

"Celibacy," according to Brother Arnold, "is a struggle you make even before you say you're going to make that commitment." Although he first visited the Shakers at age eighteen, he did not actually come to live the Shaker life until twenty-one. For three years he agonized over his decision.

Meanwhile, he fell deeply in love.

He thought he had met Ms. Right. "There was one time when I thought I was definitely, definitely in love and I thought that this girl was *it* and everything was all around that. And it had a very bad, bad ending to it. And it wasn't that I got soured on love or anything like that, that's not true."

The affair ended, but he now sees his broken heart as fortuitous. He did not come to the Shakers to escape his pain, he told me, but he did come with his eyes wide open to the life he could have had.

"So you knew something about what you would be missing?" I asked. I meant *sex*. He knew what I meant. He looked me square in the eye.

"I knew exactly what I was giving up," he said slowly and deliberately. "But . . . I don't think giving that up was such a struggle. Maybe there's something of an intimacy that's lost between two people being together that can never be re-created in any other situation." Twenty years later, I wondered if what he had just said revealed that his heart still lay broken by that young woman who had shared his love.

"And heaven knows I can still be infatuated," said this man, to whom telling the truth mattered much more than trying to maintain a holy image. "But I think what I've learned in my life is that the intimacy that is for me, that is the most strong, is that which I have with God."

And suddenly I realized what had happened. This man had ended up falling madly, madly, in love with God. "There is not a human being that I could ever have as close in my life, if I weren't a Shaker—I could never in my life be as intimate with another human being as I can be with God," he said in measured tones.

"There's something in me that calls me to a deeper understanding of God all the time. It's really something like seduction." When he first came to Shaker Village, "There was so much uncompromised love being shown to me, as a stranger," that he responded to the call to Shaker life with—well, joy.

"When I joined," he recalled, "I was by far the youngest person. The next youngest person was Brother Ted, who was as old as my father. There was no one else between us in age. Actually, that made for a very lonely kind of life for me. You know, no peers. No one around. Except for two things.

"One was, there is an incredible euphoria when you first set out. In anything. You know, if you've been working in college toward being a journalist and right after school you get the job. You've reached your goal," he smiled at me. "It took me a long time—it took me three years to make a decision about coming here to live. And once that decision was made, in August, I didn't come back until January.

"All I could think about was being here. I was so ready. It seemed like an eternity. And so, coming here was such a high. It was such an incredible feeling and joy, that . . . I never left the confines of this community from the time I arrived in January until, I think it was the end of March, when I went to Portland.

"And there was so much to do. I was really the only able-bodied person. We had such incredible amounts of snow. I had to shovel roofs and I had to take care of sheep. I didn't know how to take care of sheep. So I had to learn how, and I worked very hard all day long. I'd never probably worked so hard and I was never so happy in doing things like mucking out a barn. That should give you joy?" he laughed at himself.

"But it did. And you know, that would sustain me. And, really, the community really did show me a great, great deal of love. So I didn't have a chance to feel lonely or apart or just think, like, well I wish I could share this with somebody else or tell them about it. Because I had them. And it was more than enough. We were very, very poor in those days. Unbelievably poor in those days," he recalled.

"I think that helped. I mean, I don't wish for anybody coming in now to have to go through that, but I think it made me a stronger Shaker because it made me appreciate what we now have. It's probably not a lot by some people's standpoint, but what I've experienced in eighteen years, it just seems quite nice that we can actually afford to have restoration work done." Brother Arnold gazed out over beds of bulb gardens, in full spring bloom, to buildings whose window trims were freshly painted white. "The Village is looking good."

For Brother Arnold, the purpose of celibacy is the single-mindedness it allows. Like an athlete the night before a game, he wanted to channel all his energy into that one goal—for him, life eternal.

"If you let go of more of the world—and when I use the word *world*, I really mean it in all of its meanings," he explained. "I mean, you can use sexuality as a lust. But the lust of things is greed. Love of power is a lust. Those represent the earth and the earth plane. That's the world. And the more you let go of those things, you're aiming for something else. . . . If your mind is filled with thoughts of peaches, you can't think about apples anymore. If you're in a continual stream of consciousness with God, yes, that will always happen. Am I there? Nay, I'm not. But for the most part, I just find that everyday living sort of takes care of itself."

At the end of that week, after such wrenching talks with the sisters and brothers about love and lust and God, Sunday morning came quietly in Maine. I awoke at 5:30, when my baby began to stir and chirp his protests of hunger in the crib next to my bed. He had had a fretful night. He was cutting a tooth. Before dawn he cried and whined, flouncing about his crib, intermittently falling back asleep, till I picked him up and nursed him. Rain fell on the lake outside, and day struggled to lift light into the thick, gray skies.

Now we lay together, encircling one another with primitive need and maternal response. He slept through the feeding, but even in his sleep his little hand reached out for mine, and his chubby fingers tightly grasped my thumb.

Utter contentment flowed through me. I felt warm under the covers, happy to be sustaining this child and grateful for the chance to cuddle with him before dawn, when nothing else could interrupt. I also felt grateful not to be celibate. And I wondered, what would life be like without such physical contact?

What would happen to the need to be held and comforted—the need simply to be warmed by a child's hand or a husband's arms? My sister and I embraced tightly whenever we came and went from one another. We built up each other's strength by the power of that hug. My other sister and her husband had been married many years, yet they were still cuddlers at night. They slept all wrapped up together, and woke in the warmth of security that only body heat and love together could bring.

Where did that need go, for one who tried to live in the spirit yet remained embodied in this life?

Later that day, for the noontime dinner after Meeting, I sat across the dining table from a seventy-year-old virgin. I saw the warmth of her love for humanity shine through her eyes. I had expected to find psychological scars on this woman, who was given away at age ten by her mother and raised by various Shakers, loving and firm yet changing as one died or another left the community, ever since. Yet what I saw when I looked at her was seemingly one of the most healthy, balanced people on earth. She walked quickly through her morning, responsible for directing the activities of cooks, cleaners, carpenters, and volunteers. As she passed each one, she offered a kind word or humorous comment. She knew how to reach them, how to challenge their best work while affirming their intrinsic value. And she looked happy—happy to be in this particular tiny spot in the universe, happy to be awake for another day of the endless chores that served her God.

I looked at the brothers, all of whom were attractive and young, and I must admit I often forgot they were men. They did not impose their masculinity upon those around them, as did men of the world. They carried broad shoulders and full beards and muscular strength, to be sure, but they needed to prove it to no one.

I envied Ricky, Sister Frances's young grandnephew, the chance to spend part of his childhood here. Later, whether he chose to be Shaker or remain in the world, he would have learned a rare lesson: how to be a man without being aggressive about it. There was all the camaraderie among the brothers of men with men, no doubt of that. They laughed in deep voices as they walked down to the sheep barn together. They talked about the "very cool" Camaro with racing stripes that Althea, a staff member, had driven to work that day. They jumped in the back of the pickup truck with little Ricky and rode around Shaker Village, laughing, hoisting bales of hay with gusto. But there was no need to prove one's manliness, and no need to outdo those around them in order to "be a man."

When one was Shaker, perhaps, one had no need of the guns and jacked-up trucks of the world. I was not sure what removed the need. Maybe it was their chosen simplicity; the macho symbols of men I knew became unnecessary trappings to these brothers. Or maybe it was that their testosterone got channeled into work and worship rather than into bullying around proving their manhood.

Other times when I looked at them I thought, What a waste. What a waste of glorious manhood.

Men are meant for far more than love, I knew. And these men fulfilled their lives in ways worldly men had no energy to do; their celibacy gave them a certain single-mindedness for the spirituality at hand. They focused on their farm, Bible readings of the day, and the soul cultivation of their lives, in a way they simply could not do if distracted by lust, love, and family responsibility.

Still, I loved men with abandon, and when I looked at these brothers as *men*, I lamented the stilling of their libidos. These brothers had a lot of love to give. My sadness for their locked-up sexuality was purely selfish, and worldly, and would shock these brothers if they knew what I was thinking. Yet to me, they would have made dear, lovable, wonderful men of the world.

If that had been their choice.

CHAPTER SIX

WORK

Work while the angels work, make no delay!
In our Father's vineyard work, while it is day;
The Lord of the harvest in fullness will repay,
With peace and blessing, in the bright coming day.
Oh, work in earnest, while the sun is shining clear!
And slacken not your hand till the fruitage doth appear;
You will have a full reward for all your toil and pain,
Your labors in the Lord will not be in vain!

—*"Work While the Angels Work"*

"Work is very important to Shakers," Sister Frances told me one morning, her arms elbow-deep in flour as she dipped trout fillets into bread crumbs and herbs. Her claim did not surprise me. The history books portrayed Shakers as fanatical in their long days of labor, meticulous in their slow attention to detail, and ceaseless in their efforts to clean, cook, harvest, build. What books could not show me was how work *felt* to a Shaker, and how it became worship throughout the mundane chores of the day.

Such a lesson cannot be taught. If I came away from Shaker Village knowing how to fold twelve loads of laundry to the tune of "Simple Gifts," smoothing every crease and placing fresh piles in tidy drawers, and get it right every time thereafter, I would have found magic—not worship. For here lived flesh-and-blood human beings, who sometimes caught a cold or suffered arthritis or headaches, whose hands slipped on the weaving loom or the straw rake, whose energy and enthusiasm for their labor ebbed and flowed, as does any worker's, through the days of the year.

Shakers may work more or less hard than their non-Shaker neighbors in rural Maine. The difference is in the use of work to purify the soul, to cleave the soul ever closer to God. All Shaker life becomes opportunity for divine intimacy.

In labor, when a Shaker focuses her or his mind on the here and now, any chore becomes a chance to serve God and community. Any task becomes beautiful, meaningful, worth the effort. Devotion infuses the pies, ordinary as they look, shaped by Sister Marie. Meditation pulls together yarns of rich earth colors on Brother Arnold's loom. Prayer seeps between the lines of a column written by Sister Frances for the Shaker newsletter. Hope smoothes soft blankets knit for unknown babies by Sister Ruth's gnarled hands. Praise lifts the hoe of Brother Wayne high into the air for hour upon sweaty hour of repetitive motion. Joy lights the library as Sister June hunches over another pile of catalog cards to be carefully sorted for researchers' use. And serenity floods the sewing workshop where Brother Alistair sorts through a cardboard box of fabric scraps to plan his next craft for the Christmas fair.

Buddhists call this mindfulness. Managers call this focus. Shakers call this the practice of their most important motto: "Put your hands to work and your hearts to God." According to the *Testimonies*, Ann Lee, who was known to wield an ax and sweep a floor with the humblest of them, promised that nothing but blessing would come upon those who followed this simple way.

Ann Lee, who could see through the haze of the corporeal

to the realm of spirits beyond, loathed the dust of earthly life as much as she did its bodily passions and secretions. "There is no dirt in heaven," she proclaimed, and so her heaven on earth should have none, too. Spirits of the dead, whom she saw and heard daily, found filth offensive; all the more reason for Shakers to keep their family home sterile.

So began a lifestyle of absolute cleanliness that involved daily scrubbing and ironing, polishing and mopping as no other American utopia has known. The purity of the inner soul must be reflected in the purity of the outer environment. Sister Frances remembered that, when she was growing up at Sabbathday Lake in the 1930s, she and the other children organized their built-in clothing drawers every single Saturday morning.

The simplicity for which Shakers have long been renowned couples naturally with cleanliness. Ann Lee remonstrated her first followers: "Never put on silver spoons, nor table cloths for me, but let your tables be clean enough to eat from without cloths." Shaker cleanliness, an attempt by humans on earth to respect the spirit realm and reflect heaven as best they can amid the clutter of now, has much to do with the Shaker idea of utopia.

Just as there should be no dust in the house, there should be no blemishes in behavior. Self-control reigned supreme: "Ye shall have no talking, laughing, sneering, winking, blinking, hanging and lounging on the railings, hugging, fumbling, and fawning over each other, when going to the table . . . or carried on at the table," commanded the Shaker *Holy Orders* of 1841. Reading this, I felt relieved that today's Shakers no longer adhered to such rules, but talked and laughed freely.

Order, employed today for efficiency and harmony in daily life, was tightly embraced in centuries past, when hundreds of believers filled communities throughout the Northeast and the Midwest. Even meals were carried out with careful steps, like a Shaker marching dance. Henry Howe, who traveled to Union Village in 1847, described the precise choreography of a Shaker meal:

"Two long tables were covered on each side of the room, behind the tables were benches, and in the midst of the room was a cupboard. At a signal given with a horn, the brothers entered the door to the right, and the sisters the one to the left, marching two and two to the table. . . . They all fell on their knees, making a silent prayer, then . . . took their meal in the greatest silence.

"They eat [sic] bread, butter and cakes, and drank tea. Each member found his cup filled before him—the serving sisters filled them when required. . . . The meal was very short, the whole society rose at once, the benches were put back, they again fell on their knees, rose again, and wheeling to the right, left the room with a quick step." They returned promptly to their work.

Building a heaven on earth took care, and hard work. Ann Lee used to say that faith alone was not enough: One must pitch in and work hard, believing all the while, yet striving forth in effort. And so Shakers, beginning by laboring alongside the ship's crew on their journey to America and then building their first New England community by hand, established a precedent for hard work that made them one of the most prosperous religious communities. By their peak in the mid-nineteenth century, two dozen communities of about 6,000 members (thousands more were uncovenanted friends) crafted furniture and handiwork, harvested canned goods and herbs, shared inventions and pharmaceuticals until the Shaker name became a household word—one associated with superior quality.

Because Shaker communities grew prosperous and nearly self-sustaining, sisters and brothers could concentrate on the quality of their work rather than time schedules or quick productivity. Work equaled prayer, because one could achieve a meditative state of worship while sanding a chair leg or peeling an apple, and because all work was done for God.

Visitors to Shaker communities found the harsh scrubbing and toil repugnant. Charles Dickens, stopping by the New Lebanon Shaker community on his American visit in 1842, called it a "gloomy silent commonwealth." He dismissed the Shakers and their orderly farm as grim. Although the Shakers were honest and fair in business, to him they destroyed the innocent pleasures of life. He accused them of being "among the enemies of Heaven and Earth, who turn the water at the marriage feasts of this poor world, not into wine but gall."

I found other protestations against the Shaker work ethic, which seemed more Puritan than the Puritans themselves. Ralph Waldo Emerson condescendingly dismissed the Shakers as "a set of clean, well disposed, dull & incapable animals" living in a "protestant monastery."

Nathaniel Hawthorne, who at first thought "a man could not do a wiser thing than to join them," later changed his mind. He wrote fiction about star-crossed lovers escaping the shackles of Shakerism, and he took fault with the hygienic practices of the believers. "The fact shows that all their miserable pretence of cleanliness and neatness is the thinnest superficiality; and that the Shakers are and must needs be a filthy sect. And then their utter and systematic lack of privacy; the close function of man with man, and supervision of one man over another—it is hateful and disgusting to think of; and the sooner the sect is extinct the better—a consummation which, I am happy to hear, is thought to be not a great many years distant," wrote Hawthorne. If only he had known, I thought, that these people would prove as long standing as his own fiction.

The Shakers also appeared in Herman Melville's *Moby Dick*, in an eccentric prophet named Gabriel who had come from the Niskeyuna Shakers; in a series of *Vanity Fair* cartoons by satirist Artemus Ward; and in dances, plays, and articles that offered a romantic or grotesque view of everyday Shaker life. Everywhere I looked, they seemed like caricatures, figures who swept floors and pitched hay and prayed to God with a maniacal level of zeal.

Two hundred years later, Shakers get a mixed review on their penchant for housework. Some, like theologian Marjorie Procter-Smith, believe that "Shakers developed religious rituals that valorized housework, especially 'women's work' " such as sweeping and cleaning. Shakers "anticipated some more contemporary feminist concerns about the value of housework."

For Shakers, the cleansing of outer buildings reflects the same purifying work they are attempting deep within their hearts. Brother Arnold told me that, in the mid-1800s, Shaker brothers and sisters alike took part in sweeping rituals, in which all would arise at midnight to sing and "spiritually sweep the whole household. But they didn't use real brooms," he told me. "Sweeping, like any other act you would do in the community, can have sacred proportions. Remember that all work is worship."

Although some Shaker women assumed leadership roles unprecedented in colonial America, for the first two centuries it was the men who managed the money, real estate, business, and official theology of the sect. Eldresses usually simply governed groups of sisters doing domestic chores—canning, cooking, crafting—for the community.

That Shaker women supervised women's work was the first step away from patriarchal convention, Stephen Stein wrote from his twentieth-century perspective. And one woman I talked with, a Shakerism author and museum curator who had actually lived among the former New Hampshire Shakers during the 1970s, saw great value in the partnership of women with women. "You had the power of the sisterhood," said June Sprigg. "You had your own businesses that were women-run, women-operated. Women outnumbered men well before 1850, and women were making economic decisions."

"Women's work" was no light load. Besides the ceaseless plucking of chickens, kneading of bread, washing of pots and pans, and all that kitchen work entailed, sisters sewed and mended, washed and ironed clothing. They cultivated gardens and scrubbed clean the dwellinghouses. They also tackled rotating monthly chores: In January and February they did spinning, braiding, and sewing; in March "ketcheling" flax, carding tow, and spinning mops; in April spring cleaning and making soap; in May making starch, sewing the brothers' clothes, shearing sheep, and painting the buildings; in June making wool and in July spinning; in August and September processing corn, pickles, and apples; in October boiling cider and finishing up the wool; in November cleaning up dwellings and shops and preparing for winter; and in December butchering hogs and making applesauce.

Some jobs were rotated on a regular basis, such as four-week kitchen stints for the sisters. The sisters prepared meals for families of up to one hundred people; for example, thirty-five chickens were killed and plucked for just one meal. A five-acre garden plot was cultivated just for kitchen vegetables. At one village, in Hancock, Massachusetts, sisters produced 875 pounds of butter in three months in spring 1863. Sister Frances, who grew up in the candy-making era of the mid-twentieth century, helped her eldress, Sister Mildred Barker, spin taffy and dip peppermint patties every day, all day, every summer.

Shakers today still follow the seasons in their farmwork. In springtime the Shakers gather sap from the maple trees to produce limited quantities of syrup, which sell fast at the Sabbathday Lake gift shop. Herbs are tended for the packaged garden seed and pharmaceutical herb businesses. Meanwhile, peaches, pears, plums, and cherries bring forth their fruit. Today's Shakers also raise grapes and melons, and strawberries.

Orchards of McIntosh and Cortland apples, as well as Baldwins, Northern Spies, Astrachans, Winesaps, Ben Davises, and Winter Bananas fill 12,500 bushels of apples per year. Thirty-five acres of the orchards are leased to an outsider, but the Shakers are able to take as many apples for their own consumption as they wish. Each autumn, they set aside individual duties to come together and harvest the herb and vegetable gardens. They can foods and make cider and preserves. Sister Marie makes some of her famous apple pies, and enough Shaker applesauce to last through winter.

In addition to heavy seasonal labor in past years, the daily lives of Shakers ticked with unending hard work that filled every waking hour: gardening, weaving, cleaning, canning, cooking, laundering, ironing, and so on. Shaker sisters did escape the isolation, and sometimes abuse, of their previous nuclear families. Yet theologian Susan Setta said Shakers honored so-called women's work by elevating it to a new level comparable to men's.

"All work was equally sacred," wrote Setta, "because it contributed to God's new creation on earth. . . . The question you have to ask is not so much 'What were they actually doing?' but 'What was the *value* of what they were doing? Would they survive the winter if the canning didn't get done?' " Both in the past and now, would Shaker communities survive if not for the selling of handiwork and culinary items that financially sustains them? As I read volumes on the agricultural and industrial labor of Shakers past, and then spent time working among those who remain, I changed my mind about "women's work." What Shaker sisters did, both past and present, literally sustained the life of the community. They fed, clothed, housed, and nurtured their spirit families. Moreover, they engaged in craft and food manufacturing that earned money essential to survival.

"Men's work," meanwhile, was no mean task. Brothers generally took care of all farming and village maintenance. They also did blacksmithing—nearly every village had a shop to sharpen plows, shape and nail horseshoes, and mend copper pots and bridle bits. They worked in Shaker mills grinding grain, sawing wood, or pressing seeds. They manufactured brooms, baskets, buckets, churns, tubs, carpets, cloth, yarn, shoes, and mops. And they did carpentry, from buildings and cabinetry to chairs and other furniture; younger brothers served as apprentices to older brethren until they learned a trade.

Still, Sundays were for meditation and rest. By sundown Saturday, all workshops would be cleaned, food was prepared for simple Sunday meals, and all sins had been confessed to the elder or eldress, so that members could feel unshackled in worship Sunday morning.

Early Monday morning, it was back to work. "If you improve in one talent," Shakers believed, "God will give you more."

Most sisters and brothers were skilled in one or two areas, but could do fine work in as many as a dozen occupations.

Shakers eagerly embraced technological changes and adapted them for their own use. Being Shaker did not require that one do work the hard way. Rather, Shakers always sought more efficient methods, employing such labor-saving devices as extracting, carding, threshing machines, and washing machines; and mechanized looms, pumps, and lathes. I noticed at Sabbathday Lake the same easy approach to work. As Brother Arnold told me, "We adapt when we see something that's better. That's why we have a dishwasher, we have a microwave. We get the gadgets that seem to work." The library inventory was being computerized, to give speed and focus to research. The kitchen sisters used their microwave with friendly familiarity and the brothers adopted any new tools that aided their barn chores and farmwork. And, as for those many-pleated Shaker dresses that I had worried had been painstakingly ironed by Sister Frances late into the night before Meeting, well, they were sewn from wrinkle-free fabric.

Around Sabbathday Lake, I noticed that traditional gender roles still apply. Generally the women work inside and the men work outside, although today's Shakers seem to feel more free to cross gender lines. Thus it was Brother Alistair who sewed a fine seam, and Sister Marie who refilled the birdfeeders. It was a woman—Sister Frances—who lumbered about the farm, consulting with contractors and writing checks for the hired help. It was a man—Brother Arnold—who knew how to bake a lemon pie that left the others daydreaming about its flavor.

"Today," said Sister Frances, "whatever has to be done is done. Sister Marie, who is the community baker, also loves to be with the animals. I'm so grateful to have Alistair, who can help out in the kitchen. And Brother Arnold is a real treasure. Every once in a while he'll say, 'I'm getting supper this evening'. . . . We're not limited in any way to work, whether it be for a man or a woman."

Whatever the division of labor—no matter who sweeps

wood shavings from the workshop floor or who lights the wood-stove to warm the kitchen—Shakers still approach their work as worship. The most mundane tasks create opportunity to do something perfectly for the sake of cleanliness and order, for the sake of the Shaker heaven on earth, for God. "A man can show his religion as much in measuring onions," said one Shaker brother, "as he can in singing hallelujah."

The work and daily life of Shakers has also been evident in their governmental basis of communism. German economist Friedrich Engels, cofounder with Karl Marx of socialism, called Shakers "the first people in America, and actually the world, to create a society on the basis of common property." He extolled the symmetry of their barns and the plentiful stock of their grain and cloth. They "owned an abundance of everything," he re-marked. No one had "to work against their will" nor to "search for work in vain." Engels, writing in *Deutsches Burgerbuch* in 1845, believed this made Shakers "free, rich, and happy."

The American historian John Humphreys Noyes said Shak-ers demonstrated the success of communism. Other utopian ef-forts of the nineteenth century merely echoed their success. "Thus it is no more than bare justice to say, that we are indebted to the Shakers more than to any or all other Social Architects of modern times," he wrote in 1870.

What could be proclaimed as political could also be per-sonal, I realized. Shakers may have explained their government and their division of labor as the result of one large family work-ing together, laboring as equals, side by side.

"They have shown," Horace Greeley wrote in *The Shaker* in 1850, "how pleasant may be the labors, how abundant the com-forts, of a community wherein no man aspires to be lord over his brethren, no man grasps for himself, but each is animated by a spirit of devotion to the common good."

Not everyone agreed that communal work suited the human soul. Like any other system, it had its disadvantages. Journalist Elizabeth Peabody, writing in *The Dial* in 1841, noted the price paid for submission to Shaker society. She lamented the loss of *self*: "The great evil of Community, however, has been a spiritual one. The sacredness of the family, and personal individuality have been sacrificed. Each man becomes the slave of the organization of the whole." Yes, I thought as I read. That concept chokes us modern Americans as we try to swallow it. Yet in other countries and cultures, individual self-will does not rank as the highest value. And in Shaker community, it truly stands as an obstacle to be overcome for the sake of union. The Shakers I had met had lost none of their personality nor individual convictions. But somehow, through shared ambition toward God, they became as one.

Whether or not Ann Lee consciously set out to build a communist utopia, her own social politics show in a statement she made at Nathan Goodrich's in Hancock, concerning the poor: "If I owned the whole world," she said, "I would turn it all into joyfulness; I would not say to the poor 'Be ye warmed and be ye clothed,' without giving them the wherewithal to do it."

More than two hundred years later, Brother Wayne restated this conviction with his characteristic bluntness. "OK, let's say you see this person starving," he told me. "This [idea] comes from the epistle of James. You go up to him and you say, 'Well, keep warm, and I hope you'll find something to eat.' Well, big deal. You've done a lot for him."

Instead, "go up to him and give him something to eat, and give him a blanket or coat or whatever. Now what is that person going to remember more? Is he going to remember the person who just spoke kind words to him, or is he going to remember the person who did kind deeds for him? That's the aspect of Shakerism that really speaks to me the most," he rested his fist on the table in front of him. "It's more of what we do than what we say that counts."

Today's work at Sabbathday Lake includes hospitality to whomever comes to the door, and often they are people needy of spirit and of food. The Shaker family donates time to the hungry at a nearby soup kitchen, the elderly at their Sister Minnie's nursing home, and to local children at Christmastime. They still believe, as did their Mother Ann Lee, in the practicality of love.

The work of Shakerism has always begun with scheduling. Daily life at Shaker Village followed the clock with the greatest precision and efficiency. By 1790, a fixed schedule for the day was set, with allotted times for meals, meetings, and chores. Only six hours were permitted for sleep. The *Millennial Laws*, which governed every detail of labor and behavior, listed 125 separate laws. For example, the laws forbade brothers and sisters to "pass each other on the stairs" and prescribed that the right thumb and fingers should be above the left when one's hands are clasped. The overriding objectives were to live by the law of Christ, obey one's elders, and love all others.

William Plumer, of New Hampshire, visited several communities in the 1780s and concluded that Shakers seemed overly concerned with trifles, such as the length of their hair, cleanliness, and neatness in "houses, dress and food." And truly, Shakers were fastidious about their villages, for the *Millennial Laws* required proper disposal of garbage and "filthy" substances of any kind. Buildings were to be kept orderly and in good repair inside and out, and even the streets near their buildings should be cleaned regularly.

In times past, books were censored by one's elders, who were spiritually sanctioned to monitor and approve all reading matter. The *Millennial Laws* stated that "No Books, Pamphlets, or Almanachs of any kind, are allowed to be brought into the family, without the knowledge and approbation of the Elders." Perhaps it was an echo from the days of Ann Lee, who was illiterate and vastly suspicious of the printed word. These laws also showed an inherent distrust of the judgment of believers in choosing their own information sources. Did this kind of censorship go on today? I felt so curious that I asked outright. Brother Arnold and Sister Frances shook their heads and chuckled at the thought of checking up on members' bedside reading material. They left discernment in the hands of each individual. "We're all adults here," said Brother Arnold.

During my time at Sabbathday Lake, I had noticed blatant disregard for many of the repressive rules I had encountered in the *Millennial Laws*. Pets were forbidden; yet Sister Ruth had her precious poodle, Sister Marie had an eccentric cat in her workroom, and the entire family fawned over the two Shaker dogs.

Sister Frances put this into perspective for me. "The *Millennial Laws* were very, very brief in their tenure," she said. "And most people, most Shakers even at that time felt that many of them were completely ridiculous. In my lifetime I don't think we have ever followed any of the *Millennial Laws* that have that ridiculous meaning attached to them." She explained, for example, that Mother Ann Lee admonished against taking dogs and cats as pets because people in those days felt that animals could be possessed of spirits or even demons. Shakers today no longer believe so, and their pets have become a beloved part of the family.

Without a document such as the *Millennial Laws*, though, how would one know how to conduct oneself? What continuity could be sustained if all flowed fluid through changing time?

"One learns by living in community day by day," Sister Frances simply stated. The practice of kneeling in front of one's dining chair to pray before and after each meal, prescribed in the *Millennial Laws*, was followed at Sabbathday Lake up until her youth. "We would march into the dining room," Sister Frances remembered, "sisters and little girls in their entrance, brothers and little boys through their entrance. And we would kneel behind our chair for the grace."

However, not all members had such physical agility. "There were already many, easily two-thirds of the community at that time, who were elderly. And it became difficult for many of them. And in Shaker community, in Shaker life anything that is not going to be in union—the gift is taken away."

Now I saw the guiding rule for today's Shakers. "Union is

the strongest, one of the strongest points in Shaker life," Sister Frances shook her dark hair as she nodded in emphasis. "One of my very favorite early Shakers, Mother Lucy, wrote that union is like a golden chain, and if even one link of that chain is broken, then the whole chain has to suffer. This is so, so true. Whatever we do, it has to be something that everyone in the community is able to join in."

Much of the work of Shakers has always taken place outside. A Shaker garden manual from 1843 said, "The garden is said to be an index of the owner's mind." In other words, the one who plants should memorize every seed and season, every row and ripening. Not only order, but attitude mattered. Every act of labor opened up the soul, if willing, for worship of God.

In 1867, a Shaker elder told *New America* writer Hepworth Dixon what differentiated Shaker farming from secular farming. While the commercial farmer sought profit, the Shaker farmer wanted to "beautify" the soil "by his tilth," he said.

"A tree has its wants and wishes," said the elder, "and a man should study them as a teacher watches a child, to see what he can do. If you love the plant, and take heed of what it likes, you will be well repaid by it. . . . I am sure it feels when you care for it and tend it. . . . Thee sees we love our garden."

He sounded to me like a Shaker who listened to the earth even as he planted and tended it.

But Dixon the journalist saw a pitiful misdirection of affection. "Is it strange that a celibate man," he wrote, "who puts his soul into the soil—who gives it all the affection which he would otherwise have lavished on wife and child—should excel a mere trading rival in the production of fruits and flowers?"

Dickens, who disliked nearly everything else about the Shakers, admitted to admiring their agricultural work. "They are good farmers," he confessed, "and all their produce is eagerly purchased and highly esteemed." He saw more than just a decent work ethic. Shakers labored, in their gardens as elsewhere, to please God. As the song goes:

Just as we sow life's garden, So will the harvest be;
Just as we nurture the blossom, 'Twill bloom in eternity.
If on the barren hillside, Or in the fertile vale,
Sown in the gift of the Spirit, The fruitage will never fail.
Just as we sow, Just as we sow life's garden
We'll reap in eternity.

The work done here on earth lays the very path to heaven.

Shakers began to package and sell seeds in the 1790s, and this became a major source of income in the nineteenth century. Sabbathday Lake, among other villages, made a bulk of income during the winter months, when believers went on tour selling seeds in bulk and packets. The Shaker herb business began in the 1830s. Shakers sold wormwood, sage, spikenard, catnip, boneset, mandrake, horehound, and skunk cabbage for cooking and medicinal uses. The Sabbathday Lake community has, in recent decades, rebuilt their herb industry and turned it into an international catalog business. Sister Frances's cookbook, *Shaker Your Plate*, includes an educational section on how to use natural herbs in the simple, wholesome cooking of the Shakers.

Outside, Shakers also tended livestock, and they were known for their gentle treatment of their animals. The farming work of Shakers exemplifies the same values of love and non-violence that compelled early brothers to sit out the Revolutionary and Civil Wars. In 1838, Nathan Williams of the New Lebanon community received a vision in which Mother Ann was stretching out her arms toward the animals and saying:

> All the creatures gathered here in union . . . belong to the New Creation. They do not belong to the children of this world; they are under my care, and my eye is upon them and I know when they are abused and suffer cruelty. Poor dumb creatures were made for the use of man, and were put under his care and dependent upon his mercy and kindness.

> . . . You must have comfortable places for
> all the creatures you keep and see that they do
> not suffer in any way by cold, hunger or abuse.

In the June 1910 issue of *Harper's Bazaar*, a recent visitor
to Sabbathday Lake testified that the Shakers "never abuse or
speak a harsh word to their horses, which always look sleek."
And the chickens were so well housed and fed, she wrote, "that
their white feathers are always a degree more snowy than other
fowls, and their yellow feet almost appear to have been polished."

The values of simplicity and worship in work also reflected
in the architecture and design styles of Shakers. Shaker furniture
equaled simplicity plus perfection. Early in Shaker history, converts brought whatever they had from home when they came to
live as Shakers. As membership began to swell, communities
needed large-scale furniture, so they began to build long dining
tables, large cases of drawers for storage, tailoring counters, and
so on. The first furniture produced in Maine was much like the
country cabinetry of the day. Brother Theodore Johnson later
wrote about its style: "Primitive Maine Shaker furniture may be
characterized as substantial, even heavy, yet vigorous and emi-
nently practical. It bears all the marks of the Maine soil to which
its creators' lives were so firmly attached."

Scrolling through the artifacts of his own past heritage,
Brother Ted noted, "Obviously Maine joiners of the period saw
little beauty in the natural wood itself," because virtually all
early pieces were painted or color-stained with indigo-based
blue, mustard yellow, a dark forest green, or various reds.

The period in history of what we now consider *Shaker design*
spanned from the 1820s to 1860s, also the period of "Mother's
Work," when Shakers received visions and inspirations for music, art, and poetry. Furniture developed during the "classic era"
included Shaker chairs and rockers, tall cupboards and cases of
drawers, trestle tables and simple candle stands. Painted surfaces
gave way to polished wood surfaces that highlighted the natural

tones of cherry, pine, maple, birch, chestnut, and other fruit-woods. Shakers sometimes used contrasting woods to achieve color and pattern. Design continued to develop after the Civil War, by such Sabbathday Lake Shakers as Elders Henry Green and Delmer Wilson, who used some late-Victorian elements and ornamentation.

Thomas Merton wrote in 1966, "The peculiar grace of a Shaker chair is due to the fact that it was made by someone capable of believing that an angel might come and sit on it." This comment, quaint as it sounds at first, conveys truth. I think Shakers really did build and bake as though someone were watching over their shoulders at all times. They believed so intensely in the spirit realm that they felt constantly surrounded. Thus, their chairs had better be worthy of superhuman presence.

Shakers looked at the graceful lines of a rocker or a barn and saw the underlying spiritual motives of its beauty. Sabbathday Lake's former eldress, Sister Mildred Barker, tried to explain: "People look in upon us and that's the first thing they say. 'Oh, they're the people that made that nice furniture, they made nice chairs and tables.' And I say, 'I know it, I almost expect to be remembered as a chair or a table.' But the people that come in feeling that way, they forget there's something special behind that work. There's the religion that produced the good chairs and the good tables, because everything they put their hand to was well done."

Despite marked changes through history, "Shaker furniture, architecture, dress, and song were remarkably alike," wrote June Sprigg and David Larkin in *Shaker Life, Work, and Art*, "in villages as far apart as Maine and Kentucky." Hallmarks of Shaker architecture are double entrances and parallel staircases, for the sisters and brothers to enter separately, as they still do at Sabbathday Lake. Once, when hurrying upstairs to meet Sister Frances, I forgot and used the brothers' stairs. My stomach lurched and I blushed, though no one was there to see me. I felt I had violated a private taboo.

Shakers were also well known for peg rails for hats and

cloaks, and built-in storage cupboards in the walls, where no dust could gather. They took great care in architecture, even to the graceful construction of attic spaces, which few would ever see. Shaker style evolved over many years, beginning in the rural styles known to the community's first converts and slowly becoming more distinctive, more deliberately simple.

The *Millennial Laws* commanded simple architecture: "beadings, moldings, and cornices, which are made *merely for fancy* may not be made by Believers." These prohibitions gave way to current style in the Victorian era, when several buildings sprouted bric-a-brac and fanciful millwork. Still, various buildings in a village usually bore certain colors: wood buildings alongside a street took "a lightish hue," and other back houses were painted a darker hue, such as red, brown, or "lead color." Only the meetinghouse was pure white. These guidelines, too, have given way. At Sabbathday Lake the library, museum, trustees' house, and several work-buildings, as well as the meetinghouse, are white.

As for textile style, "Fashionable visitors found both Brethren and Sisters hopelessly unstylish," wrote Sprigg and Larkin. Cartoonist Artemus Ward described one sister as "last year's bean-pole stuck into a long meal bag." But from the Shaker perspective, it was the worldly who looked silly. "Shakers ridiculed the fickle outside world, which seized on new fashions with every passing year," they said.

Ironically, the cloaks Shaker sisters made for their own use became the fashion rage in the late nineteenth and early twentieth centuries. Worldly women clamored for them, to wear to the opera and out about town. Shakers sewed these cloaks in brighter colors such as pink, red, purple, bright blue, and green, and lined the hoods and cloaks in satin. Also, "The Canterbury Shakers," explained Sprigg and Larkin, "developed a good market for their original 'Shaker knit' sweaters, mostly to New England college boys, in the early 20th century."

Today I still see Shaker-knit sweaters hanging in department stores and boasted about in the junk mail that stuffs my mailbox.

And a company whose factory sits near Sabbathday Lake, in Portland, fabricates a whole warehouse of Shaker reproduction candle stands, peg rails, furniture, and knickknacks. I thought, as I perused their catalog's numerous pages with garish "Shaker Style" claims, that the consumer market had come a long way from the authentic craft and intention.

"What does remain of Shaker work testifies to the makers' conviction," concluded Sprigg and Larkin, "that what they did really mattered. The humblest, most mundane objects—a coat hanger, a clothesbrush, a wheelbarrow—reveal a concern for excellence and grace. . . . Work and worship were not separated in the Shaker realm." Yes, I thought. Here lay the kernel of Shaker style that our glitzy world had forgotten. I remembered the Shaker saying, "Trifles do not make perfection, but perfection is no trifle."

Meanwhile, the work goes on at Sabbathday Lake. Work has changed from the days of backbreaking labor toward unachievable standards of perfection. "I wonder," I asked Sister Frances one day, "why you all seem so carefree to me. I think I expected a rather solemn collection of people, walking about this farm. But you seem lighthearted. You know, there's a happiness coming through."

She laughed at the image of solemn people, which seemed to her incongruous with Shaker life. Then she looked at me. "I think that we can't be unhappy people if we have that gift of salvation," she said in a quiet, even voice, "if we have the gift of the gospel," she murmured.

"God wants us to be happy. That doesn't mean that there aren't times when we're not carefree. When burdens come into the community, or when I have personal burdens to deal with and cares, I know what it is like to be unhappy," Sister Frances looked down as her hands clasped and unclasped. Knowing what little I did of her biography, I could picture some of that pain. But I also had seen that the soul of this woman was innately optimistic. She would always bounce back.

"I just don't allow myself to sink into that," she continued, "because always, *always* there is the gift of salvation. There is the gift of having a Father/Mother God to care for us, and that can't help but make one happy."

This I accepted. Yet early Shakers had claimed their way to be true, and said they would "labor" in prayer till the whole world was saved. "Do you not feel terribly responsible," I asked the eldress, "for sort of bringing the rest of the world to a re-alization of that salvation?"

She shook her head. "Nay. We pray for the world, always. But I don't think that it is my personal burden to 'save.'" She took an utterly practical approach to salvation. "I pray, and I leave it to God."

Still, even Shakers get tired some days of the repetitive work that ties them to earth for cycles of years of endless chores. "You know," Sister Frances told me frankly, one day as we chopped and sautéed in the community kitchen, "you're bound to be burned out. I have worked in the kitchen or with food ever since I was nineteen years old. It has been a part of my daily life, except for brief periods when I have been away or when I have been ill and couldn't do it.

"And that's OK," she admitted. "I still feel, and I don't want to sound like Ms. Pollyanna or a goody-goody, but I still feel after all these years that I want to present a meal that will look colorful, is pleasing to the community, and is what they're going to enjoy. I take great pleasure in that and I enjoy it." She loaded her rosemary chicken onto a serving platter. "'Hands to work and hearts to God' is the official Shaker motto," she reminded me. And cooking has become for her a lifetime of handiwork for God.

"We also live very closely to Mother Ann's other very well known saying, 'Do all of your work as though you knew you were going to die tomorrow and yet as if you were going to live a hundred years.' I think that really has very, very much influ-enced the work that we do here in the community," she mused.

"From the very beginning, no matter how revered, no matter

how high a position people in Shaker communities held, everyone was expected to have some physical labor. See, *labor* is an important word in Shaker theology. You labor to feel the gift of God. You labor to feel the love of God. You labor to do the right thing." She turned to face me. "It's not something that just comes easily because you're a Shaker. You really have to work to bring forth these things. So labor has always been very important in Shaker life, whether it be physical labor, or more particularly spiritual labor."

Next day, Friday, the Maine sky formed a thick soup of clouds. Chilled, damp air penetrated one's clothing and skin, too. Sister Marie and I, shivering in the kitchen after breakfast, agreed the chill got down into our bones. Outside, the painter, wearing a baseball cap and sunglasses despite the gray skies, seemed perfectly content in just a sweatshirt, reaching up from the scaffolding to touch up the dwellinghouse window frames. We women, inside, clasped our arms around our middles or moved about quickly. Spring, it seemed, would never come to Maine.

Again I found myself, the antithesis of a Shaker sister, sweeping the floor. That day it was the bedrooms and hallways of the trustees' house, where two men had come to stay a couple of nights en route to a Rhode Island business trip. This building, where the elderly yet independent Sister Ruth had an apartment and privileged guests take lodging, was built in 1816. I stepped in the side door onto graceful wide-pine floors, painted in a peculiar shade of pumpkin. The front hall walls were lined with Shaker pegs for coats and hats, and bedrooms boasted classic Shaker built-ins—cabinets and drawers built flush against the wall and finished with simple wood knobs.

The guest bedrooms, I knew, had housed untold numbers of the curious and the kindred from the world. People who arrived with stuffed luggage and stereotyped preconceptions had discovered with delight an authentic Shaker chair in their rooms, next to a 1950s plain wood twin bed, and a travel clock on the nightstand. Linoleum floors and clean white coverlets turned the rooms back a generation or two. Really, except for the Shaker pegs and built-ins, the place felt like any grandmother's house in the country. The sense of timelessness a guest might feel here was offset only by the noise of trucks on the rural highway just outside, and the list of mealtimes for which the Shaker bell would be rung posted on the bureau.

I swept and the broom I used, knobbly and stiff with time, may once have been a smart Shaker invention but was now a worn-out tool. The mop I borrowed from Althea, the woman from town who labored every day to keep the buildings clean, was old and raggedy and black with use. As I wrung it out with my hands and put it to the floor, I felt that it was a privilege to be able to clean the floor for these kind people, who had allowed me into their lives.

Yet I also knew certainly that if I had to sweep and mop these floors every day, I could not maintain this sense of happy service. How did Althea do it? She sang and hummed throughout the rooms as she worked, though she must clean the same grime over and over again, with little to show for her efforts in these old buildings. Maybe she was—in her mission of quiet, willing service—a bit Shaker, too.

So I, in my citified garb, dabbled for a few hours in the housework of the sisters. Having stayed here long enough to see the reality of the Shakers' everyday life, I now knew deep in my heart how unlike them I was, after all.

I had feared coming here because I feared loving them so much, and seeing enough truth in their faith, that I might stay. And now I saw, as I swept the floors where hundreds of humble Shakers had walked, that I easily could leave. Not just easily, but gladly, with relief. Though I fully saw the irony of myself, this pampered, materialistic, suburban woman making a show at mopping Shaker floors, still I longed for my own home. I could not live up to the height of Shaker values. I knew that now, as I had never known before standing among these people.

It was time, a voice spoke from someplace below my conscience as my mop swished to and fro, to get back to my own "real" life. To restock the groceries in my family's fridge, to hold my boys tight and read piles of the same storybooks over and over again, to cook and clean and write and talk again, in my own beloved home.

For all the lessons of my time with the Shakers, I would feel relief to come away from this place in which I constantly watched to be sure my words were gentle and not too prying nor blunt, constantly smiled and strove to please others. The striving for perfection just seemed too much for me. These people seemed to live that way all the time. Yet I could not. Or, perhaps too lazy, would not.

I wanted my independence again.

Later that day, a rather festive feeling spread throughout the community. It was Friday afternoon. Like office workers soon to be let out for the weekend, the Shakers finished their chores with aplomb, closed up the library an hour early, and took a break from hoeing to give a child a ride in the back of the pickup truck.

Ricky had come for the day, and that lifted everyone's spirits, too. He reminded them to play. His "Aunt Fran" took him shopping for trout that morning at the market, and they stopped to watch the lobsters swim in the tank, and then got sidetracked at the doughnut shop on the way back to the farm. And so we all had doughnuts for dessert at the noontime dinner. "They're not just for breakfast anymore," Sister Frances sang, joking. And things got a bit silly when little Ricky and I began making towers out of doughnuts and the brothers threatened to separate us so we could behave at the table.

You see, I was feeling right at home here.

The Shakers have a great sense of play, and they brought that to the day. One does not, of course, have to be Shaker to do this. But playfulness reigned right alongside work that day at Sabbathday Lake.

Charlie, a friend of the eldress since her birth and now a weekly volunteer at the farm, came to wash up the breakfast dishes. Soon after, I saw him sitting at the kitchen table opposite Sister Ruth, drinking coffee and gossiping about the health and doings of neighborhood people. He was munching on some baked treat she apparently saved for him.

Brothers Arnold and Wayne mixed up formula for the lambs and took little Ricky with them to help feed. The scene at the barn looked like bedlam, for all the sheep were yelling "BAAAAAAAA" at the top of their lungs while three large dogs barked their protest and a dozen sparrows hopped nervously about on fence posts, squawking for spare bread crumbs. The brothers smiled widely and patted the heads of petulant lambs and their mothers alike, and they gave Ricky a garden hose to fill the sheep's buckets with water.

Brother Alistair had come, too, still sniffling from a cold that would not let him go, yet nodding good-naturedly at the others and clearing a path when Ricky came running past him. Sister Frances had noticed on her farm a twelve-year-old boy, the son of one of the cement workers, and so she promptly introduced herself and then took him by the hand for an adventure here in the barn. Soon the boy found himself patting woolly heads and passing out straw.

Sister Marie, working in the kitchen, stopped to savor an extra cup of coffee. Usually too busy for a break, today she paused to watch activity out her window, to comment on the cold weather, and to give the dog Jason a few extra scratches. Brother Alistair soon finished in the barn and was on to the next chore. He brought in old crockery from the "Girls' House"-turned-office next door and washed it in the big kitchen sink.

"Some of these pieces," he confided to Sister Marie, "I'm going to try and persuade Sister Frances to donate to our white elephant sale next Christmas. There are some plastic bowls with lids from the 1970s that are truly the most hideous things I've ever seen," he laughed. "Wait till you see them."

His task seemed endless, Sister Marie commented, as Brother Alistair continued back and forth with piles of dusty dishes brought out from storage.

"Oh, yea, it's a big job," he admitted, conjoining the Shaker "yea" with his native Irish lilt, "but these will be lovely in the new dining room upstairs."

He explained to me, as he washed and I dried the assortment of dishes and silver, that the family was creating a second, smaller dining room on the second floor of the dwellinghouse, nearer to their rooms and more cozy for the evening meal, "when it's just family," he nodded.

Whereas friends and staff joined the group sometimes for breakfast and always for the noon dinner, the Shakers had a simple meal for supper: salad and sandwiches, soup and bread, or the like. Or, if they really did not feel like cooking, they would grab a pizza from the Pizza Paddle down the highway.

Just like any other American family.

Saturdays, the family spent their time on their own. The brothers and sisters may sleep "late," Sister Frances told me, which meant they might eat breakfast around 8:00 rather than 7:30. And breakfast seemed a bit less formal on weekends, too, with members getting what they like. Maybe no one had to wait and hold the back of their chair, or spend an hour cooking omelets and bacon.

Then the community would spend the day as they liked, running errands, making visits, and so forth. Tomorrow Sister Frances would shop for supplies, and Brother Wayne would go to visit his two-year-old nephew in town.

And, as we already had peeled carrots and potatoes and soaked beans for Saturday and Sunday dinners, the kitchen work would lighten for the weekend. The Shakers still slowed down on Saturday evenings to take note of the Sabbath, resting and meditating at the end of the week.

Still, many other archaic Shaker laws had given way here. Like the mortar that had crumbled and now literally needed new cement to bond the bricks, the guidelines of Shaker life had been patched over with new.

The sisters and brothers still perched in separate waiting rooms just before the mealtime bell rang, and they still entered the dining room by separate doors. But once inside, they no longer knelt down before and after their meal, and they no longer dined in utter silence. Brother Alistair brought round mugs of coffee, and Brother Arnold always came to refill water glasses. There was no sense of women nor men's "work." The two genders took turns being first to the buffet line, and although they did not hug and touch one another, they certainly did not scurry away from physical proximity.

The sense of distrust that pervaded the *Millennial Laws* no longer existed here, and perhaps that was the crux of the difference. Now the community members were trusted—to do their work, to keep their chastity, to cultivate simplicity, and to nurture their souls. It seemed taken for granted that everyone had come of his or her own free will, as adults, and may either remain committed to the Shaker life or choose to leave. Harsh rulings and fearful admonitions no longer girded the Shakers in; they cherished their freedom to choose the Shaker way of their own accord.

The result was an almost palpable sense of union among the brothers and sisters. Oddities and traits were taken in stride. "Everyone has their gifts," as Sister Frances said, meaning that no one has it all. Two sisters may work together to follow a recipe, one multiplying the portions to feed their large group and the other grating onions and fetching butter. No egos clashed for power here. Two brothers may have their distinct ways of getting milk into the mouths of young lambs, yet they just chuckled at one another and carried on, each in his own way getting half the babies fed.

And in prayer, when the table of women and the table of men lifted their voices in psalms, the sound was almost that of music. The deep voices of the men shouted out the words with precise pronunciation, and the lilting voices of the women extended the pitch and gave waves to the steady sound of words that filled the room.

Late in the afternoon, we toured the ministry shop building. We saw artifacts of work past, and workrooms full of tools still in use. There were old weaving looms and skeins of yarn from the Shakers' own sheared sheep, dyed in rich shades of teal green, slate blue, cocoa brown, and magenta. There were drying racks for homegrown herbs, and the scent of rosemary and sage filled the air. There were roomsful of old Shaker baskets, woven from poplar in the fashion taught by Sabbathday Lake's first inhabitants, the Native Americans, to early Maine Believers.

One workshop housed a couple of sewing machines and boxes of fabric and trim. Hundreds of crafts and gifts awaited the summer season in the gift shop a couple of buildings over to the south. And another, smelling of fresh-cut wood, was filled with tools and saws used once again by the Shaker brothers to make poplar oval Shaker boxes, finished in a pumpkin-orange color and polished to shine.

Everywhere the old artwork of the Shakers seemed to thrive. To resurrect dying crafts of the Shakers' past has been an important mission of current Sabbathday Lake Shakers. Still, with so few hands to mind the farm, and so much business attending to the world, art has become a luxury here. Traditional craft-making can take place only in one's spare time.

Today, however, the family quickly finished up what they must, so that they might get on to the business of the weekend.

"What do all of you do on a Friday night?" I asked Sister June. We stood at the edge of Highway 26 and waited for the trucks to pass so we could cross over to the library for one final hour of work.

"Oh, maybe watch a little TV," she mused.

Sister Frances and Ricky came to visit us researchers in the library. They tried their best to whisper but no need, for it was just Sister June and me. Sister Frances bent down toward Sister June, who was busily continuing the ancient process of card cataloging.

I thought I heard Sister Frances ask Sister June if she would be interested in going to such-and-such place tonight. "Oh, sure," Sister June replied with a bright, wide smile.

The Shakers, it seemed, on this Friday after a long week of hard work, were going out that night to do the town.

CHAPTER SEVEN

SPIRITS

Hark! from the mountaintop a voice is heard crying,
Watchman, watchman, what of the night? what of the night?
Thro' the valley the echo comes rolling,
Like a mighty vol-ume comes roll-ing and re-echoes,
Watchman, what of the night?
And a voice is heard from heaven, Angel bands in chorus
blending,
Prophets, martyrs, all the saints, The word of God in pow'r
proclaiming.
My house upon the mountain is established strong and firm,
From which my law goes forth for the nations yet to learn.

—*"What of the Night?"*

Twilight at Shaker Village falls in folds, thick velvet. Lights
laugh out across the dark cloak of night. The chilled air seems
charged with the rustling of a thousand whirling skirts, ancestors
of this land, long since dead, still dancing their fierce, one-
pointed love of God. A brother walks up the path from the last
chores of the evening, and he almost shivers. A sister stares out

her window near the top of the looming brick building. She moves the lace to gaze unafraid at what lay beyond in the uncontrollable night.

The Shaker sense of reality spans two realms. Concurrent with the tangible, three-dimensional life of the body exists a drama of the unseen. Spirits surround us, perhaps all of the time. Buildings at Sabbathday Lake seem to vibrate with the life of past believers who linger still. Spirits can guide the living, if we allow them, but to Shakers they are not sacred beings to be worshiped. Rather they, like we, are souls along the way, on a path toward salvation. While not divine, spirits know more than we possibly could, living as we do in our three-dimensional shadowbox. Spirits know dimensions we cannot explain. Shakers believe, in a way that resembles the Native American respect for deceased ancestors, that spirits from the past can teach, inform, warn, inspire, and guide. They are the grandmothers and grandfathers, brothers and sisters, mothers and fathers, gone before from a spirit family that takes care of its own, even from beyond the grave.

Early in the history of Shakerism, throughout Ann Lee's lifetime and well into the nineteenth century, encounters with the spirit realm occurred often. Ann Lee and others saw spirits and conversed with them as though the veil between earth and beyond had actually lifted.

The spirituality of the early Shakers shined through their very faces and clothes. One young New England woman, Jemima Blanchard, said that she could see "the power of God visible on their faces" when she first met the Shakers. Even their clothes looked "perfectly white and run in veins." When she went into the kitchen to meet Mother Ann Lee, the matriarch turned to look at her with a gaze that "absorbed my whole soul." Ann Lee's voice "seemed to me like the voice of God," said the young woman, who soon became Sister Jemima.

The Mother of Shakerism commonly saw beings not of this earth. One of the first Shakers, Abijah Worster, had a sort of fit in which he involuntarily thrashed about and threw himself against the wall. Later, he wrote that "the mighty power of God in Mother" allowed Ann Lee to see what caused his fit. "I felt that my blood was boiling," Worster reported, "and every bone in my body was being torn asunder, my flesh pinched with hot irons, and every hair on my head were [sic] stinging reptiles."

Ann Lee walked right up to him and said that "some of the worst looking spirits I ever saw in my life" were on his shoulder. Worster begged for mercy, and Ann Lee prayed over him from head to foot. "I was relieved at once," wrote Worster in an 1850 unpublished history of Shakerism, "and I have never doubted since."

Many Shakers testified to this kind of physical writhing and pain. One follower felt consumed until his very skin turned purple. Needless to say, all who wrote such accounts converted. For me the question that loomed was, did they convert as a result of miraculous healing or sheer terror?

John Cotton, another of the first Shakers in those spirit-filled years at Niskeyuna, explained a mystical experience that overtook his entire body. "The power of God came upon me," he said, "filling my soul and controlling my whole being. It raised me from my chair, and under its influence I turned around, swiftly, for the space of half an hour." Now come on, I thought as I read. Assuming a person *could* spin around for thirty solid minutes, what would be the medical results to blood circulation, inner ear equilibrium, and the man's basic sensibility?

"The door of the house was open. I was whirled through the doorway, into the yard among stones and stumps, down to the shore of Mascoma Lake, some rods distant," Cotton wrote. "On reaching the shore of the lake that same power that led me to the water whirled me back again in like manner, and I found myself in the same chair that I had been taken from. This was a seal to my faith and baptism of the Holy Spirit, and I promised to obey it to the end of my days."

How convenient that he was whirled right back to the spot from which he originated, snarled the cynic within my brain. Likely it was all a dream. Still, the experience loomed as life-altering to Cotton. He gave praise for the power of the Spirit God and converted to Shakerism.

The past resounds with stories of people who looked at Shakerism and encountered therein the supernatural. Ann Lee's connection with the spirit realm inspired some of her strong views about the physical world. Could it have been that she, in some way a psychic, built an entire religious system not on moral principles nor political convictions but on raw truths garnered from her glimpses into the "other side"? She had visions of those who went to their death without the saving power of the gospel. "Souls that go out of this world, and have not heard the gospel, do not know God, nor where to find him. I have seen them wandering about," she told her followers, "weeping and crying, until, to appearance they had worn gutters in their cheeks, as large as my fingers." Perhaps the sight of those pitiful wisps, with faces engraved by endless tears, inspired compassion so great Ann Lee wanted to save the world.

She also wanted to save the persecuted in our land. Her spirit visions showed her what came next for the souls of African Americans enslaved and abused all their lives. "I have seen the poor negroes," the 1816 *Testimonies* reports her saying, "who are so much despised, redeemed from their loss, with crowns on their heads." The visions she had when awake, as common as night dreams to us mere mortals, showed her that when all else got stripped away at death, all souls stood equal, and nothing else mattered but merciful love.

Other Shakers experienced spiritualistic "gifts" throughout the next decades, long after the death of their Mother Ann Lee.

After Lucy Wright died in February 1821, Sister Lucy Smith, who had loved her dearly, had a series of visions of the dead woman. In one, she had gone to bed and suddenly saw Lucy Wright laying down face-to-face with her, looking "very butiful [sic], her handkerchief and Collar appeared very white pure and Angelic." Sister Lucy felt deep healing from the loss of her spirit family mother. "My soul," she said, "felt refreshed."

After David Darrow, elder of Union Village, died in 1825,

Shaker funeral goers reported that his corpse appeared "beautiful beyond discription [sic]" to them; the "brightness of heaven" seemed to rest upon it. Some said his dead body "surpassed any thing they ever saw of the kind," because it scarcely showed signs of his seventy-five years of age. Also, it emitted no odors. This Shaker legend involved many people witnessing the same mystical experience, in which their beloved elder's body hovered somewhere between here and the hereafter. Certainly other religions contain stories of masses experiencing miracles. They could, I realized, by their very nature never be proved.

A twelve-year-old named Emily Pearcifield in 1835 had a vision in which she traveled to the spirit realm, where she saw Jesus, Ann Lee, and some of the deceased first Shakers. Soon thereafter, a widespread wave of spiritism descended upon the Shakers in the mid-nineteenth century. Fifty years after the death of Ann Lee, thousands of Shakers, in communities now spread from Kentucky to Maine, began a period of intense communion with the spirits of the dead.

The "Era of Manifestations" or "Mother's Work," as Shakers call it, lasted from the 1830s to the 1850s. A rash of messages from the grave and "gifts" of inspiration for music and art filled meetinghouses and dwellinghouses to such a frenzy that daily work could not get done. Spectators from the world flocked to Sunday worship, eager to catch a glimpse of someone in a seizure or vision. Non-Shakers became so intrusive and mystical experiences so powerful that, for many decades, Shakers closed off religious ceremonies to outsiders. The visions and inspirations of that era, however, built an artistic and spiritual legacy that still sustains the Shakers who remain at Sabbathday Lake.

The Era of Manifestations began among some young adolescent girls, aged ten to fourteen, at Watervliet, New York, in August 1837. Several became absorbed in trancelike states; their "senses . . . appeared withdrawn from the scenes of time." They claimed they communicated with angels and took journeys to heavenly places.

The next month, Shakers began to see spirit manifestations

at their religious meetings. A female spirit dressed in white appeared and proceeded to kiss all the sisters, dance with them, and sing songs of mourning for sinners and encouragement for the obedient. From that point, more and more Shakers began to report experiences of visions of "the happified state of the Saints in light" or the "dark & dismal dungeons" where the wicked groaned in "awful distress."

Those who received visions were called instruments. They saw leaders from the past, dead members of their Shaker or birth families, angels, and unknown figures. They often reported that parts of their visions were beyond description. They sometimes saw heaven itself, or saw "Holy Mother Wisdom" or "Heavenly Father," the two sides of the face of God. Often, the "visionists" had to be carried to their retiring room "like a lifeless person." No consistent record was kept of the visions, but one writer estimated the number as "certainly in the thousands, perhaps even tens of thousands."

I wished I could travel back to those years and see for myself. Were these Shakers describing dreams that made strong impressions, ephemeral glimpses that may have been visions—the kind of chance meeting with the beyond that I myself, and countless creative and intuitive people, had had? Did they record such sensory perceptions only to have history exaggerate them? How far, really, was their experience from the hunches and peripheral visions I have had all my life? And if I shared some level of intuition with the Shakers, I wondered if that meant that I, too, intrinsically believed in spirits. Or perhaps we all merely suffered from overactive imaginations.

It was young people, especially young girls, who were especially prone to visions. According to Benjamin S. Youngs, they spoke in "unknown tongues" and underwent "extraordinary exercises," including "Powerful *shakings & quakings*, testimonies, promises, threatenings, warnings, predictions, prophecies, *Trances*, revelations, visions, songs, and dances." He said the trances often lasted as long as seven hours. The most frequent *gift*, as Shakers called the content of the visions, was that of repentance—"the most earnestly taught and the most earnestly sought for." All agreed that during the vision it was "as tho the veil between this & the other world was made almost transparent."

Sometimes Shakers received imaginary spiritual "things" like colorful balls, golden chains and jeweled necklaces, fine clothing, musical instruments, birds, flowers, and "other wonderful presents the likes of which the Shakers did not possess in everyday life. In fact, some were items the Believers explicitly condemned as worldly," reported the journals of the Shakers.

As instructed by the spirits, Shakers began a tradition of outdoor "mountain feasts" in which members would spend full days outside singing, praying, giving sermons, receiving spirit gifts, and feasting. People received sacred songs in their dreams, or visions of artwork to be produced, or new dance movements. At this time, each Shaker village received from beyond a spiritual name. Sabbathday Lake became known as "Chosen Land."

One Shaker took extraordinary measures to try and record the wonders he saw all around him. Brother Philemon Stewart received a series of special revelations and published them in 1843 as *A Holy, Sacred and Divine Roll and Book*. The book contained more than 400 pages of spirit messages, given by an angel at the Holy Fountain at the New Lebanon community. He thought the messages represented "the sentences of Eternal God and Creator" as read to him from a sacred roll. The book, which claimed divine status equal with the Bible itself, contained moral counsel, biblical quotations, historical and theological commentary, testimonies by ancient prophets, and a defense of the character of Ann Lee. At the time, seventy living Shakers in various villages publicly stated that they believed in the truth of these spirit communications. Today, however, the book is viewed with great skepticism, as a sort of mythology of its time.

Some stories of visions from this period seemed humorous, even though their content was taken seriously. A Shaker medium told a comical story from the spirit of Sir Isaac Watts, a dissenting English minister and hymn writer who had died in 1748, about his hard luck in heaven. Watts arrived in "the Spirit land, and could not find a soul I knew; I was so disappointed about heaven I sat down on some old rubbish and began to cry." Eventually, he "received the gospel." Mother Ann Lee "made me shake most of the time for three months," until he rid himself of "the old Anti-Christ—he stuck to me like wax, the blood-sucker!" All this was told in good humor, through the medium, and the Shakers laughed and began shaking, too, singing and dancing and laughing all at once, reported an 1850 unpublished Shaker history.

Throughout the Era of Manifestations, normal life turned inside out, as strange spirits presented themselves day after day during work and prayer. There were daily visits from angels with unpronounceable names. Native Americans, Africans, and Arabs came seeking to learn the Shaker gospel. Such historical figures as George Washington, Benjamin Franklin, Napoleon Bonaparte, and Pocahontas came forth, as did such biblical prophets as Jeremiah, Abraham, and Moses.

The Shakers felt a strong bond with Abraham Lincoln. They wrote letters back and forth; he permitted Shakers a conscientious objection from the Civil War; and he received from them a "very comfortable" Shaker chair. Just before Lincoln's assassination, a sister at Mt. Lebanon had a prophetic dream about the crime.

Spirits instructed Shakers to learn new songs and new dances, to spend days sketching and painting "gift" drawings, and to hold special rituals that interrupted their daily work and sometimes lasted well into the night.

I read these accounts, as I did the most unusual of Shaker testimony, with more than a little skepticism. Something about the psychology of large groups seemed to foster fertile ground for exaggeration, storytelling, and wishful thinking. It could be that the adrenaline coursing through Shaker communities during these decades pumped members up so much that they really believed they saw and heard these spirits. As with all such intangible mysteries, to prove these accounts would be impossible. I wondered if even the current Shakers believed.

During the Era of Manifestations, Native American spirits reportedly would knock at the front door and ask permission before entering the abode as a tribe. Taking a sort of possession of the Shakers, they would (through the Shakers) yell and whoop throughout the house, speak in Native American languages, and dance Indian dances. Sir Arthur Conan Doyle wrote of these possessions in his 1926 *The History of Spiritualism*. The spirits had come to be taught in the ways of Shaker faith.

The outbreak of spiritualistic manifestations "shook the society to its foundations," declared Stephen Stein. The revival caused confusion: people spent night and day entranced by their visionary scenes. Children and adults switched roles, because it was often the youth who wielded the spirit power of dead elders and ministers over the living adults. To those who did not receive the gift of visions, I imagined, these years could have seemed nightmarish; one never knew when some pipsqueak would command the entire community. Lines of authority frayed, and rules snapped, leaving one nothing much dependable to hold on to.

"From this religious commotion," Stein concluded, "Shakerism never fully recovered." Tensions developed between those who supported the visions and those who wished for a return to structure and order, and between the self-appointed spiritual mediums and the official Shaker ministry, each of whom claimed to speak the will of God.

Even in a utopia such as Shaker Village, factions battled one another for the upper hand. All believed that their own view, from conservative disbelief to liberal spiritism, ought to guide the fractured community. As in other cultures and times, spiritual visions brought power to the heretofore unnoticed, and that power was sometimes abused. Mediums sometimes faked messages to gain control over others or disrupt the harmony within their community.

A young brother at Enfield, New Hampshire, for example, pretended to be speaking in tongues but was found to be swearing in Latin. In 1850, Elder Freegift Wells reported that he had had a bad experience with a "vision" from another Shaker. "I once swallowed down without doubting everything that came in the shape of a message from the heavens," he wrote. "But after a while I got confounded by receiving a message in the name of Mother Ann, which I knew was a positive lie! From that time I found it necessary to be more on my guard."

I read that Shaker ministers tried to discern which spirit messages were valid by checking for consistency with other inspired writings and consulting the Bible. Still, to sort out legitimate from phony visions and gifts must have seemed, at times, impossible. How could they know what really motivated each visionist's heart?

The spiritual revival faded in the 1850s. Sacred drawings were stealthily hidden away, in shame, for a century. Yet that was not the end of spiritualism. The movement had taken root in American culture. Experiences with the occult became, for Shakers and many other Americans, a "scientific" defense of religious faith and a proof of the existence of the afterlife. Shakers remained interested in the spirit realm, even to the present day.

For Shakers, unlike many other Christians, the occult cannot be divorced from the divine. Shakers have been called the first modern American spiritualists. In the nineteenth century, when all of sophisticated America dabbled in spiritualism, Shakers eagerly joined in spiritualistic conferences and in private demonstrations of spirit power, including materializations through mediums, clairvoyants, and séances. They found a spiritual link with other religions worldwide, for example at the World's Parliament of Religions in Chicago in 1893, in the spiritism of Hindus, psychics, and pagans; and in the universal view of the Christ-Spirit, which they now saw in the leaders of many world religions.

Those who visited Shakers all too often bumped into the

spirit realm there. "They live with angels," Dixon wrote, "and are more familiar (as they tell me) with the dead than with the living." He told of one Sister Mary, who sat in his room "not an hour ago," leaned upon the Bible and confided in him that "the room was full of spirits; of beings as palpable, as audible to her, as my own figure and my own voice." The journalist grew alarmed at her "dreamy look," her "wandering eye," and would have feared "for her state of health," he quipped, "only that I know with what sweet decorum she conducts her life, and with what subtle fingers she makes damson tarts."

The *Atlantic Monthly* reported in 1876 that "they are all spiritualists" and "they claim to have been the first spiritual mediums." Spirits who visited the Shakers had "animated so many table-legs" and taken such "phantom shapes" that Shaker families were "in full communion with the other world."

What had Shakers to say about the outcome of such spiritual frenzy? Many Shakers felt that by communicating with the dead, they could help rescue the world from evil influences. Also, visionary Shakers contributed an abundance of hymns and music from inspiration beyond the grave. Sisters and brothers who received such gifts, explained the Shakers, had little training in science, poetry, or music, and so they "chiefly relied upon the teachings of the Spirit." This was the simple music, the Shakers explained, of a simple people.

In 1884 the Shakers published a book called *Shaker Music: Original Inspirational Hymns and Songs Illustrative of the Resurrection, Life, and Testimony of the Shakers.* "We claim that the words and music, are not *all* of Earth," the editors explained, "nor *all* of Heaven; simply inspirational gifts that verify their religious testimony." Daniel W. Patterson, a Shaker music historian, concluded that as many as ten thousand Shaker songs existed in manuscript form, with an untold number more songs, unrecorded, from the oral tradition.

Shaker "gift" songs ring out Shaker beliefs about doctrine, trust, thankfulness, love, and union. They describe the evil of the world, the condemnation awaiting those who deliberately sin, and the comfort and joy awaiting those who struggle to be faithful. Most gift songs sound "irregular and strange," reflecting the lack of musical training among the Shakers and the inspiration process of fleeting visions and tunes. Some songs reflect the tunes and styles of secular music of the day. The well-known Shaker song "Simple Gifts" was a gift from this period.

Writing from a twentieth-century perspective, Sabbathday Lake Brother Theodore Johnson claimed the power of this sacred Shaker music. "The hundreds of inspired songs and the so-called spirit drawings of those years," he said, "bear eloquent testimony to the depth and power of God's revealing of Himself to those who were open to the gifts of His spirit. . . . God continues even today to reveal Himself." I felt sure that Mozart, too, felt the power of God flowing through him when he composed. And could not the same kind of spirit infuse Shaker music as gives harmony to history's masterpieces?

Visual art, too, abounded. Many drawings were said to be concrete representations of visions from heaven above. Like Shaker music, the art is crafted in a folk style—heartfelt rather than academy-trained—and depicts everyday objects such as balls, boxes, baskets, trees and flowers, horns and harps, crowns, cups, clocks, and birds. Sometimes the drawings contain geometrical forms and strange machines. Often, sketches are surrounded by extensive inscriptions; for example, one dedicates the gift to "Beloved Sister Anna. Receive this, with my never ending love and blessing, Polly Laurence. Given by Mother Lucy's permission, *with a bright Jewel of her love. June 1853.*"

The best-known work of Shaker art is Hannah Cohoon's *The Tree of Life,* with intensely colored orbs of fruit hanging from the branches of the spiritual family "tree" in heaven. Other spirit drawings were more ominous, showing "prophetic signs" of "cataclysms of nature" that would strike the earth, such as fire, wind, hail, and earthquakes.

The two hundred extant pieces of "gift" art lay now sprinkled about the country, in Shaker museums and libraries and in private collections. Through the effort of such historians as Patterson and the Andrews, hundreds of songs and pictures have been reproduced in books. I pored over these, noting patterns in symbol and language, wondering what had finally stopped the flow of inspiration from beyond the grave.

One afternoon at Sabbathday Lake, I sat in the upstairs prayer room with the elder and eldress, talking about spirituality and spiritism. Having been together long enough to begin to feel comfortable, we drew our chairs in together, to form a small circle. Brother Arnold, in his blue jeans and bare feet, stroked his goatee as we talked. Sister Frances gracefully folded herself down into the sofa, cupping her chin in her hand while she thought. They both seemed open, and honest, yet the topic proved difficult, for they did not know how to educate me in the unseen, and they did not even have words to express some of the deepest ways that they *knew* the spirit realm existed.

Perhaps I still wished to find that tabloid story, about spirit possession at Sabbathday Lake, or angelic visions, or some such drama. In reality, Shaker life seemed much quieter than all that. Ecstatic whirling, spirit mediumship, divine visions, and occult messages all had waned within this community of plain faith. They still believed, no doubt about that. They simply did not have the spiritualistic hysteria of centuries past.

Although he had not actually had visions, Brother Arnold felt certain that he had "sensed" the presence of founder Ann Lee as well as many Shaker saints. "I have never seen them," he said, but others had.

He hesitated. "I'm trying to think of the last time I had heard of anything like a message coming through anybody, but I can't really think of one off the top of my head. But there are a lot of times when we'll have Meeting that people will sense a presence or sense the room being filled. Like when we did the CD, there was no doubt that the meetinghouse was very much filled." When the community celebrated their two hundredth anniversary at Sabbathday Lake, too, they had felt surrounded by the spirits of Shakers past. "There have been a lot of times," according to Brother Arnold, when the eight current believers have sensed the presence and support of angels.

"Sister is very sensitive about these things," he added.

"Yea," Sister Frances nodded, although she pointed out that she, too, had not actually "seen" those beyond the grave. "I truly feel very, very close to people I have loved here on earth who have gone on," she said.

"And sometimes I find myself talking to them, speaking to them. I always ask that their spirits be with me, to guide me, give me wisdom. That's just a part of my daily prayer, too. I don't think I have ever really seen spirits, had a vision. But I certainly feel very close to people who are in the other world. If I go into the Meeting room for Sunday service, that place sometimes is just alive with the spirits of those who have gone before. It really is. I feel that."

The whirling of the spirits has quieted at Sabbathday Lake. Many of today's Shakers have had only the most vague, transient experiences with the beyond. But one of them has had the vivid kind of spirit visions of Shaker past. It was the youngest, Brother Alistair. And it was what had brought him across an ocean to Shakerism.

He remembered the time, not long ago, when he wrestled with the decision to come join the Shakers. He grappled with the pull of the world, he told me, versus the pull of the quiet life. In the end, it was a series of visions that convinced him he was making the right choice.

"Torn in two is a very apt way to describe the way I was feeling," he said. "It was almost a physical feeling of being pulled, part of me being pulled into monastic life. And it had to be traditional—a traditional monastic life. There could never be any compromise for me."

The young brother had undergone a series of transforma-tions, from Anglicanism to Catholicism to a study of spiritism. He sought some sort of marriage between the gospel and the spirit realm, community and monastic prayer, that he found culminated in one within Shakerism.

"I was working with this woman who was a spiritualist and started going to spiritualist meetings," Brother Alistair said. He brushed light brown bangs back away from his eyes. "And that really was the next major step in my spiritual development. From there I went to mediumship development classes for three years." Three years, I noted. For this man of intense curiosity, who had studied so many approaches to faith, that was a long time.

"I got a tremendous amount from that. I would say that development, I think, enhanced my prayer life more than anything since I was in the abbey. And my father had been a spiritualist. Before he married my mother, he was involved in the Spiritualist Church in Dublin. My great-grandmother and my great-great aunt also were mediums. So, I had that tradition in my family. And I knew," he nodded, "that it was nothing to be afraid of within certain limits and boundaries. And the Christian spiritualism that I was involved with, I think, was very sensible." Those who believed in the psychic as a very real realm, I supposed, would say that young Alistair had intuition in his blood. That the power to perceive had been passed down for generations.

He began to attend spiritualist as well as Christian churches and Quaker meetinghouses. Then he told a story of being called into the Shaker way, actually *called*, by early Shakers who had been dead nearly two hundred years.

"Being very open to the Spirit, I had some exciting experiences which influenced me profoundly, particularly with Father Joseph and Mother Lucy."

He admitted that he did not literally, visually *see* these spirits. I had to ask, "So how did you know who they were?"

"I'm clairsentient," he answered, "rather than clairvoyant. I'm a little bit clairvoyant as well, but clairsentient means just that you have a very strong sense of the person's presence. And you communicate—you get communication but through your feelings. You feel what they're saying to you. But it's very, very strong. It's not that I have visions. I've never needed to have a vision. But I have a very strong sense of their presence and a strong sense of them supporting me and calling me.

"Later, last year, when I was making the final decision to come here, I sensed their presence in quite a general way, but they were very definitely offering a choice—wanting me to make a choice from what *I* wanted. And not pushing me, do you know what I mean? But I had a sense of them supporting me, and of them saying, 'Look, if you want to do this, we'll be with you.'"

A series of similar experiences showed Brother Alistair that, in his thirty-year spiritual search, he finally had stumbled upon the right path for him.

Brother Alistair told me that his most extraordinary experience took place at Stonehenge, the ancient pagan rock formation in the countryside of England. A friend of his, a counselor who was also a medium, had connections to get them into Stonehenge for personal and group meditation on a full, midsummer moon. "By ourselves, just six of us there in the dark at night. Which was an immense privilege," he recalled with a broad smile.

"And that was where I had a very strong sense of Father Joseph leading me. Ultimately leading me here . . . pulling me. He pulled me outside of the circle down to another stone and I just had to follow. I felt an overshadowing of him, really." Although the spirits clearly had left it up to him, the young Christian eagerly followed. And the faith into which he was led felt just right to him.

Brother Alistair told me he prayed to both Jesus and Ann Lee as teachers, not redeemers: not for salvation but for guidance. "I pray to them as I would pray to Father/Mother God or to the saints. I pray to the saints. I talk to them, and hopefully I listen to them," he said.

How in the world, I wondered, did he know that anyone heard him?

"Yea. Well, experientially I know it. I'm aware of individual spirits being around at times." Some are the souls of people he ministered to on their deathbed at the AIDS hospice where he worked in London. "I have visits from people I've known, especially through my HIV work. The person will come into my mind and I might go into an ecstatic state. And have just a very strong sense of their presence. I shake a bit, from the spirits, you know. And I may feel some communication from them."

He looked straight at me, this highly intelligent, sensitive man, and smiled the warmth of his love for me, which came freely whether I should end up believing him or not. "So, this, of course, can't be proved in any way, but I *feel* they're around. I feel attached to them and supported and helped by them."

I wanted badly to understand what this felt like, to feel the presence of spirits and to shake in spiritual bliss.

"Well," Brother Alistair told me, "you must know by the gift of God. You feel by the gift of God that you have the power of God. Then you feel strong. I see the ecstatic state as a longing in some way.

"It's kind of dangerous for us to talk about this, but I think it's important. Some religions play down the part of feeling and the emotions in worship and in prayer life and say you mustn't trust the emotions, it's the will that's the important thing. And that's certainly true. Without a strong will, committed and consecrated, then the feelings can get out of control," he said firmly. "Still, the feelings are important to my being sustained in the Gospel way.

"And the state of ecstasy. For years I had this, from the time I was a child, and I didn't know what it was called. I would just kind of shiver with delight and would feel it in my body. It's like a surge of power going through me. It can sort of be induced by breathing and prayer at the same time, or by visualization. I think more people have it, but perhaps they just don't call it that. You know, but they have it. It's a feeling quite unlike any other feeling," he smiled.

Was he saying that anyone could have such experiences of ecstasy, even nonbelievers?

Brother Alistair admitted that, because so much of his religious belief emerged from occult experience, he felt more closely tied to the spirits than to God. "The experience of the saints and angels, and the reality of other benevolent entities," had led him to believe. "Yea," said Brother Alistair, "I think faith in God is harder for me than faith in the spirits."

Taken aback, I stared at him.

"Because God is so much *pure* spirit and so totally unseen," he continued. "I think perhaps I know that there is a God because my prayers are answered and because I do get glimpses. In a wonderful book I read, *Tapestry from the Wrong Side*, Benedictine nuns and monks are talking about their religious lives. And the idea is that God is weaving a tapestry of our life and through all the things that happen to us and we only see the wrong side—we see the knots and the cross-stitches and the mess—but God sees a perfect picture. Occasionally, one gets a glimpse of the picture emerging, even though there are lots of threads crossing over each other. So I know from looking at that that God exists. But I *know* I experience the spirit realm."

People today, I reminded him, might see the Shaker belief in God and spirits as rather quaint. People today, in the world, believe in the tangible, the scientific, the universe.

"Actually, the universe, and the force of all of these things," he said quietly, "are not such a long step away from the kind of God that we believe in. Father/Mother God is a spirit, and God is love." As he spoke I felt that he tried only to answer my questions with honesty and respect. He did not try to sway me, nor convert me.

"It's very pure, not an anthropomorphic view of God that we hold. I think our God is an awful lot easier to believe in than the God of the average orthodox Christian."

Not all the members at Sabbathday Lake have seen or felt spiritual visions. When Brother Wayne joined the Shakers, he had an experience at the other end of the spectrum, not at all ethereal. Having grown up Protestant, with "no real understanding of the idea of religious order and what it meant," he felt his Shaker choice "was certainly a radical departure" from the path he would have followed. Still, his surety about Shakerism came not from spirits nor visions but from common sense.

"It wasn't a bolt of lightning that hit you on the head?" I asked.

"No," he chuckled. "It was so gradual that I think probably by the time I made the decision—or seriously thought about it— it was still a surprise to me because the decision had just come about so gradually. I wasn't aware that I was seeking something."

During my stay among the Shakers, Brother Wayne frequently pointed out to me that "the door's right there," and that if he chose to retract his Shaker vows he could walk out any day, into romance, marriage, the corporate life, the American dream, the world. Nothing held him there, he reminded me. He freely chose each day to stay. And I wanted to know: Why?

"Shakerism is a fulfillment of my Christian faith," he said, with arm extended and hand outstretched. "This is what I feel is the best way I'm spending my life, serving God. I think I'm as close to God, living a God-centered life as I would ever be. It's nice having the discipline or the structure of the religious life. That's really good in keeping me centered."

He talked and talked, and right-sounding phrases rolled from his tongue. But what about your heart? I asked. I could see that his head was there, but where did his heart dwell?

The Shaker brother stopped short, listened to himself, and grew quiet. "My heart is *here*," he said, finally, softly.

He struggled with himself, seeming out of his domain yet wishing to answer honestly. "Faith is something that's hard to articulate. And I don't know what would be the best way to spell it out for you, but it's just something you know from inside of you is right."

And so, for a moment, I could see the link between the spirituality of this pragmatic farmer with that of the sensitive Brother Alistair. They both felt their faith, not from their heads but from their hearts, and therein lay the bond of their brotherhood.

For Sister June, a sense of the mystical came as naturally as breathing. She trusted in the way a little child trusts, and she believed that God and Jesus were, literally, her best friends. "God was the most important person in my life," she said, "and has been since I was a child."

She remembered, as a girl, feeling a playful sort of connection with God. "Sometimes after I was put to bed at night, I would just think about God. And I tried to play little games with Him, like I'd tried to think of what was going to happen the next day and then all aspects of it and different things that might happen. And after I thought about everything that might happen, I'd say to myself, 'Well, God can't come up with anything else that would happen.' And He always did."

God felt like a grandfather, all-powerful yet very friendly. During her "ordinary Protestant upbringing," Sister June read Bible stories and received her own copy of the Bible. "I thought of Jesus as my friend and started to have a personal relationship with him when I was still a child," she recalled.

"I've had spiritual experiences all my life," she told me, "and I've come to depend on Jesus totally for everything, really. Even when I was in high school I felt very close to God. When I was about fourteen or fifteen, I joined the Christian Association. And in college I just felt that God was someone who loved me and I could depend on him."

Her path toward the Shakers took half a lifetime. Sister June was fifty when she came to Sabbathday Lake. One reason for the delay was intentional: She would not leave while her aged mother still needed her care.

"I made the decision to try and help my mother. It was something that God wanted me to do." Later, after the death of her mother, a friend brought her to Shaker Village for a weekend, and again she felt God calling her. "It's kind of hard to describe. It was kind of an inner feeling, somehow. Sort of an inner attraction to this place."

She had begun to read about saints, but not until her encounter with Shakerism did she understand "that you could communicate with people in the next world." Reading into Catholicism and Shakerism, "I discovered that I had quite a personal relationship with the Blessed Virgin Mary and with Saint Theresa the Little Flower, particularly. And other saints."

Although she did not actually see these saints, she had direct experiences of their presence. "You know, personal help in my life. Things would happen that I realized meant that they were there."

I smiled at her, thinking how innocent she looked when she talked about divine coincidences in her life. "Now," I asked, "how do you know that's not just in your imagination?"

"Because I've had enough spiritual experiences, so that I know," she replied. "You know, after a while, when things keep happening, you begin to *know*. If you ask God, Jesus, perhaps the Blessed Virgin Mary, something and then something happens shortly thereafter which is an answer to what you have asked, and, you know, if this keeps happening to you throughout your life. I mean, after a while, you'd be pretty dense not to catch on that somebody up there is listening and really cares about you."

That sounded like what I would call the power of positive thinking, I told her.

"Well, I call that faith," she maintained.

Given such emphasis on heaven and the spiritual realms beyond, Shakers welcome death with open arms. This did not surprise me. Death, to a Shaker, represents a passage of the soul forward, toward the ultimate goal of God. Shaker funerals include "set songs," emphasis on the life and witness of the deceased, and personal testimonies by family members.

A strong sense of the spirit of the deceased pervades the

funeral. Sometimes, as with Sister Mildred and Brother Ted of the previous generation at Sabbathday Lake, the sense of presence lasts years and years after their death. "You can feel them still here," Sister Frances told me. "Their presence is almost palpable." The community did not seem to deny, however, their feelings of grief. They longed for the presence of their former eldress and elder. They missed particular personalities, dear idiosyncrasies, mentoring love. However, while they lamented their own loss, they staunchly believed that dead Shakers were much better off than they.

Brother Alistair and I talked about death, and what happens to a soul in the afterlife. He shared his rather unique Shaker view. I was learning that, in some ways, there are as many Shaker theologies as there are Shakers.

"I believe that eternal progress is open to every human soul," Brother Alistair began. "That is the first of the seven principles of the English spiritualist church: eternal progress open to every human soul. I believe that our ultimate purpose is to *become* God. We may postpone this until we get to the other side of life, and so we're doing ourselves a favor if we start now."

"What would heaven look like?" I asked.

"I hope that the next stage beyond the veil for me will be a perfectly ordered Shaker community which is practically harmonious but has all the joys of community life here. I think that the spirit world is communal. We shall enjoy earnest, loving relationships with other spirits. I believe that friendships continue beyond the grave."

Heaven, to him, seemed a sort of idealized Shaker Village, where no human frailties stood in the way of perfect union. What Shakers on earth tried, worked perfectly there.

And hell?

"I believe that people can make definite choices for evil and cut themselves off from grace," said Brother Alistair. "I don't believe in the kind of God who will judge anyone harshly or damn anyone because they have behaved badly. But I do believe that people will be damned. There is a process of damnation."

Heaven and hell, for him, are "states of existence, not physical places—but when you're there, they feel physical." And, for many of us middle-roaders, there is an in-between.

"Mother Ann definitely believed in purgatory. She didn't call it that, but she would labor with loved souls often, their bodily sufferings and mental anguish. And I think it's very important for us to pray for them," he noted.

"Purity is an important standard in people to work toward on the other side of life," Brother Alistair added. "There is no marriage in heaven. There is connection of souls, you know, but you have to let go of the carnal nature—and it's probably easier to do it in this life than in the next."

For Sister June, faith in the afterlife seems to come as easy as faith in God. At death, said Sister June, "I would expect to go home to God."

Home. She said home, and she meant to use that word for a plane whose existence cannot even be proved. As I longed for the shelter and grace of my own home in California, I wondered, Did Shakers ever truly feel at home in this world?

"Actually," she explained, "I think of Heaven as my home, and I think of this life here as just sort of being a transition, an opportunity to grow spiritually. I remember reading somewhere that Heaven is like a garden and we're living in Heaven before we're born. After we die, we go back to Heaven. This life in this world was just a parenthesis between the two."

She gazed at the library, which she had spent the last decade helping to build, and she looked at me with clarity in her shining eyes. "I'm here to grow as much as I can and learn how to be close to God, and how to serve Him and so forth. So that when I get back home to Heaven, I'll be better able to serve God and do what He wants."

She sounded like a child, yet steady, sure of what she wanted. "By living in the community," she continued, "of course we're supposed to obey. Sister Frances is head of the community. So you learn to be obedient, to do what she asks of you, and not to run off on a tangent and do what you want. I think that's good training for doing what God wants, which I think is what everyone does in Heaven. And I've read that in Heaven there is unconditional love from God and all of his creatures." The trust in the unseen, the longing for the next life, shone clearly in this small woman.

Still, something was missing. What I expected would go hand-in-hand with the longing for Heaven—a distaste for this life, an impatience to get on to the feature presentation—I did not see in Sister June. Rather, I saw contentment. Whether she was clearing dirty dishes off the table or sorting through endless piles of cataloging cards, Sister June emanated joy.

She claimed this joy came from God.

We were approaching the end of my stay at Sabbathday Lake. Many questions still burned within me, and I became bolder in my need to know. "I want to know why," I asked bluntly. "Why are you so happy?"

"Well, I think it's just living my life for the Christ." She blushed and looked down. "You know, just being with Jesus Christ and being with people."

I remained unconvinced. "Have you always been this way or is it just since you've become a Shaker?"

"No, I think I've always been happy. I learned I could depend on Jesus for everything I have ever since I was child. That conviction has been growing more and more so, and getting deeper and deeper the older I get. The circumstances in my life," she said, "have brought me closer to Him."

She hunched over toward me and told me something as though it were a secret. "I know He loves me. And I like the way I become when I'm close to Him. Because He just gives me this great joy."

Even Brother Arnold, the matter-of-fact intellectual, had felt himself at the threshold of the realm beyond. What he described sounded like Shaker bliss. "There's a kind of feeling of excitement," he told me, "that you get sometimes when you're least expecting it. Just walking around. Just doing the normal everyday things. And then suddenly it's the realization of the presence of God, and that's it. I mean, it's a joy that I can't express. And I don't necessarily know when it's going to happen."

Perhaps I had little to compare this to, but I thought of orgasm. Could he have somehow mastered the art of mental sexual release?

"Is it emotional," I asked him, "or physical, or both?"

"A little of both," said Brother Arnold. "I don't know."

Still, the joy he felt differed from the happy feeling one got on a radiant spring morning, or the general gladness in being alive. "Yea, it's very different from that," he mused. "But it also brings an understanding that your relationship with God has to be shown. When my prayers get to be so darned redundant, I mean, my external prayers, I forget about this joy." Bliss fed true faith, perhaps, but spiritual bliss could not be sustained during the vicissitudes of daily human life.

"See, there's this light, there's this love that is God that has to not just be visible to us but that we have to make visible to others. We can act as a conduit for God. That's our life. I mean, if we're called to be Christians, to be Christ-like, to live for Christ's life, then we have to not only inhale it but exhale it. We can't just hold it in till we blow up."

Brother Arnold assured me that without a doubt God existed, and that spirits dwelt around him as he labored toward purity in this life. "Faith gives substance to the things that are unseen, and the things that are unseen are eternal," he tried to explain.

I could not agree. "But that's like the chicken and the egg to me," I protested. "You're telling me 'I know there's a God because I have faith. And I have faith because there's a God.' I don't know how to get out of that circle."

He laughed, with delight. "Well, you shouldn't get out of the circle. The circle is that which represents eternity. There's no beginning and no end to a circle. Brother Ted summed it up so well when he coined the phrase 'living in the eye of eternity.' That's where we are." Then he paused. Silence filled the room where we sat. I breathed in the scent of wood shavings in this carpentry workshop, and I waited.

"I can't *make* you believe," Brother Arnold sighed. "I can tell you I believe. I can show you, I can give you actions of what faith is about, and if you don't want to believe, then you can pick it apart. Absolutely. That's your free will."

It was a human instinct, he thought, to believe in a beyond. "I think the more you believe," he told me, "the more you see reasons to believe. Most of the people I've met who were non-believers didn't really want to be nonbelievers. They wanted you to be able to prove to them something that was better and was there, beyond humanity," he said.

"And they want to believe in an omnipotent creator. But because they can't touch it, and because they are so materially bound, they can't in their own heart accept," he said. "I see Christianity as having a great deal of hope to it—the hope for that which is better. The hope for our eternal home. To be totally and absolutely one with God. And that's the goal that we're working on. As Shakers, we're willing to give up all to follow Christ in the regeneration. We're getting back a glimpse of that hope, here and now."

And for him, as for all Shakers, the hope that is gained through faith must be put to work. "Christ is always telling us about how to give and you'll be given, seek and ye shall find, knock and the door will be open. . . . That just doesn't mean sit here and meditate on my word and I'll come to you. He's saying, 'Do it!' Mother Ann, too, was always saying, 'Do it.' Labor for a gift of God. Go forth. Work with your hands, produce for yourselves, *do* something. Lay up the store of the Kingdom and provide for those who are in the here and now who need you, who need help, and who need to be shown a good example."

For Brother Arnold, everything—even a simple feeling of bliss—carried with it moral responsibility. He felt compelled to turn that joy back to others, through his living out of his beliefs.

"You know, God's expecting that no matter what he gives us, we have to give back. And we do it by the kind acts and deeds in our lives. By the way we live our life. This life is a joy as well as a labor," he declared.

Brother Wayne had his own unique view of death. We had not meant to talk about it—on a warm spring afternoon when all the earth seemed bathed in life—but we had been pondering the purpose of a human lifespan, and what he said felt so far away from my understanding that I could not find even the ricketiest bridge between us.

Unlike the men I knew in the world, men with lusty phalluses and looming egos, this virile Shaker man had no desire to propagate the earth with his seed, to impregnate women, spawn children, to propel his DNA code into immortality in the blood of his children and their children. Men I knew and loved in the world had a ceaseless craving for competition, and a rumbling hunger for more money, more power, more of the life that money could buy. Yet this man would sweat all day in the barns and fields, and be up at sunrise to work on weekends, never to take a Florida vacation nor buy himself a sportscar nor get promoted to an easier desk job. Men of my world all seemed to want to leave behind a legacy of sorts: a well-managed restaurant, a home in impeccable repair, a product they had helped build, a family they had reared well, a foundation to build a wing of a museum, or a treehouse to be shared by generations to come. Brother Wayne, however, sat across from me and looked me right in the eye and claimed he cared nothing for legacies.

I pointed to him. "Is there no ego in there?" I demanded.

"Ego?" he said. "Oh, believe me, there's an ego in here!" He laughed in scorn at himself, as though he wished it were not so.

I looked out the window to the Shaker graveyard beyond, where one plain marker spoke for all the individuals who ever had died on this soil and were buried beneath it. Shakers did not use individual grave markers, because even in death they wanted to achieve union. I realized that Brother Wayne, with all his vitality and conviction, would turn to dust in a field of anonymity, without even so much as a grave marker, when his brief years on earth came to an end. Unknown, he would be consumed by worms and disintegrate into unwritten history.

This bothered me. A lot. Life felt so fleeting anyway, and history lost nearly all the lives of people past. Did Brother Wayne have to surrender his sense of self even in death? Did he not see that he was setting up his life to end in oblivion?

"What will happen to you after you die?" I asked.

"I'm going to be cremated."

"No!" I nearly yelled at him. Was this man just that stubborn, or did he really only look at that one side of things? I caught my breath and vowed to listen harder. Perhaps I was missing something here.

"I mean, is there a rest of you that will go somewhere, besides the body?"

"Oh yea," said Brother Wayne. "I believe very strongly in an afterlife."

"What do you think will happen?" I prodded.

"Oh, I don't know. I hope I'll go to Heaven." There, again, was that maddening matter-of-fact surety. How could he be sure of Heaven? I challenged him to tell me about such a place.

"I think Heaven is a very hard place to describe," he said. "And I think probably the reason people get so many misconceptions about it is because for the last—well, let's just approach it from the Judeo-Christian point of view—for the last 6,000 years, we've been trying, in our own temporal way, to describe God and Heaven and an afterlife. And of course then we are a spirit." And the twain body and spirit, according to Brother Wayne, never shall meet.

"Everything that's a reality to us now has very little bearing on a spirit. . . . But I believe very strongly in an afterlife. And I think, in the more traditional Catholic approach and certainly in the Shaker approach, that there is a middle ground. That there certainly is a Hell, there is a Heaven, and there is a middle ground for those who were trying but didn't quite do it. Whether you call it Purgatory or the Land of Spirit, whatever. I would like to think that I'm going to Heaven. I would certainly hope so."

In the end, Brother Wayne claimed a different measure for success than would the men of my world. In the end, when he came to draw his last breath, he would mark his days on earth with a standard not held by many others.

"We aren't put on this earth to make monuments to ourselves," he said emphatically, as the rays of sun pouring in our windows began to slant toward dusk. "And, if I do nothing better than live a good Christian life here at this community, that's more of a monument or tribute I can leave to myself, to leave a positive message behind for the next generation of believers that comes along, than probably anything I could have done if I were President or a famous attorney or dictator for life of some third-world nation. Because, I mean, the gift of a good example and of love lasts and does more than any sort of grandiose thing that you can do otherwise."

And, as for the anonymity of the Shaker graveyard, he welcomed that. "I'm glad there won't be a gravestone for me," he said, smiling wryly, "because I hate mowing cemeteries."

I dreamed that I was at Sabbathday Lake, and someone took me by the hand and led me into the dwellinghouse. Up, up the stairs we went. I do not know who led me, but it was more than one person, and they felt like friends, though I could not see their faces. We laughed together with glee as we seemed to float up staircase after staircase, down stretches of long hallways, and up, up, to the top of the building. The red brick dwellinghouse has six stories, and finally we came to the top and into a wide open room. Its ceilings slanted under the eaves of the roof, and light poured in from paned windows, bounced off gleaming wood floors, and lit the room with the color of our laughter.

"Is this where you do the dancing?" I asked, knowing in my

heart what the answer would be. Somehow I knew a secret: that today's Shakers did, in hushed privacy, continue the whirling ecstasy of their ancestors. Over in the corner stood a Shaker rocker. It was empty, but it nearly bobbed to and fro with the power of the air that rushed throughout the room.

Then the spirits who had led me suddenly became quiet. The room transformed back into a dusty, closed attic as Sister Frances ascended the stairs behind us.

"You know," she shook her head back and forth and smiled ruefully, "it really does go against the rules for you to be up here."

"Oh, I know— I didn't mean— Of course I'll come down right away," I stammered, feeling that I had overstepped the deepest privacy of their faith. The spirits, or sisters, who had led me up became bashful and shamed, and they scurried down the steps like children. But as I came down, too, I knew they had given me a precious gift, for I felt I had seen that the mystical heart of Shakerism still beats.

CHAPTER EIGHT

WORLD

Farewell! farewell! vain world farewell! I find no rest in thee.
The greatest pleasures form a hell too dark and sad for me.
Alas! alas! I have too long prefer'd thy sinful crowd:
I listen'd to your Syren song, while mercy call'd aloud.

Farewell, vain world! I say once more, I'm bound for
Canaan's land.
I see a happy world before—prepar'd at God's right hand.
On life's tempestuous sea I sail, while countless billows roll;
But Christ my pilot will not fail, with him I trust my soul.

—*"Vain World"*

Afternoon stretches toward the close of the workday at Sabbathday Lake. Weariness settles in my bones, aching, pulling my
mind away from the present moment. Having awakened well
before dawn, I fed the baby, read Shaker tracts in the motel
room, and rushed into the sisters' waiting room just minutes
before the 7:30 breakfast bell. It has been a long day, full of my

household chores and theological research that have rippled into a sort of pattern during my time here.

It has been a long visit, and I fight fatigue. My head feels as though I have been in a museum too long: absorbing endless data, scrutinizing myriad images, memorizing too many details. Nights have been spent reading what I could not fit within days, and writing in my journal the colors, smells, gestures, and stories of Sabbathday Lake. My head reels with it all.

I want to go home, to rest. I realize I shall never know the fullness of this faith. Life has given me only a glimpse. My heart aches for the rest of the family I left behind. As I had promised, I have called home every day, at the same time, from a pay phone a mile up the road from the motel. Only once have I heard anger and pain, when my eldest screamed into the phone instead of talking to me. Otherwise, I have heard from my sons of their adventures, feeding bits of bread to the ducks at the park, going to the beach with Daddy and his friend Jeff. And, sharing my life back with them, too, I have told them about the baby sheep in the barn, the big dogs in the dwellinghouse, and the exciting new foods I have tasted.

They have survived the time apart; they have thrived. Yet I hunger to feel their little arms about me, and to see the stead-fast love in my husband's deep brown eyes. I wish to take up again the sacred commitments of my own life.

More than I thought I would, I feel torn in two. If not for the ties that bind me to my husband and children, my home and work, I perhaps would stay longer among these gentle, prayerful people. They have taken root in my heart.

Around me, the daily activity of Shaker Village swirls. I wait in a downstairs hallway for Sister Frances. We will go and sort linens in a moment, but first she must consult with the foreman on the mortar-and-foundation job. I swerve quickly out of the way as Michael, the fresh-out-of-college museum curator, barrels through a nearby door. His arms encircle a stack of old Shaker prints and portraits. He has sorted through dusty roomfuls to design this year's exhibits for the tourists. Close behind him follows Brother Arnold, with another load of framed artifacts. They toss each other jovial comments about their progress.

Across the flower garden, in the new administrative offices, I hear the voice of Muriel as she answers a telephone call from a Midwestern antiques collector seeking advice. Brothers Wayne and Alistair have teamed up with local farmers who come seasonally to shear the Shaker sheep. Lenny walks down to the print shop to check on the volunteer who lays out copy for the quarterly newsletter, and Sister June shows the new librarian around the old schoolhouse library. As I stand, tired and dazed in the hallway, I attempt to smile at passersby. I hope that Sister Frances will come soon, that the linen sorting will go quickly, and that I might squeeze in a bit of rest before an evening full of baby care and research.

I realize that only because I have spent some time here can I tell who is really Shaker and who is not. When I had arrived the first day, I remember, I waved to some men working on the roof, thinking them brothers. The line of differentiation between the covenanted, the salaried, and the volunteer is blurry indeed. An outsider would have to squint hard to see where the world leaves off and Shaker begins.

Past Shakers seem to have protested loudly the influence of the world. Books and print material were sources of ill intent. Not only was Ann Lee illiterate, but she rejected all writing. There was an early prohibition against writing, and an antipathy toward formal theological documents. Conventional forms of Christianity that surrounded the Shakers seemed to fester with apathy and hypocrisy. Shakers condemned clergy and laity as structured in society.

Wishing to achieve separation from temporal affairs, early Shakers harvested their own crops, raised livestock, produced cheese and butter, baked their own bread and wove their own fabric, to minimize the level of commercial interchange. Still, from the beginning Shakers needed some supplies from the world, and in subsequent centuries they found themselves buying many items that eased and simplified their lives, and selling products crafted with unmistakable Shaker precision.

Shakers have worried throughout history about the world creeping in to their haven. Near the time of the Civil War, Isaac N. Youngs protested that the increased business ventures of the Shakers with the world had begun to impede their "spiritual travel." Shakers were becoming "more & more tasty," Youngs wrote in *A Concise View of the Church of God*, "about clothing, and articles of fancy, the use of high colors, of paint, varnish, &c . . . than is virtuous or proper."

All this hiding from the world seemed to me a rather unpleasant denial that we humans *do* dwell in the here and now. By purpose or accident, we have ended up on Earth. All this rejection of temporal life chafed at me. Having spent decades studying the Shaker faith, however, Brother Arnold offered a different perspective. He looked back to a time when early Shakers despised the world and all its trappings and viewed that within the historical context.

"Don't get Mother Ann wrong," said Brother Arnold. "First of all, she *only* lived in the world. I mean, she never lived a secluded life.

"She traveled from place to place and she met people head on, in every situation. You know, from the low to the high. I think her fear of the world was worldliness itself. She was trying to get people to understand what was important and what wasn't important."

And the point was, for both Mother Ann Lee and for Brother Arnold, that a person cannot honestly live in two places at once. One could embrace spiritual values wholly, or live in the tangible here and now.

"If you're thinking about your own vanity," the elder explained, "if you're thinking about how good you look and how you're dressed and all, you start thinking very highly of yourself as a self—instead of the giving up, the cleansing. . . . A lot of those [eighteenth-century] people were very haughty, very proud that they were very early consumers.

"And Mother saw as much spiritual advantage in the poor people as she saw in the wealthy, and she had to unify them, too." Hence Ann Lee used a rejection of worldliness as a way to level Shakers of all socioeconomic levels to one of simple faith.

Total isolation from the world never really was the intention. Shakers did not build their communities far from the reach of civilization. Rather, they set them physically in society—near towns and villages—yet somewhat removed, poised atop a hill or tucked a few miles from town. And technology brought the secular realm into Shaker life, because Shakers, unlike some other utopians, always welcomed industry and invention. As early as 1873, the Sabbathday Lake community used a steam engine. Toward the end of the nineteenth century, even the most conservative Shakers embraced modern technology: power, transportation, machinery, telecommunications. The Sabbathday Lake group bought the first Shaker car in the United States, a Selden, for $2,100 in late 1909.

Still, Shaker elders must always have felt pulled between the outside world, with which they must conduct business, and the inside utopia, in which they strove for higher values. Their temporal and spiritual responsibilities weighed heavy: appointing new Shaker leaders, managing the society's finances and industry, giving inspired public testimony and compassionate individual counseling. Meanwhile, elders were expected to uphold Shaker values, to the letter, in their own personal lives, and to pitch in with the daily chores: cooking, washing up after, chopping wood, tending the animals and gardens, answering letters, and recording the community journal. Today, not just the elders but the entire community feel that level of interaction with the world. Various members participate in lectures, workshops, and fund-raising activities. And all contribute to the simple, gracious Shaker hospitality that hundreds of visitors each year find in the museum, meetinghouse, and dining room.

Perhaps because so many of the current Shakers have come from the world, and have known well what they willingly give up, there is no looming sense of temptation that could sweep over one when one least expects it. A certain naïveté exists, but it is a chosen innocence. And in many cases, it is a postworldly innocence. This enables ease in the exchange of friends, technology, media, goods, and information from the world.

The Shaker marketplace has become international with the opening of a Shaker store in London, which sells books, herbs, crafts, music, and gift items. This allows more Brits to discover the faith that originated in their country. Also, the store helped bring Brother Alistair to Maine, for this is where he delved into books on Shakerism. Ironically, the commercialism of the world led a convert to the shores of Sabbathday Lake.

Sister June saw a sharp contrast between the closed doors of Shaker past and the doors of today, flung open to the world. "There were times when Shakers pretty much stayed to themselves and within their little communities," she told me as we worked together to wipe down the tables after dinner. "Shakers were quite separate from the world.

"Of course, that has changed. We have people coming to us from the world who stay nearby, but they eat with the community and share a lot of activities with the community. And there have been times when Meeting wasn't open to the public," she recalled, "but it is now."

The Spirit, according to Sister June, "is very flexible. And Shakerism follows the Spirit according to the community leaders, especially Sister Frances now and Brother Arnold. They're the leaders." And because "they're both very outgoing, friendly people, they like to welcome visitors."

For Sister June, opening the door to the world can enhance, rather than impede, the divine. "You know," she said, realizing this as she spoke it, "having meals is a sort of a spiritual communion as well as a physical meal." Then she laughed. Part of this, she added, was due to a heavenly level of culinary talent. "Sister Frances has the gift of being a good cook as well as being very spiritual," she said.

Among the Shakers of today, I noticed, the fear of the world has dissipated. Members come and go from errands, lectures, and trips so easily that I was shocked. My stereotype Shakers would have ducked their heads, averse to the temptations that lurked at the shopping mall and the downward pull of the local pizza pub.

In reality, I had seen Sister Frances go into town to get her hair cut, and come back like a shy schoolgirl hoping for a compliment. I had seen the whole family pile into the car and go out for dinner on a Friday night. I had heard stories of trips, on airline tickets sent by friends who wined and dined and theatered Sister Frances for a week at a time.

"How," I asked her, "can you come and go so easily from town, travel all around the country, and hobnob with wealthy friends, but not lose your sense of the simple?"

"I guess," she answered with a ready smile, "because I never forget my roots, I never forget my life. I can be with friends who, as you put it, are quite wealthy, and I enjoy them. That does not upset me. It never has made me want for something more than I already have. I can enjoy the world. I don't want to be in it for too long at a time, and I'm always very happy to come back to Chosen Land and what my life is here."

Sister Frances told me a story of one time when she visited a family in Cincinnati with whom she had become good friends. One evening they planned to go to a dinner party and take her as their guest.

"Well," the husband asked her, "shall we introduce you as Sister Frances or just Frances?"

Not wishing to belabor a lot of explanations about the Shaker way, and perhaps wishing for a night off from holiness, Sister Frances decided to throw off her eldress title and mingle as just "Frances." As soon as she was introduced, however, another party member announced, "I know who *you* are. I just saw your picture in *National Geographic*. You're *Sister* Frances." Sister Frances never had her chance to try an evening as a secular woman. He asked a hundred questions and quickly became a friend of the Shakers himself.

Sister Frances had, it seemed, come a long way from Ann Lee and her penchant for asceticism. She had come a long way from me, too, and my deeply embedded Catholic guilt. I had spent an adulthood trying to learn how to enjoy an extra slice of cheesecake, how to bask in a bubblebath, or linger in the lingerie department without feeling overriding guilt over the self-indulgence of it all. Guilt, to this Shaker eldress, was a foreign experience.

"But do you not feel guilty," I asked, "when you take that second glass of wine, or feast on lobster—such worldly pleasures?"

"Oh nay, oh nay, nay, nay," Sister Frances resounded with good humor. "Another thing that has helped me an awful lot in my life is the saying that *the Lord loves a cheerful giver.*

"I think God wants us to be happy. And most of the time I'm happy. With the blessings I have, with the beauty of the gospel, with every—Why should I not be happy? God has made everything in the world, and he wants us to enjoy it."

Although Sister Frances would not "use the wherewithal that belongs to the community and spend it for something that would be a luxury, if these other people are happy spending money for lobsters for us and that sort of thing, I'm happy."

So, there it was. A gift was a gift, whether from nature or from the world, and all derived from the goodness of God. For a Shaker, one had simply to give thanks for it, not to scourge oneself for the receipt of it. And I, having learned how much the Sister loved chocolate, then resolved to pick up a box of truffles for her from a famous San Franciscan candymaker back home. Already I could imagine the relish with which she would tear open the box, and the delight with which all the brothers and sisters would choose their favorite morsel.

Later, I asked Brother Arnold, too, about the ease with which members lived near the world. "Here it seems," I said, "that you can come and go into that realm without it getting into your soul."

"Uh hmmm," he thought for a moment. "Yea. Well, hopefully, that's the way it should be, because you can't mix oil and water."

The community now lives much closer to the world than before he joined. "This community was very, very cloistered into the 1960s," Brother Arnold recalled. "It was a very, very real sense of division between the world and the community. And there are some who wish for that to be reestablished. I don't wish for that, even though in a very real sense I'm probably far more cloistered than anybody else here. I mean, in my interior mind view."

But Brother Arnold does not wish a return to the early days of world aversion. "I don't think you can go back. I think it's wrong. Because what we've done is, we have opened up our lives to let other people experience it to the degree that they can and will experience it. I think it's very important for us to share our life. So it means opening our doors more.

"I do believe that there should be separate community life, too. I mean, we can't just live our lives out in public all the time. But I believe that it's important for us to continue to practice hospitality of having people dine at our table and worship with us. And, for short periods of time, to allow people to work with the community and see its goings on. I don't know how else we ever hope to attract anybody if we don't.

"A lot of people have benefited by being able to come here for a week at a time and experience the life and be part of it. And it helps them renew themselves a little bit, it just helps them."

Shakers took a long time to come around to the kind of openness of today. Yet "The early Shakers," said Brother Arnold, "had no blueprints to go by. They had no other experiences. They were trying something radical and something very new in what they were doing. And they just also trialed and errored.

"I mean, Father Joseph had a great system, but he forgot to include one important thing. How do you get more people?"

Through time, "Shakerism grew and it changed. And they introduced this, and they subtracted that. And they changed this and they changed that. If it didn't work anymore, get rid of it. Try something new. If it works, keep it. If it doesn't, you get rid of it."

Despite the Shaker willingness to adapt and innovate, the world has long been wary of them, and incredulous that they could survive even a generation without the staying power of reproduction. The media, for example, has been reporting the imminent extinction of the Shakers for at least a century. In 1911 the *New York Times* ran an article entitled "The Last of the Shakers—A Community Awaiting Death," in which the reporter described the twenty-two Shakers at Enfield, Connecticut as a "quaint, ghostlike colony of religious fanatics." Since then, nearly every piece written on Shakerism has proclaimed the end of the faith. Seeing only a few converts straggling over to their meetinghouse each week, the world has looked on in smug surety of Shaker death.

Meanwhile, Shakers have always responded with zeal. They would not, could not believe that the Father/Mother God had brought them this far for naught. Early Shakers looked to the Bible for the promise of the future. Elder Joseph Meacham, who led the Shakers after Ann Lee's death, pointed to the example of Noah in the Hebrew Bible. "If there is but one called out of a generation," foresaw Ann Lee, "and that soul is faithful, it will have to travail and bear for all its generation." And Shakers believed the promise of Matthew 18:20: "For where two or three are gathered in my name, there am I in the midst of them." Not just numbers, but the fidelity of the few mattered.

Strong promises made by the founders of the faith have sustained Shakers for centuries hence. "This gospel will go to the end of the world," prophesied Ann Lee, "and it will not be propagated so much by preaching, as by the good works of the people." As for the future, there need only be a faithful few to carry on. "If there are but five souls among you that abide faithful, this testimony will overcome all nations," proclaimed Father James Whittaker.

Shakers have responded to dour prophecies about their extinction that have been proffered by the world since the death of Ann Lee. "Are Shakers Dying Out?" asked Shakers Anna White and Leila Taylor at the turn of the twentieth century. "Yea! dying out and up," they answered with more than a little sarcasm. "Men and women die—advance, go to higher planes, to spheres of greater radius than earth, where we hear of them actively engaged along the same lines as on earth—the spread of truth among humanity." So, while the bodies of individual Shakers may die, the faith itself never would. "Is Shakerism Dying?" they continued. "Nay! Not unless God and Christ and eternal verities are failing."

They felt that Shakerism had survived because of a willingness to change, not tenets but tradition, over time. The two sisters declared that Shakerism had little to do with mere custom. "The Shaker may change his style of coat, may alter the cut of her gown or cease to wear a cap," they said, "and no harm will be done. Vital harm may be done by retaining either . . . merely to preserve old forms and customs, when the time is crying out in vain for action."

I could imagine how society might react to these ardent sisters today, in a political debate, given their repugnance for custom merely for custom's sake. Perhaps I lived in a more conservative time. I saw debates being waged with anguish over the church's acceptance of homosexuality, ordination of women, empowering of lay ministry, and the ethics of abortion and birth control to genetics and euthanasia. Clinging to old forms, I had seen within my own church, could preclude the possibility for growth.

White and Taylor, however, believed their progressive faith held possibility for the future. Shakerism embodied "the underlying truths of God-life in all ages." Its universality would appeal to people more and more as worldly people discovered how many of the ideals they held dear were embraced within Shakerism. "A new age of spirituality is at hand," they prophesied in 1904, "and the conditions now existing in embryonic form . . . will develop in a manner perhaps as startling to the Shakers as to the world." And the Shaker faith, they said, would be ready to accept this explosion of faith.

Eldress Anna White told her fellow Shakers that this was a time in which "we realize profoundly our duty to be zealous in all that makes for righteousness." So, in the twentieth century, Shaker leaders lobbied for women's rights, fair labor laws, animal protection, temperance, and peace. They hosted a 1905 international peace convention of meetings, addresses, and Shaker songs. They talked of reduced armaments, an international police force, a central world court, and neutral waterways for commerce, according to Flo Morse's *The Shakers and the World's People*. As I read this account I thought about the century that had proceeded with such developments as the United Nations, the Peace Corps, the League of Nations, the European Community, and other attempts at preserving global peace. Shakers saw, long before international television news was invented, how countries must work together to preserve our world.

Sister R. Mildred Barker, the eldress at Sabbathday Lake just before Sister Frances, once said that "The principles and ideals which the Shakers were first to expound have gone out into the world and, like a pebble dropped into the water, we cannot measure the distance of the influence they have borne. First in so many things we now take for granted—sex equality, religious tolerance, and so forth—Shakerism is not dying out, nor is it a failure," she declared.

Not all Shakers agreed. Some began to believe they *were* a dying breed. Gertrude Soule, the last eldress of the former Canterbury, New Hampshire, community, called the Shakers "an endangered species." Another eldress said, "Oh! I know we're disappearing, but what of it? We've done our work. . . . We've served our time. Yea! and if we go, something else that's maybe better will take our place."

Tired resignation sunk down to the bones of Shaker communities in the second half of the twentieth century. And indeed, Shakerism might have died, I discovered in the carefully couched language of history books, over a bitter battle that took place between the last two Shaker communities—Sabbathday Lake, Maine, and Canterbury, New Hampshire. The fight was over membership, and money. And if the elderly Canterbury sisters had had their way, the covenanted Shakers of the past generation would have died with both clenched firmly in their hands, and with the memory of Shakerism hung upon museum walls.

In 1965, a proclamation declared that membership into the society was closed. It seemed the Shakers had become fairly well-to-do, and had stacked up a sizable pile of money into a Shaker Central Trust Fund. Gertrude Soule, then an eldress at Sabbathday Lake, worried that the assets would attract new members interested only in the money, and so she declared Shakerism a closed faith. Soule held that no new members ought to be accepted, partly because there were no living brothers to train male converts, and partly because young people in that day had not the self-discipline nor stamina required for Shaker vows.

But other Shakers protested that this stance was unnecessary, as the Shaker covenant protects the community from financial predators. Worse, it went against the very core of Shakerism, which welcomed all who would come to it. Shakers at Sabbathday Lake had, throughout history, welcomed inquirers and kindred spirits. They took personally the suspicions of Gertrude Soule, because in their midst already lived a new man, the first male Shaker in some time, who wished to take vows as a brother.

Soule left Sabbathday Lake in 1971, never to return. She took up leadership at Canterbury. Mildred Barker became the leader of Sabbathday Lake, and she declared, "No one has the right to shut the door of the church on anybody who sincerely seeks to enter it." From what I could gather in my research, it seemed to me that Shakerism then split into two faiths, with only the barest level of public civility shown between New Hampshire and Maine.

Amid the painful dispute over money and membership, Sister Frances wrote in 1979 to the editor of *Portland Press Herald*, publicly stating her dismay over the New Hampshire decision not to admit new members. She said the Maine Shakers had no such worry because their covenant "contains stringent safeguards" protecting their properties. "The Covenant," she wrote, "also requires that the door must be kept open for the admission of new members of the Church.

"To be a Shaker in the last quarter of the twentieth century," she wrote, "is to take on a great personal burden; it is not an easy life. We have been impressed by the personal integrity and courage of those young men and women who would make their spiritual home with us. We prefer to be encouraged by the admonition of our leader, Mother Ann, who said, 'Open the windows and doors and receive whomsoever is sent.'" I knew firsthand that Sister Frances still lived by that challenge: She had, after all, taken the chance of letting me in the door, and she welcomed each year's cycles of the faithfully curious with her same optimism for their future.

Those at Sabbathday Lake defied the New Hampshire ministry by accepting Brother Theodore Johnson into their community. For years, until the death of the last Canterbury sister and the subsequent closing of that community, Sabbathday Lake was apparently cut off from nearly all funds. These were the years of poverty that Brother Arnold remembered, for he came to Sabbathday Lake not long after Brother Ted.

Ironically, it was this brother, whose right to be a Shaker seemed in question, who launched what historians now call the "Shaker revolution" of the 1970s and 1980s. Having earned a graduate degree at Harvard Divinity School and studied on scholarship at Oxford University, Brother Ted spoke many languages, loved theology, and embraced Shakerism with a deep enthusiasm that still echoes in Maine today. He helped rebuild a stuffy Shakerism into a more flexible format that would sustain itself into the twenty-first century.

A rebirth of Shakerism then began at Sabbathday Lake. During the 1960s the straggling few believers in Maine began to fight extinction. The "new Shakerism" of Sabbathday Lake differed from the past in its liturgical, biblical, and ecumenical emphases. The Bible became the focal point at worship services. Shakers read about the saints, prophets, and teachings of other faiths, and deliberately reached out to other Christian groups in the spirit of unity.

Brother Ted wrote in 1963 that the Shaker church is "but part of *the* Church." Shakers were called to live in humility and love. "Shakerism has a message for the twentieth century," he wrote, "a message as valid today as when it was first expressed . . . Shakerism teaches God's immanence through the common life shared in Christ's mystical body."

The Sabbathday Lake Shakers have committed themselves in a prayer, "All Things Anew," to carry the torch of their truth into the future:

> The light kindled in that first [Maine Shaker] meeting in Gowen Wilson's farmhouse has not yet been extinguished. We pray God that it may never be. Although it may not seem to burn as brightly as it once did, it is still alive. It has the latent power to kindle within human hearts the warmth of divine love and peace. It has the power to bring light into the minds of all those seekers who are open to divine truth and understanding.
>
> Although few in number, it is our resolution that we be caught up more and more in the blessed work of God. We pray that with heavenly Guidance we may so make ourselves in-

struments of divine truth and light that the way
of Believers may once again appear to the children of God as a meaningful, vital and challenging way of life.

Now, no one questions the openness with which the eight
Maine believers approach their faith. "Shakerism has always
prided itself on continually moving towards something better,"
Sister Frances told me. "As the world around us revolves, if we
refuse to move ahead we would find ourselves very stagnant and
set in a place where there would be no room for growth or
improvement."

I could see the flexibility with which the Shaker faith had
responded to a changing world. Yet, I asked, "How do you draw
the line between progression and transformation? What if you
change so much that you lose the essence of Shakerism?"

"Some things about Shakerism will never change," Sister
Frances said. "We refer to them, jokingly, as The Three C's. No
matter what exterior changes may occur in this Shaker Village,
we'll always have the Community of goods, we will always have
Celibacy, and we'll always have Confession.

"Those three things are rock bound. They are part of the
Shaker life, they are the essence of the Shaker theology, and
they will never change or be taken away."

The rift between the Maine and New Hampshire Shakers
set a precedent for the openness of Sabbathday Lake toward the
world today. It is not with fear or suspicion that those at Sabbathday Lake open their door to whomever may knock.

And somehow, some way, suddenly the outside world began
to take great interest in the mythos, culture, and artifacts of
Shakerism. There had always been some who had felt drawn:
Even by 1878, *Shaker* editor George Lomas reported that the
"Shaker influence" was felt around the world in various reform
movements, and through "thousands who claim they are 'more
than half Shakers.' "

Yet in the 1960s and 1970s, a group of devotees—Shaker

antiques collectors, museum curators, and spiritual kinfolk—began to grow and surround the community. For the first time, non-Shakers thronged to Shakers not for morbid curiosity but for what they could learn, hold in value, take as truth.

Some, admittedly, have wanted not much more than furniture. Fever for Shaker antiques began in 1923 with Edward and Faith Deming Andrews, collectors who stopped in at a Hancock, Massachusetts, village because they had heard what good bread the Shakers baked. They ate their bread and had a good look around at the graceful, plain lines of Shaker tables and trestles, and decided that "our appetite would not be satisfied with bread alone."

The market has come a long way since the Andrewses paid, in their early collecting days at Sabbathday Lake, $6 for a table, $25 for a bureau, $10 for a yellow sink, $15 for a workbench, and $5 for a spool bed. Recently, an eight-foot-tall cupboard with drawers sold to Bill Cosby for $200,000, a Benjamin Youngs tall clock sold for $165,000 to businessman Ken Hakuta, and a pine work counter sold at auction to Oprah Winfrey for $220,000.

Some believe that those who come from all corners to consume Shaker furniture and faith take a parasitic toll on the living Shakers themselves. Shallow co-opting of Shaker ideas and artifacts certainly exists, and the American marketplace swells with flimsy imitations of "Shaker style." Still, today, people from all corners of the country feel a magnetic pull toward the spirituality of the Shaker way.

"There is a great deal of interest in Shakerism in the world," Sister Frances said. "And I'm not talking about the interest in furniture. That doesn't concern me. I mean, I'm not going to waste my energy on their interests, although some of my very good friends are Shaker collectors."

But for others, the appeal lay elsewhere. "The people we mention in our daily prayer as being friends of the Holy Spirit are very, very interested in this life. For one reason or another, they are not able to commit themselves fully to this life. Most of them are married. Some have families they have to look after. Many, many reasons. But they are terribly drawn to the Shaker life. This happens with so many people in the world."

She looked up and smiled in her way, a way that engaged her whole face. "And I think that's good. I encourage that. But I also feel that right here at Chosen Land, we have to maintain this core of true, real Shakers to be able to counsel, to help those others who, hopefully, some time or another, might come and make the full commitment."

Hope ran high at Sabbathday Lake that increased interest may bring vocations. "There's a lot of interest among young people today," Sister Frances continued. "Hardly a week goes by—oh, goodness, I would say almost every two or three days, Brother Arnold and I receive a great deal of mail and endeavor to answer every one of those letters, particularly concerning people who are interested in joining the Shakers."

She stopped to consider the weight of all those letters of inquiry. "I think, I truly think, that when people have a chance to really consider what it all means, that more people will be coming. We already have a new brother. There's a possibility of a female novice coming. So I really feel—I hope and I pray—that forever there will be a core of Shakers here at Chosen Land to continue to keep the faith alive, to nurture the people who hopefully may make that decision."

Today, the line of differentiation blurs between those who embrace and those who covenant Shakerism. Who carries on the faith? All may agree that it is the eight who vow their lives to the Shaker way. Still, often it is the friends of the Shakers who raise needed funds, offer moral support, and carry the message out to those beyond.

The friends of Shakerism play a vital role, according to the eldress, in translating the message to the world beyond. "We ourselves are not able to go out and preach the gospel to the world. We're barely able to take care of what we have to take care of here," she said wryly.

"Many, many people really and truly do try to portray to

the world at large, wherever they come in contact with people, the real spirit of Shakerism. And I'm very grateful for that," Sister Frances said.

Some friends of the Shakers have lasted a lifetime. Gerard Wertkin, a Manhattan lawyer, drove up the back roads of Maine thirty years ago to inquire about this religious community. He went back, again and again, and again. He wrote a book about them, *The Four Seasons of Shaker Life*, and still visits them at least two or three times per year.

"You go to Sabbathday Lake as often as—maybe more often than—I visit my family of birth," I confessed to him when we met.

Now in his fifties, Wertkin had a wife, three grown children and one young granddaughter, a high-profile job at the Museum of American Folk Art, and a Jewish religion of his own. Still he returned to Shaker Village in every season.

Was he something like an unconvenanted Shaker? "I would never be so arrogant as to think of myself that way," he spoke in the quiet, measured tones of one who knew himself well and cared little if others did. For him there was no blurring of the "line" between Shaker and non-Shaker. "Some entirely well-intentioned people make facile declarations of their identification," he told me, "with the Shakers or the faith. But to paraphrase Sister Aurelia Mace, 'One is either a Shaker, or one is not.'"

Rather, he told me, it was the stillness that drew him year after year. The respect for those who live their faith round the clock. The order of measured days of prayer and chores, prayer and chores. The commitment to time-honored tradition and to a lively, still relevant belief system that few are willing to adopt.

Did few adopt, I wondered, because Shakerism required celibacy?

"No," he answered, almost with disdain. Not only was celibacy not what kept prospective members from becoming full-fledged Shakers, but, he said, celibacy was not a looming frustration for the Shakers either. Celibacy was almost beside the point. The point was submitting oneself to a Higher Will: first, God, twenty-four hours a day, and second, your elders, present and past. Wertkin was the first of many I would meet who, though entrenched within other faiths and families, came frequently to Shaker Village to take a share in its spiritual treasures.

France Morin, a contemporary art curator from New York, spent an entire summer at Sabbathday Lake, organizing a project called "The Quiet in the Land: Everyday Life, Contemporary Art, and the Shakers." She and ten international artists lived on site, working and eating and praying with the Shaker family, and filling journals, canvases, film, and sculptures with their impressions of this sacred, simple life.

"They were so courageous to let us come into their lives and try this partnership," Morin told me. "Each of them has had a unique interaction with each of us. We will never be the same."

She marveled at the way the Shakers opened their home and hearts to these unknown artists who came very much from the world. How could they have known it would be safe to welcome such people, who were not necessarily religious nor celibate nor simple, into their haven? "Maybe there was a swarm of angels floating over their heads, telling them it was OK to let us in, and to try this," Morin shook her sleek black hair, laughing. Yet, she remarked, she had been profoundly touched by her time among these people.

One of the ten artists, a photographer named Sam, told me that he found the Shakers to be courageous people. The artists had resurrected an old Shaker tradition, that of evening Union Meetings, with the sisters and brothers. And so they would meet once a week and engage in debates over politics, religion, and art. "We ask a lot of questions," Sam told me, shaking his head with a crooked smile, "and they are very honest with us."

I spoke with another, an installation and performance artist named Domenico, about his reaction to Shaker life that summer. He had spent merely a month with these eccentric Christians halfway round the world from his home in Australia, yet in Meeting I had seen him sing forth nearly all the songs, and in testimony he had dared speak up. He blushed as he did, but he seemed compelled by the strength of what he had to say.

"This will be my last Meeting here, as I leave next weekend to begin the journey home," he told the group. "I can tell you honestly that my experience here has changed my life deeply, and forever."

Later he explained to me that he had been born in Italy and grown up in Australia, and had known nominal Catholicism as a child. "My parents weren't really that much into it, so as I grew up it sort of faded out of my life," he told me. "But when they talked today in Meeting about the image of the tabernacle, it brought back so sharply for me the image of the eucharistic tabernacle."

"Oh yes," I interrupted, "it was always in gold, and quite ornate."

"And all shut up," he added. "Ann Lee said that her gospel could not be enclosed into a tabernacle, because the light should go out to all who sought it, at whatever cost."

"But in the Catholic church," I remarked, "not only did we put it in that case, we locked it up. Did they do that in your church, too? Lock it up?"

"Yes," he said. "With the Shakers I have had the opposite experience. There is such an openness here."

The recent decades' revival of Shakerism, the gathering of several young brothers and a sister from the world, and growing enthusiasm from non-Shaker supporters have given those at Sabbathday Lake grounds for hope in their future.

Sister Frances told me she felt certain that Shakerism would survive far into the next millennium. "Remember, for over two hundred years, God has blessed Shakerism right in this very spot where we are. I don't want to sound like I'm passing the buck to God—that's quite a statement, isn't it—but if He has kept this work going for all of those years, through some very difficult times, I think He/She has plans that we may not even be aware of yet."

"Do you honestly think that this community will survive?" I asked Sister June in the library one day.

"Yes," she replied unwaveringly. "I think it will continue certainly past my lifetime, I expect it to. Actually, it's all in the hands of God. I mean, if He wants it to continue, it will."

This sort of passivity, which she would have called faith, made the hairs on the back of my neck bristle. "But why wouldn't God want to continue it?" I asked. "Because if Shakerism has a specific message, you know, a specific truth to offer to the world, then—"

"Yea," Sister June shook her small head. "Well, that's why we're still here. Sister Mildred said that Shakers do not have the right to close the covenant and to stop accepting new members. So that's why this community is still alive and well. Because she had that belief and others shared it." We both realized as she spoke that Sister June would not have been accepted into the covenant unless Sabbathday Lake had refused the elders' order to close their ranks.

"Shakerism doesn't have a specific set creed or anything. It's quite flexible. And it changes for whatever the working of the Spirit is in a particular time. And I think God works in different ways at different times. So, Shakerism has a specific message which is, I think, very relevant to today."

As for the future of his small community, Brother Alistair believed very strongly in the prophecy that when there are as few Shakers as could be counted on a child's hand, a surge would swell the community with countless numbers. "We may never grow to a huge movement," he said, "but we may grow into a reasonable-sized religious community. And that would keep me happy."

The way the prophecy would come about, in true Shaker fashion, had to do with God's blessing but also Shakers' effort. "I think it would come about by the grace of God and God actually calling people. But I think there are certain things we can do to help God along," said Brother Alistair. "Like producing good Shaker literature, and this is something that the community has done since Brother Ted began reproducing the *Testimonies*. I'd like to see more good, solid, orthodox Shaker literature reprinted. I'd love to see the Shaker Shop in London carrying them, for example, as well as their books on Shaker art and artifacts.

Brother Alistair believed that their new web site—which features information on their history and faith, library, museum, herbs, and upcoming events—would draw interest from the world.

For Brother Alistair, movement into the future meant keeping an open mind. As more and more members would join, it would be "important for me to come to terms with the theological diversity within the community. And the fact that we can have union, we can have unity, without uniformity." He thought that prospective novitiates ought to understand clearly the kind of life a person would be entering.

"The way forward is definitely monastic," to Brother Alistair. "We need to be very clear what we expect of people in terms of their personal regimen on top of the common prayer." The future would continue the Shaker emphasis on personal, private prayer, the study of Shakerism, and perhaps a "more ordered regimen in the house."

He explained why he longed for more, not fewer, rules. "The preceding generation is glad to get rid of an awful lot of rules that had lost their meaning—but I think that my particular generation needs rules if you're going to give up the world to come to a religious community and seek God."

Brother Arnold saw the simple faith of Shakerism as firmly entrenched in this time of computer technology, space travel, and genetic engineering. "There's nothing quaint about this lifestyle at all," he told me flatly. "It requires a great deal to become a Shaker. It definitely is not a lifestyle for everyone, because very few people are willing to give up everything for the sake of the Kingdom.

"Especially in this day and age," reflected the elder, "people are less and less likely. We have many friends who are in other monastic communities. You know, everyone's crying the same thing, about vocations, vocations, and lack of vocations."

He saw two reasons for the general decline in spiritual communities. "It's first about commitment, and second of all we're looking at fully a second and almost into a third generation of non-church-attending people.

"If children don't have the basics," he cried, "how can you expect them to come to religious life?" He lamented the many American families today who, wishing to permit their children to choose their own beliefs, end up giving them no basis from which to choose. "Parents who are so afraid of their children becoming members of cults later on," he warned, "should look back at how they brought their children up. Nine times out of ten, you're going to find out it's a lack of a faith they finally had to find somewhere else. But if you bring up your children well grounded in faith, then when people who are charlatans or deceivers come into their lives, you give them the better opportunity of understanding and seeing and knowing."

"How do you see Shakerism," I asked, "in the twenty-first or even twenty-second century?"

"Oh, I see it as always evolving," said the elder, "so it will adapt to the time. And if it doesn't, then we'll die."

Shakerism, he told me, "is organic; it has to be changing and adapting. You have to keep the principles of the church alive or else we are no longer Shakers." The "Three C's"—celibacy, confession, and community—would always remain at the core. Yet "other aspects will depend on whether the faith remains in America, if it goes to another country, if it goes to another world. Now, it will adapt itself to a time. As for what we do for our living, we'll adapt to the place where we live in and the time we live in."

The last weekend of my season at Sabbathday Lake, Shaker Village thronged with visitors from all over the country who came to learn and embrace the faith. A nonprofit organization called The Friends of the Shakers, which hosted the annual weekend gathering, had grown to include seven hundred members, and more than one hundred of them came.

People traveled from the west coast to the east, from California and New Mexico and Texas and all the way up the eastern seaboard. I met a woman from the Washington, D.C., area who worked as a lay minister in a "very progressive" Catholic church, and a man from Connecticut who had become a self-taught historian of Shaker ephemera. Some brought their children. One man told me he had been bringing his son and daughter, now teenagers, since they were four and six. Another said he had first come when he was twenty-five years old, and that now his youngest son was twenty-five.

We spent the day conducting the business of electing new volunteer board members and approving constitutional amendments. Sister Frances brought the group up-to-date on events at Shaker Village in the past year, and Lenny and Michael offered news on library reconstruction and museum development. Despite the business at hand, no one seemed too businesslike. Rather, an air of camaraderie filled the historical room in which we sat. Men and women from the world, dressed in shorts and sundresses against the humid Maine heat, laughed and applauded easily. And the morning passed quickly.

After lunch, Shaker brothers, sisters, and staff members led visitors through exhibits and workshops, to the lake and around the farm. And that evening, after we friends had shared doughnuts and meetings and presentations and museum tours and hikes, we all sat down together at rented tables under a tent and shared a barbecued feast.

Miriam, a Reform Jew, sat at a table full of Christian women. She felt free to tell us what, to her, was the essential flaw in Christian faith. "I could never be Christian or Catholic," she said, "because I cannot accept the idea that someone else died to atone for my sins. In Judaism, we are taught from early on that we hold full responsibility for our actions. If some Savior died on the cross to make up for whatever horrible, evil things I might ever do in this life, then what is the implication there?"

Three of us shook our heads at her. That, I was thinking, sounded like a line from fundamentalist or evangelical Christianity: Jesus died to save you, so don't you worry about a thing, you're saved. It doesn't matter what a scoundrel you've been, it's all forgiven because of Jesus.

Well, Miriam realized the cause and effect: If you are saved no matter what, then what's to stop you from doing "no matter what"? And to me, she had a good point. Had we not seen Christians committing unspeakable evil in the Nazi Holocaust of the closing century, and calling themselves not only saved but "righteous" all along the way?

"I don't know, Miriam," I shook my head, "I've been Christian all my life but I've never thought of it that way. I don't feel Jesus takes responsibility for my actions." Rather, I believe that somehow, the energy created by good or ill-intentioned acts eventually cycles back toward oneself. This I tried to explain. The other two women at our table chimed in, more forcefully, defending their faith.

"No, this whole Jesus-Savior thing is a real turn-off for me," contended Miriam.

Wanting peace to reign over the New England baked beans, I pulled out of my conversational deck the trump card: union. At a dinner on holy Shaker ground, more than anything one wanted union. And there was a way to achieve it, by reminding ourselves of what we shared in common.

"You know, what I really like in Shaker theology is the view of Jesus as the Christ-Spirit," I began. "He was not the first, nor the last, to embody it. Was it Sister Mildred Barker who said that Jesus was just one of many, including Plato and the Buddha, to open himself to the Spirit—"

"Yes, I can live with that," murmured Miriam.

"Yes, that's lovely," nodded someone else, and before we knew it we were once again buttering and breaking bread together.

People filled their plates and their bellies and milled about, talking with one another under the tent, and near the coffee urn. Many knew one another from having converged here in the past. Others smiled a greeting or initiated conversations about things Shaker.

When the large serving platters had been whisked into the dwellinghouse kitchen, and the grill smoked down to an ember, we ambled across the street to the meetinghouse for an evening concert by two musicians, Barry and Shelley Phillips, who specialized in Shaker music. They happened to be married to one another. He played the cello; she a neo-Celtic harp. They set up orchestra in the 1794 meetinghouse, with just one small lamp to light their sheets of music. The building, with neither air-conditioning nor electrical lighting, felt apt for a concert of early Shaker music played on instruments crafted in the ancient manner.

The Shaker benches brimmed with people eager to hear the faith they loved set to music. The couple began, and as they played the sun set outside the windows of the old building, on the brothers' side. The sky turned periwinkle blue, against chartreuse green herbs with yellow and purple flowers waving in the soft August breeze.

We poured out through the sisters' and brothers' doors at intermission to drink in the cool air. We chatted and pulled sweaters around our shoulders until it was time to return for the second half. Now Brothers Wayne, Arnold, and Alistair lit kerosene lamps and set them in the deep, painted-wood windowsills. Their flickering light sent soft, dim rays about the room and into the night beyond.

The musicians played song after song, with their hearts in their throats. They had studied Shaker music for years, and the wife had loved it since she had first heard a number of Shaker songs at age ten. They stood in the center of the room, yet respectfully he on the south brothers' side and she on the north, and they played in the sacred space of a people who seemed, on the surface, to be as different from them as east is to west.

The musicians were folk artists; the Shakers were plain farmers. The musicians, with long, overgrown hair, had dressed formally for this concert but elsetimes wore Birkenstock sandals, tie-dyed T-shirts, and bandanas. They hailed from a bohemian town in California. The Shakers, neatly dressed in their dark slacks and button-downs for the brothers and permanent-press skirts and pullover shirts for the sisters, looked like hearty stock New Englanders.

At the end of the concert, Barry said that there was a song that he and Shelley wished to sing in tribute to the Shaker family themselves.

"The rest of you can listen, if you want," he joked, "but really this is for the Shakers themselves."

Then the couple stood in the middle of the room and joined voices in a harmony of intimacy that only years of singing together could bring, and they sang to the Shakers about their respect for the purity and faith these people had chosen. Tears shone in their eyes as they sang.

More than one hundred people crowded the benches at Meeting the next morning. The Shakers sat in the two benches nearest the podium, brothers and sisters opposite one another. Sister June read from the psalms, then Brother Arnold and Sister Frances did scripture readings.

The communal testimony went on and on, because so many of the crowd felt moved, and comfortable enough to say so. "What brings us together," said Elaine from Chicago, "is love— the love we have for this family and this place. We are such a diverse group of people, and yet there is such a feeling of acceptance for one another."

Yes, I thought. Being here at Shaker Village, whether for a summer or an hour, gave us a chance to dabble in Shakerism. We may never reach the level of depth that a Shaker commits to, but we came together from many places and lives to experience union. It was love that held us together, although we did not even know one another. And that, I suspected, was what Shakers would call the presence of the Spirit.

I watched Barry close his eyes in silent prayer, seeming to

absorb the sacred essence of the hour and place in which he sat. His wife, Shelley, sat directly across from him on the sisters' side, and during testimony she rose to speak. "We are meant to be conduits," she said, "of light. And then again we are like electricity—the power that flows through us is meant to be light to others, if we let it." She laughed at herself, swung her long, wavy brown hair, and added, "I know this probably sounds a little flaky." A whole roomful of people looked at her and smiled.

"But no, I really mean this," she said, thrusting her hands outward. "I totally see us all as tabernacles of light, of the Spirit. I want to become a more efficient channel for that light."

"Last night's concert moved me so deeply," said a woman from her wheelchair in the aisle. "When we listened to the Shaker music, the light from that one lamp shone so softly on the wall, and little shadows formed from the Shaker pegs as if to say 'Welcome to all of you, come, more and more, come and hang your hats upon the wall.' "

Even during the sacred time of Meeting, some joking passed between Shaker family members and those who knew them best. A young intern named John, who had spent the summer working in the print shop with Brother Arnold, expressed his regret that he soon would move back home to continue college. He teased Brother Arnold about the stereotypic cleanliness that he had not found at Sabbathday Lake. "I thought Shakers were supposed to be tidy." Everyone laughed. Brother Arnold nodded his head in a tilted, good-natured way.

Once during Meeting, a man tried to launch the singing of "Simple Gifts," but he was singing in too deep a bass voice. He looked around, wondering why no one else would sing, then flushed deep red. Everyone then joined in laughter, including him. So, as we started the song over, chortles and chuckles accompanied the well-known song.

During testimony, Brother Alistair rose to speak from his heart, and as he did so he looked around the room and met steadily the eyes of people to whom he spoke. This moved me, for I had seen some people in the group stare blankly at the meetinghouse wall as they delivered rather dry, didactic messages. One did not get that from this young brother; one got the humble truth from one human to another.

"The passage from today's scripture that most touched me," he began, "was in Corinthians, when Paul said, 'Where the spirit of the Lord is, there is freedom' [2 Cor 3:17]. Well, I have been thinking very much in these last few days about freedom. And for me, there is nothing that is quite so freeing as a good confession." Brother Alistair let out a deep breath.

"When one comes to this place," said the newest Shaker, "one doesn't suddenly shed the tendency toward attachment. It's not easy, just because we have given our lives to this faith; it's still very, very hard. I find myself becoming attached to the simplest experiences and possessions."

I knew just what he meant, because I, too, have an addictive personality. A certain coffee cup, a particular routine before bedtime, a beloved soft sweater or a cherished volume of poetry— I knew that one may more easily substitute benign for harmful addictions than to become nonaddictive.

Maybe Brother Alistair was saying that, although he had given up smoking and daily drinking, nightclubs and friends, cherished foods or pet habits, still here he found himself hooking in to a whole new set of addictions, "simple" as they may seem.

"So what I wish to work on, in myself," he told the roomful of people, "is to come above the need to hook onto things, to come clean of attachment altogether. And that will be freedom."

Walking back to the dwellinghouse lawn, where a large, white tent sheltered twenty picnic tables from the searing sun, I met a woman who had in some ways become a Shaker without having signed the covenant. She lived in a nearby village, and had come to Meeting every Sunday for months. Slowly, she was transforming from conventional Episcopal faith into this radical new Shakerism.

"Do you know," Paula told me as we walked, our long dresses swishing across our ankles, "I have lived right up the road from this place for sixty years and never had any idea it would become so important to me. Why, I'm only a few years younger than Sister Frances. We lived so close together for so many years, but I didn't know how much she would come to feel like kin to me."

A Hindu friend of Paula's, who had discovered deep spirituality at Sabbathday Lake, convinced Paula to come with her "just once." And now Paula, who had been a dutiful Episcopalian all her life, found herself starving for the stark, unpretentious faith she found on the farm just a few miles from her home.

The transition proved painful, for her identity had long been wrapped around her active participation in her neighborhood church, and her nonchurchgoing husband had recently converted—diving headfirst into the Episcopal faith from which she now felt herself being pulled away.

"And tonight," she had told us over dinner the previous evening, with tears in her eyes, "my husband is in charge of a lobster dinner, full of pomp and circumstance for five hundred people, to commemorate the history of the church I've always attended. And I sit here eating Boston baked beans off a paper plate with the Shakers."

The pain of following her own path seemed to rend her and her husband in two, but she remained convinced that he must honor his own spiritual growth and she hers. "And," she said, looking around at the crabgrass below her feet and the clear, open skies above, "I am so happy here."

The depth to which Paula had been drawn into Shaker spirituality astounded me. I sat that evening under a tent with a hundred people from Jewish, Christian, Universalist, Buddhist, New Age, and humanist backgrounds who came to Sabbathday Lake not to convert away from their own religious heritage but to nourish the Spirit within. Shakerism did not require them to melt into one pot. Their hosts did not speak of any need for these friends in spirit to come into the fold. They neither convinced nor cajoled.

Sister Frances and Brother Arnold, in fact, told me they

believed they had "no corner on the salvation market." They felt certain that Shakerism was not the only true path. They were not even certain if it were the surest or quickest way to God. "It is just that it feels right to *us*," Brother Arnold said. "It is not for everyone," Sister Frances added. "This is just our way. That's all it is. Our way."

Their way to God, however, had so touched this married Maine neighbor that she now found herself attending Meeting every Sunday. She had braced herself and tearfully explained to her husband that she had found her true spiritual home in a church that was not complicated Episcopal ritual but simple Shaker realism.

And she had been shaken, yes shaken, to her very soul.

"Something happened to me on the way to Meeting this morning," she confessed in the middle of communal testimony. "In fact, it has been happening to me more and more often these days. As I was driving along, I looked out the window and saw the sun shining so beautifully on this perfect day, and a feeling of incredible happiness just flowed through me. I can't explain it, but this sort of thing has happened several times lately. It's a feeling of sheer, unexpected joy."

Paula's sheer joy. Brother Arnold's moments of bliss. Brother Alistair's clairsentient visions. Early Shakers' whirling into ecstasy. A common thread wove together these stories, told haltingly in language inadequate for expressing such encounters with the divine. Paula had discovered union with God. The woman of the world, who lived right down the road but had spent a lifetime searching everywhere else, had come to Shaker Village and had found God.

EPILOGUE

When I arrived at Sabbathday Lake, I felt I had come with a clear purpose: to live among the Shakers and learn what I could of their way. My clear purpose, though, soon washed down the drain of the old Shaker kitchen sink where I washed parsnips for noon dinner. I had expected drama from people who believed so strongly in their principles of celibacy, confession, and community that they would cast all worldliness—including family and sexuality, money and material goods—aside. I expected a certain harsh toiling in the ceaseless farm chores and relentless housekeeping, a poignant loneliness for the embrace of lovers and babies they would never have, and a somber martyrdom in the praying for a world still asleep to the kingdom of God they felt already in our midst.

What I found at Sabbathday Lake was a group of flesh-and-blood human beings, who suffer from winter flus and family squabbles and disobedient dogs, much like any other American family. I found people who struggle daily to cultivate the best in themselves, to love one another, and to honor their God.

I found reality: the smell of wheat bread steaming through the house, inviting. The sound of women's voices merged with men's in the laughter of conversation, the reverence of prayer. The plainness of clothes and dishes and furniture, not poor but simple. The openness of eyes, all colors, as they peer straight into yours without convention nor role playing. Hands outstretched to receive, not to pull in, only to welcome in as far as I want to come. Barns outside, and workshops waiting, work without end. Hair uncombed and faces wrinkling into smiles, sometimes with self-consciousness but never with pretense. Hands reaching hungrily to platters of hot food, color and scent arranged like art on the old wood table. Herbs grown across the way drying on the racks, then sifting softly to the bottom of barrels, swelling the storehouse with scent. An endless row of jackets hung upon pegs in the downstairs hall, windbreakers and raincoats, overcoats and sweatshirts. The slow, steady drip of rusted water from a century-old washing machine in the basement, matched in rhythm by the rumble of the Kenmore in the other corner. Voices, ever polite, calling out greetings or bits of news about the day's progress as Shakers pass one another along the way.

The Shakers of the flesh did not resemble the strange, ethereal beings of the history books any more than I lived or looked like a Catholic immigrant from prerevolution America. Times had changed.

The sisters and brothers still called one another by title, "Sister June" or "Brother Wayne," and they still responded "yea" or "nay," as did their Shaker ancestors. They still sang some of the ten thousand Shaker songs given to their nineteenth-century predecessors by spirits beyond the grave. And they carried with them the Shaker sense of respect for work and worship: No one ever came late to the three prayer services per day, nor to Wednesday evening prayer meeting or Sunday morning Meeting. No one approached their work with a hurried or loathing attitude, for the most mundane floor sweeping or garden weeding can become an act of devotion to God, communion with others, meditation within oneself.

Laughter rippled across the buildings and grounds at the top of the hill where Shaker Village stands. Joy lived here.

"You are not what I expected," I told Brother Arnold as we

sat together in his woodworking shop, where he had resurrected the craft of the Shaker oval box. "I expected a pretty somber bunch," I laughed, "you all walking around the farm feeling the weight of the world on your shoulders. But you're happy. You're fun."

He smiled and stroked his graying beard. He told me that, as Shakers past "toiled" in prayer to save the souls of millions, those at Sabbathday Lake today do still pray for the world. "Yet there's also an enormous sense of relief when you realize you've already been saved," he said.

Now his body shifted on the stool and his eyes twinkled. His narrow, veined hands did a drumroll on the knees of his jeans. "Maybe that's why we have fun," he smiled.

The sheer size of Sabbathday Lake farm—1,900 acres—and the leasing out of lands to lakeside tenants and orchard farmers, the ongoing business of sheep and herb and vegetable and Shaker goods production, and the daily upkeep of over a dozen old buildings, overwhelmed me. Somehow, though, Eldress Frances and Elder Arnold kept it all together with just a few hours spent in their rather cluttered joint office. The banking, accounting, stocking of goods, and repairing of buildings never ended. Then there were piles of letters to be answered, phone calls all times of day by people curious about the faith or hopeful about some old piece of Shaker furniture, the quarterly newsletter to be written and self-published in the print shop, and fund-raising activities to be coordinated and advertised.

Life looked more complex than I expected, here in the last stead of Shaker simplicity on earth. Also, life here had far more to do with the outside world.

The truth, which began to sink in as I bent over peeling the parsnips but has taken much time to fully absorb, was that these Shakers were not the antithesis of me. Not some holy, heavenly creatures fairly floating around their farm in prayer, they walked solidly on earth. They participated in the three-dimensional realm. They did live a semimonastic life, and they did preserve time for prayer and reflection, but they did not hide from the world. Visitors came and went nearly every day: evangelistic preachers, lonely rural neighbors, old friends from all professions and faiths. And the Shakers ventured out, shopping for supplies at the discount grocery store, driving into town for haircuts and stopping off for doughnuts. They had been to Manhattan, to stand on a street corner and sing their Shaker songs to whomever would listen. They had prayed, preached, and performed in cathedrals and lecture halls. They had professed their truth on national television. They had gone on tour in the world.

And, as the Shakers dressed just like anyone else from rural New England, one might not know them as foreigners to the world. Their eyes did not roll about in their heads with the glory of God, and they did not go about muttering prayers or condemning urban values. Rather, the Shakers gave thanks for the new day and all it held, and they peered into the faces of both the homeless and the elegant to find therein the Christ.

I wished I could come away from my time with the Shakers and say that they lived a beautiful, lofty life far beyond the reach of anyone like me.

I could not.

The Shakers touched my soul in a way that stays with me. Now I live again in the worldliest of worlds, in town with manicure salons and gourmet cafés on every corner, where people worry about their annual income and sagging muscle tone and their slightly dusty Mercedes. I get all caught up in the piles of laundry and dishes and schedules and end up yelling at my kids. I glare at the blank computer screen that taunts me to write something worth reading, and then end up going out shopping for something I did not really need. As before, I dwell firmly entrenched in the here and now, where we Americans look out for number one because no one else seems to care very deeply for us, where we clamor for more food, drink, and goods to fill the void that gapes with age.

Still something nags at me, something I know but will not

face, about the intersection of Shakerism with my world. As I write, I think of the Shakers eating breakfast now: the brothers digging into their eggs and bacon with zest while the sisters mind their cholesterol with their soggy, virtuous cold cereal. I imagine them chatting amiably, then falling silent to daydream, later clearing the table for morning psalms and Shaker songs. And I know a connection has been forged between us. I no longer can say that these people are my polar opposite, for I have dwelt with them and seen the truth of their personal struggles and family dynamics. I no longer can escape Shakerism by claiming it is only for the chosen, monastic few, for I have felt the spontaneous joy in whatever work the day brings and the warm love that lives among these people of God.

This small group of believers have wedged deep in my heart, and it may be that I shall feel cared for and influenced by them for the rest of my days on earth. Months after my visit, we exchange cards on holidays, and long, newsy letters in-between.

Sister Ruth grew feebler. She moved out of her independent apartment in the trustees' house, down the gravel road and into the dwellinghouse. Her spirit-family cared for her tenderly, till one morning in February she died peacefully, surrounded by them all. Brother Alistair said snow fell that morning like a soft, clean blanket of God's love. Sister Ruth appeared in my dreams around that time (before I had heard of her death) and has graced my thoughts many times since. Her life of unwavering devotion and the warmth of her open-hearted love will live long in my memory.

Meanwhile, the life of both her family and mine goes on. Brother Alistair took his vows and became a fully-covenanted Shaker. Having come to join the Maine Shakers on the same exact day I gave birth, he shared with my son his spiritual birthday: now they both were one.

Through my research and writing in the last few years, my children have grown strong, capable, both with and without me. They color, wrestle, and sing with their beloved nanny while their mom clicks away on the computer in the next room. And then, when I return to them, it is with a full heart and a joyful soul, of one who is doing a bit of her work here in the world and is now exactly where she wants to be.

One of the sweetest results of my search for God among the Shakers has been the affection my whole family now feels for theirs. My sons have sensed the Shakers' importance to me, and so, in their natural generosity, they have asked again and again, "Mommy, could we go with you to the Shakers *one day?*" They want to pet the lambs, taste the applesauce, meet the people they have heard stories about. And so next summer we do plan to go, all together, to Sabbathday Lake. The sisters and brothers will likely marvel at how much the baby has grown. I hope the older two will get a ride around the farm in the back of the pickup truck. And I suspect my husband will engage in some heated debate with Brother Wayne over politics. As for me, I shall sing to the Spirit God for the chance to return to this haven, and to bring together those I love of this earth with those of the hereafter.

Meanwhile, day to day, I sometimes cook from Sister Frances's cookbook, with the boys helping me, standing on chairs to reach the bowl and striving earnestly to measure and stir. Sometimes we bake cookies, and pack a big box to send to the Shakers. My husband has tracked down Shakerism on the Internet; my mother has roused interest in Shaker spirituality among her girlfriends; and my friend Christina gave me a book for Christmas on Shaker herb gardening. The circle widens.

The heart of Shakerism offers, even to us who would remain in the world, the chance to see life in a new way. We can consider the possibility that the Christ-Spirit, not coming in on some distant cloud from heaven, dwells within us right this minute. The spirit, already within us even now, can be freed. It becomes love—it is love—which is God.

Something about Shakerism invites me to open myself to the possibility of purity, though celibacy is not for me. It invites me to consistency, though my clock does not chime for scheduled prayer three times per day. It beckons toward simplicity, even in a world like mine. It offers a different way of loving, loving all people equally and seeing them as hosts of the spirit, loving from the gut rather than the mind, without judgment, without limit. Shakerism, I begin to realize, will change my life—not by converting me into a celibate sister on the farm in Maine, but by fleshing out the beliefs I hold dear into a way of living them daily.

Some questions I brought to Sabbathday Lake remain unanswered. I still cannot decide, for myself, whether Ann Lee was a mentally unbalanced charismatic, who surrounded herself with fearful sheep who believed her fantasies; or whether she was a divinely inspired, genuine psychic, who saw truths about this life and the next that shall send me to hell for my sins. The portrait of Ann Lee in history books shows her as a sinister ouster of secrets, a martyr for the sins of a whole lustful world, a scrap-eating ascetic, a magician of miracles, a rolling-eyed visionary. She looks like a cross between Jesus and a witch. She looks scary. And many would rather laugh or turn away than meet her steady gaze. For me, I may not know what she was, but I know what she did. By her fruits she is known. And she left a legacy of faith in God, love, and union that has brought out the best in thousands of followers beyond her lifetime.

As for today's Shakers, I still do not really know who they are either. Are they the last voice of God crying out in the wilderness, with a warning to save ourselves that the world would ignore only at the cost of all life? Are they unbalanced people at the fringe of society, secretly leading a double life of whirling ecstasy, stealthy sexuality, or otherworldly visions, that they dared not tell me about? Or are they blatantly ordinary people, glorified only because their sect happens to get today's headline news, wishing only to get on with the business of Bible reading and hay baling?

Clearly I cannot, as Brother Arnold said, see into the heart of another. Only they know what really motivates them to this life, what holds them there, and what darkness they battle on the way to God. Yet these people showed me nothing but love, and openness, and honesty, and that counts for a lot with me. We can never know the heart of another, but we can choose to trust. As I choose to trust my husband, my family, and a few friends, so I choose to have faith in the Shakers, in all their human imperfection. That does not mean that I swallow Shakerism whole. It means that I can, simultaneously realizing its historical errors and contemporary flaws, come to it in faith to learn its unique way of devotion, love, and truth.

Perhaps it is feeling that the Shakers have given me. My emotion, formerly lodged so low in my soul, now wells up easily in moments of prayer and music. The way my eyes first filled with tears in the meetinghouse, as I looked down from the rafters onto the simple human Shakers who led the way and the hundred worldly followers who had come to open their hearts to God. In this same way I find myself nearly weeping when I devote a day's work to God, or sing to my children at night.

These days my heart has come to surface. I feel what I never felt before, and it washes over me in waves whether I would have it or not. Sometimes it is a bit embarrassing, really. My composure has vanished. I am left a more honest, open woman who feels much more compassion than she knows how to express, and who believes in the unseen more than she would like to admit.

One day I found myself driving along, telling my children that I suspected that their grandpa, who had died last year, had become an angel. The old me would have laughed. "I don't know for sure," I told them, "but I think he may be near us many times, watching over us."

"And does he have wings?" they wanted to know.

Even as I spoke I felt Earl's presence in the car. It felt like love, a pure love, the kind he had felt in his heart while on earth but could not fully express. Honestly, I had felt his presence often lately, and I had talked this over with Sister Frances, who absolutely believed that my beloved father-in-law was looking after me. My educated intellect, trained to disbelieve the unseen, reminded myself that the feeling of Earl's presence was likely only my own emotional longing for him. This time, though, my heart spoke louder.

"I really don't know if he has wings," I told my children. "But I know for sure that he loves us very much."

Now I know—or at least think I know—that my deepest fear in going to the Shakers, that I may end up converting, will not come to pass. I have come and gone from Sabbathday Lake with my family safely intact. The Shakers did not wish nor try to convert me: They had nothing to prove to anyone but themselves. One who embraces Shakerism, though not requested to convert, is challenged to be most authentically themselves. As I learned when surrounded by a hundred people of different faiths at the Shaker Friends' Weekend, the Shaker way can be a gift to take home to one's own spiritual tradition, family, work, and life.

I may never be a Shaker, but I think my journey to Sabbathday Lake may help me become a better me. If I let it. Simplifying my life, absurd as that seems in my materialistic existence, can happen in small steps along the way. Not austerity, not martyrdom, but happy, conscious choices for a less complicated life. Keeping myself honest, speaking gently my truth to those around me and—most importantly—to myself, can evolve me from the pain of rigid expectations to the serenity of what really is. Sharing with others the feelings that well up from deep within, and giving testimony to the inexplicable faith I have in the unseen, can extend my own personal church beyond Sunday mornings to the weeks that follow. I suppose I have discovered that I, too, believe in a few things unseen.

I shall go on thinking, in the still moments of my life, about the lessons it will take a lifetime to learn. The Shakers themselves, I have no doubt, will go on triumphantly into the third millennium. Measured by their own standards, not by the world's, they will reap a bountiful harvest for the daily quiet toiling in the meetinghouse and on the farm. As the Shaker song proclaims, they will arise "Out of the Shadows":

> Out of the shadows cold and gray,
> Into the light of a newborn day,
> Up where the sun shines brightly alway,
> Let us be onward going;
>
> Ours is a joy which the world cannot know,
> Love that increases as onward we go,
> Peace that the spirit of good will bestow,
> As onward we're joyfully going.

Today's small family of Shakers have, indeed, kindled the light in Gowen Wilson's farmhouse on the rolling hills of Sabbathday Lake, Maine. To many of us in the world, it burns brightly, helps light our way. And thanks be to them for that.

BIBLIOGRAPHY

Barker, Sister R. Mildred. "Our Mother in the New Creation." *The Shaker Quarterly*, vol. 1, no. 1, Spring 1961.

Barker, Sister R. Mildred. *Revelation: A Shaker Viewpoint*. Poland Spring, ME: The United Society of Shakers, 1989.

Barker, Sister R. Mildred. "The Gift to Be Simple." *The Shaker Quarterly*, vol. 5, no. 3, Fall 1965.

Barker, Sister R. Mildred. *The Sabbathday Lake Shakers: An Introduction to the Shaker Heritage*. Sabbathday Lake, ME: The Shaker Press, 1985.

Brooks, Leonard. "Sister Aurelia Mace and Her Influence on the Ever-Growing Nature of Shakerism." *The Shaker Quarterly*, vol. 16, no. 2, Summer 1988.

Campion, Nardi Reeder. *Ann the Word: The Life of Mother Ann Lee, Founder of the Shakers*. Boston: Little, Brown and Company, 1976.

Carr, Sister Frances A. "Feed My Sheep." *The Shaker Quarterly*, vol. 23, no. 3, Fall 1994.

Carr, Sister Frances A. *Growing Up Shaker*. Sabbathday Lake, ME: The United Society of Shakers, 1994.

Carr, Sister Frances A. "Lucy Wright: First Mother in the Revelation and Order of the First Organized Church." *The Shaker Quarterly*, vol. 15, no. 4, Winter 1987.

Carr, Sister Frances A. *Shaker Your Plate: Of Shaker Cooks and Cooking*. Hanover and London: University Press of New England, 1987.

Chura, Walt. "How the Shakers Keep It Simple." *USCatholic*, vol. 60, no. 7, July 1995.

Confrater. (Brother Theodore Johnson.) "Shakerism for Today." *The Shaker Quarterly*, vol. 3, no. 1, Spring 1963.

Editor. "The American Shakers." A List of Tenets. *The Shaker Quarterly*, vol. 17, no. 3, Fall 1989.

Elders. *Testimonies of the Life, Character, Revelations and Doctrines of Mother Ann Lee, and the Elders with Her, Through whom the Word of Eternal Life was opened in this day, of Christ's Second Appearing, Collected from Living Witnesses, in Union with the Church.* Albany, NY: Weed, Parsons & Co., Printers, 1888.

Johnson, Brother Theodore E. *Life in the Christ Spirit.* Sabbathday Lake, ME: The United Society of Shakers, 1969.

Johnson, Brother Theodore E., ed. "Rules and Orders for the Church of Christ's Second Appearing." *The Shaker Quarterly*, vol. 11, no. 4, Winter 1971.

Johnson, Brother Theodore E., ed. "The Millennial Laws of 1821." *The Shaker Quarterly*, vol. 7, no. 2, Summer 1967.

Mace, Sister Aurelia G. *Journal, 1896.* On file at the Shaker Library, Sabbathday Lake Community, ME.

Mace, Sister Aurelia G. *The Aletheia: Spirit of Truth.* Farmington, ME: Knowlton and McLeary Co., 1907.

Marini, Stephen A. "A New View of Mother Ann Lee and the Rise of American Shakerism." *The Shaker Quarterly*, vol. 18, no. 3, Fall 1990.

Morgan, John H. "Experience as Knowledge: A Study in Shaker Theology." *The Shaker Quarterly*, vol. 14, no. 2, Summer 1974.

Morgan, John H. "On Taking the Christ-Presence Seriously." *The Shaker Quarterly*, vol. 14, no. 4, Winter 1987.

Morse, Flo. *The Shakers and the World's People.* New York: Dodd, Mead & Co., 1980.

Mount Lebanon, New York, North Family. *Original Shaker Music Volume II.* New York: William A. Pond & Co., 1893. Reprinted in Sabbathday Lake, ME: 1992, The United Society of Shakers.

Mount Lebanon, New York, North Family. *Shaker Music, Original Inspirational Hymns and Songs Illustrative of the Life and Testimony of the Shakers.* Copyright 1884 by Daniel Offord. Reprinted 1995 by The United Society of Shakers.

Newman, Cathy. "The Shakers' Brief Eternity." *National Geographic*, September 1989, pages 302–325.

Patterson, Daniel W. *Gift Drawing and Gift Song: A Study of Two Forms of Shaker Inspiration.* Sabbathday Lake, ME: The United Society of Shakers, 1983.

Procter-Smith, Marjorie. *Shakerism and Feminism: Reflections on Women's Religion and the Early Shakers.* Old Chatham, NY: Center for Research and Education, Shaker Museum and Library, 1991.

Setta, Susan M. "When Christ Is a Woman: Theology and Practice in the Shaker Tradition." In *Unspoken Worlds: Women's Religious Lives,* edited by Nancy Auer Falk and Rita M. Gross. Belmont, CA: Wadsworth Publishing Company, 1989.

Spencer, Sylvia Minott. "Next Door to the Angels—My Memories of the Shakers." *The Shaker Quarterly,* vol. 10, no. 4, Winter 1970.

Sprigg, June, and David Larkin. *Shaker Life, Work, and Art.* Photographs by Michael Freeman. New York: Stewart, Tabori & Chang, 1987.

Stein, Stephen J. *The Shaker Experience in America: A History of the United Society of Believers.* New Haven and London: Yale University Press, 1992.

Wertkin, Gerard C. *The Four Seasons of Shaker Life: An Intimate Portrait of the Community at Sabbathday Lake.* New York: Simon and Schuster, 1986.

White, Anna, and Leila S. Taylor. *Shakerism: Its Meaning and Message.* Columbus, OH: Fred J. Heer Press, 1905.

Whitson, Robley Edward. "The Spirit of Shaker Christianity." *The Shaker Quarterly,* vol. 5, no. 3, Fall 1965.

FOR MORE INFORMATION
ABOUT THE SHAKERS OF SABBATHDAY LAKE, WRITE TO:

THE SHAKER SOCIETY
707 SHAKER ROAD
NEW GLOUCESTER, MAINE 04260

OR VISIT THEIR WEB SITE AT:
WWW.MAINE.COM/SHAKERLIBRARY

ABOUT THE AUTHOR

SUZANNE SKEES met the world's last Shakers while studying world religions at Harvard Divinity School. She graduated and moved across the continent, birthing a family in the suburbs and writing theological features for newspapers and magazines. But she felt pulled back toward Maine, to explore the depth of faith she had glimpsed among the Shakers of Sabbathday Lake. She found there a loving God unlike the Almighty of her Midwestern Catholic upbringing. She found a spirit realm, rich and alive, despite our modern world's disbelief in the intangible. And she embraced a family of women and men living out their beliefs in daily, one-pointed purity. Skees returned to the world a changed person, and wrote her first book, *God among the Shakers*, to share her story. She lives with her husband and three young sons near San Francisco.